Where the Strange Roads Go Down

The University of Arizona Press
www.uapress.arizona.edu

Century Collection edition 2017

Originally published by The Macmillan Company

Printed in the United States of America
22 21 20 19 18 17   7 6 5 4 3 2

ISBN-13: 978-0-8165-1273-7 (paper)
ISBN-13: 978-0-8165-3573-6 (Century Collection paper)

Library of Congress Cataloging-in-Publication Data
Del Villar, Mary, 1917–
    Where the strange roads go down / Mary del Villar
    and Fred del Villar, with a new foreword by Susan
    Hardy Aiken.
        p.   cm.
    Reprint. Originally published: New York :
    Macmillan, 1963.
        ISBN 0-8165-1273-6
        1. Michoacán de Ocampo (Mexico)—Description and
    travel. 2. Guerrero (Mexico : State)—Description and
    travel. 3. Del Villar, Mary, 1917– —Journeys—
    Mexico. 4. Del Villar, Fred, 1900– —Journeys—
    Mexico. I. Del Villar, Fred, 1900–
    II. Title
    F1306.04 1991
    917.2'37—dc20   91-16622
                                               CIP

British Library Cataloguing in Publication data are available.

♾ This paper meets the requirements of ANSI/NISO Z39.48-1992
(Permanence of Paper).

We were dreamers, dreaming greatly, in the man-stifled town;
We yearned beyond the sky-line where the strange roads go down.

—*Rudyard Kipling*, "The Song of the Dead"

Foreword

*It is a convention of Western thought to believe all cultures are compelled to
explore, that human beings seek new land because their economies drive them
onward. Lost in this . . . observation is the notion of a simpler longing, of a
human desire for a less complicated life, for fresh intimacy and renewal. These,
too, draw us into new landscapes.*

—Barry Lopez, *Arctic Dreams*

WHAT DOES IT MEAN TO BE ENCHANTED BY A LANDSCAPE,
to have your imagination seized so completely that you will relinquish
security, material comfort, even personal safety, and give yourself over
to that place, moving with its rhythms, submitting to its severest requirements in order to discover what Isak Dinesen, speaking of Africa, calls its
"song"? Recalling his initial encounter with the Sonoran Desert in *The
Desert Year*, Joseph Wood Krutch writes of love at first sight. Dinesen, in
Out of Africa, describes "a landscape that had not its like in all the world."[1]
To find and recognize such a place is to experience the feeling of entering, awake and in full daylight, the world of dreams. Traversing its terrain, one explores not only a physical locale but the geography of one's
own being.

It is just such an experience, transporting in every sense of the word,
that is the subject of *Where the Strange Roads Go Down*. The place was the
backcountry of southwestern Mexico, in the states of Michoacán and
Guerrero, before the advent of paved roads, electricity, television, and
tourism—those homogenizing forces of Western technological society—
had transformed the centuries-old ways of life in that locale and marred
the natural landscape with a grid of highways and wires. The year was
1951. Most white, middle-class American women, responding to the

---

1. Dinesen *Out of Africa* (New York: Random House, 1937), p. 3.

renewed cult of domesticity that swept the country in the aftermath of World War II, had returned en masse to hearth, home, and housework. Not so Mary del Villar. Unconfined by traditional conventions of femininity and singularly unimpressed by domestic comforts and conformities, she would leave home behind without a backward glance to embark on a momentous journey in search of the strange roads she had yearned for all her life. In three months she would cover, on foot, nearly a thousand miles of desert, mountains, rivers, and seacoast, exploring some of the most rugged terrain in all of Mexico.

It was in part this appetite for adventure that had drawn her to her husband and traveling companion, Federico del Villar (his name anglicized to Fred in response to the ways of his adopted country). The two made a curious pair—she the cultivated, independent-minded daughter of a New England academic family, he a charming, golden-tongued Italian nobleman living in exile. They had met—in one of those unlikely encounters that was to typify the subsequent chanciness of their married life—over a poker game. It was 1945. The world was at war, and both were working as correspondents at the State Department.

By that time Federico Carrassi del Villar had long been a confirmed nomad. Born in 1900 to an aristocratic family in Turin, he had set off on horseback at the age of seventeen to fight in World War I. After the war he graduated from the Italian Cavalry School and served as a cavalry officer until he was imprisoned by the Mussolini regime on charges of anti-Fascism. Released on the condition that he leave Italy, he embarked on a peripatetic life, selling wine in France and Spain, working as a gaucho on a ranch in Argentina, and as an intelligence agent, gathering information on Nazi and Fascist infiltration in Brazil. Along the way he became fluent in Spanish. Eventually, he also became a journalist. Having worked during the war first as a correspondent for the French news agency Havas in Rio de Janeiro and later as a reporter for Agence France Presse at the United Nations, he arrived at last in Washington and the fateful poker game at which he would meet his future wife.

In the same year that young Federico left home on horseback for the war, Mary Catherine Harmon was born in New Haven, Connecticut, where her father was a professor of Classics at Yale. She had, by her own account, "a typical New England upbringing"—typical, that is, for young women of her class: boarding school, summers in Maine, the healthy life of the outdoors: "sailing old boats, picnicking on islands, and swimming in cold water."[2] After graduating from Smith in 1938, she went off to Greenwich Village, armed with a Phi Beta Kappa key, high honors in English, and a determination to live, as she would later write, "what I thought of as real life at last"—the bohemian existence of the freelance writer. Discovering like many before her that such a life provided but sporadic sustenance, she took a salaried position as what she calls "secretary-cum-publicity agent" at Kenyon College. This more conventional existence proved hard to bear: she was fired after eight months for "undue levity."

But this was the year of Pearl Harbor, and like others of her generation, she found her life transformed by the war. As a civilian code clerk with the AAF Air Transport Command in Puerto Rico, charged with getting American planes to Europe, she ran code rooms staffed by young women, many of them experiencing for the first time a heady new freedom from traditional gender codes. But after two years, in a move typical of the government's ambivalent response to women workers during and after World War II, her group was replaced by male soldiers and advised that they could either work in the continental United States or be released.

Thus began Mary Harmon's career as a journalist, a vocation she would pursue sporadically for many years. She started as a copy girl for the Associated Press, soon moved to the Transradio Press Service, and covered, in four years, "just about every Washington beat from Capitol Hill to Labor." She wound up at last in the State Department—across the poker table from her future husband. "We got acquainted," she recalls, "playing games of penny ante in the press room."

As she would later tell it, Mary was drawn to Fred by his gift for storytelling. She married him "for the same reasons that Desdemona eloped with Othello, for the dangers he had passed. He was a great raconteur and was never pompous." To her parents' doubts she responded, "At least I will never be bored." She never was. They would remain together

---

2. This and subsequent quotations other than passages from the text are taken from letters and personal communications to me from Mary del Villar Porter, who also provided the biographical information herein.

for nineteen years, their frequently trying relationship sustained by their common love for wandering the back roads of the world. In the landscapes and lifeways of rural Mexico that yearning found its deepest fulfillment. When, in 1948, they left Washington to be married under the volcanoes in Yautepec, Morelos, Mary del Villar "entered," as she would later write, "upon a lifelong passion for Mexico." This was the real beginning of the adventure recorded in *Where the Strange Roads Go Down*. Though the title page bears both their names, it was finally Mary who authored the book, based on the journal she kept throughout the trek. As his wry prefatory note acknowledges, Fred served primarily as an editor. He also did most of the interviews and, Mary would later note, "with his impeccable manners charmed all those along the way."

The del Villars had first discovered the road south to the Rio de las Balsas in 1949, while living among the Tarascan Indians of Michoacán on the shores of Lake Pátzcuaro. The "road" was in fact a mere track, virtually impassable except by burro or on foot. But its very remoteness held alluring promise, inspiring fanciful visions of *tierra caliente*, the hot lands of the south, "where all the fruit comes from, and tiger skins and rare woods and gold, where there are snakes and scorpions and fever, palm trees, parrots, buried treasure" (p. 1). Those visions became the motivating force of the del Villars' lives. Three years later, having sold virtually everything they owned in order to finance the journey, they made their way back to Tarascan country, abandoned their automobile, and set out on foot for *tierra caliente*.

They were accompanied by two burros (christened, with due ironic solemnity, Evita and Perón), on whose reluctant backs they packed their meager provisions—coffee, rice, a few pots and pans, blanket rolls, some changes of old clothing, and assorted first-aid supplies. They would survive for three months on these spare stores and on the generous hospitality of the people through whose world they traveled. By the time they returned to Erongaricuaro, they had exhausted both boots and provisions. They had also lost many pounds, a few romantic illusions, and one burro: Perón, worn out after climbing the mountains above San José de la Montaña, had been taken in by a welcoming campesino family. Fred, too, finally collapsed en route, the victim of illness and exhaustion. Too sick to travel farther on foot, he stopped for a time in Los Reyes and later took a battered country bus to Cherán, leaving Mary to complete the last major leg of the expedition alone.

What they had not lost was the adventurous spirit that had launched them on the journey. Fred having mended enough to go on, they met again in Cherán and, "feeling lightheaded and a little crazy," plunged into the final downhill trek to Erongaricuaro:

> We were a disreputable-looking pair, clothed in dust and dirt, still marked by the insect bites of tierra caliente. . . .
> But we had made it, over seven hundred miles of walking: deserts, rivers, mountains, beaches, towns, villages, and lonely ranches, in spite of fatigue, hunger, insects, heat and cold. We had set out, not to prove anything or to discover anything, but just to see what manner of people and country lay at the end of the "strange road" that goes south from Ario de Rosales.
> We might have returned with phials of gold dust, tiger skins, maps of buried treasure, parrots, rare botanical specimens, or clues to fabulous deposits of silver or copper. Instead we came back from the distant hot lands with a handful of broken sea shells, picked up on Pacific beaches, a case of dysentery, and a baby. (p. 242)

And something more: a rediscovery of that interior landscape of the spirit to which all strange roads eventually lead.

Many changes have altered the face of the landscape, both topographically and politically, since the del Villars and their burros trekked across it. The completion of the Pacific coastal highway opened the way for outsiders who have too often regarded the local inhabitants either as potential servants or as quaint curiosities. Michoacán and Guerrero are now associated in the popular imagination with tourist resorts like Acapulco and Ixtapa, gold mines of a type quite different from those in Mary del Villar's ironically remembered visions. It is no coincidence that both states have also been sites of revolutionary unrest and sporadic violence on the part of those for whom Westernized development has only intensified the split between the wealthy and the far more numerous *pobres*; Guerrero in particular has long been a locus of opposition to the country's ruling party. Even in 1952 the signs of political friction generated by unequal privilege and U.S. encroachment were already beginning to appear: the scathing portraits of the self-absorbed missionaries and the Texas cattle inspector, for example, suggest the del Villars' sympathies for the indigenous peoples whose lives were to be increasingly invaded by insensitive, ethnocentric outsiders. There is a marked contrast between the defensiveness of the missionaries or the smug self-satisfaction of the Texan—a comic epitome of the ugly American—and the del Villars' mutually respectful relations with local inhabitants whose generosity and civility literally sustained them throughout their journey. The exploratory impulse that compelled their adventure, though potentially related to the mentality of colonialism, was in fact its opposite. For where the colonist seeks an unknown land in order to possess it, the del Villars sought it out in order to *be possessed*. Given the times in which she wrote, Mary del Villar's sensitivity to the diversity and distinctive perspectives of the native peoples she encountered, her combination of respect and a clear-eyed refusal to romanticize, appears especially striking. Equally unusual is her implicit recognition of the perils of neocolonialism and the ambiguous "progress" promised by modern technologies.

Long out of print, *Strange Roads* has continued to enjoy word-of-mouth popularity as a small gem of travel literature in the tradition of works by John Van Dyke, Carl Lumholtz, Charles Lummus, Mary Austin, Edward Hoagland, and Bruce Chatwin. But for all its absorbing detail about topography, flora, and fauna, its keen observations of character, and its vivid re-creation of the sense of place, it is much more than a travel memoir. For on every page one senses the strength, character, and distinctive perspective of Mary del Villar herself. An uncommon woman by any standards, she seems all the more remarkable when one recalls the profoundly reactionary gender ideologies that prevailed in the postwar era in which she lived and wrote. Like Mary Austin, Karen Blixen, Beryl Markham, and other great female wanderers, she transcended the confining notions of woman her society would have imposed on her, living her life according to the dictates of her own intrepid spirit. Reflecting on that vigorous unconventionality, one shares her ironic amusement at the many observers along the way who—encountering her in old trousers and heavy boots, her braided hair concealed beneath a battered hat—mistook her for a man, and at their shocked disequilibrium on discovering their mistake. Ever resistant to classification, she unsettles conventional definitions.

In the years after their trek through *tierra caliente*, the del Villars—soon accompanied by their daughter Jane, who had been conceived en route—would go on to other adventures, sources of stories yet untold: working on a barge on the Erie Canal, laboring with Mexican braceros in the Northwest, running a ranch in Jalisco, living on an ancient surplus landing craft in Key Largo and in an adobe in Wagon Mound, New Mexico.

Thus it happened that they arrived in Tucson in the late 1960s. As with Mexico, so too with the Sonoran Desert: "We decided," Mary recalls, "that Arizona was where we wanted to be for a long time." But by then the marriage itself had deteriorated beyond retrieval. When it ended in 1969, Mary, now in her early fifties, had already entered the graduate program in English at the University of Arizona. She received a Ph.D. in Renaissance literature in 1970.

After a year's stint as assistant professor of English at the State University of New York at Stony Brook, she was invited to return to Tucson to join the faculty of the University of Arizona. Believing herself home at last, she bought a three-room adobe house west of the Tucson Mountains on sparsely settled land adjoining the Saguaro National Monument— "miles of desert," she recalls with satisfaction, "in every direction." But her travels were not yet over. A few years after the move to Arizona, she married Howard Porter, a professor of Classics at Columbia, and together they retired to Guilford, Connecticut, on the shores of Long Island Sound—only a few miles from where Mary had grown up.

Now her journeying had come full circle, but she could not get the desert out of her blood. In 1979, having grown increasingly homesick for the Southwest, she acquired twenty acres of land adjoining the Tohono O'odham reservation, a place to come back to for two or three weeks each year. Situated on the eastern incline of the Comobabi Mountains, the land was too steep for grazing cattle or growing crops and had been emptied long since of whatever paltry ore it once possessed. It was also, to conventional Anglo eyes, fifty miles from nowhere. For Mary, it was close to perfect.

Here she and a group of friends built a rough one-room cabin, hauling every piece of wood up the steep, waterless slopes thick with jojoba, scrub mesquite, cholla, prickly pear, and saguaro. The finished house, perched precariously on a narrow saddle where the promontory juts out of the mountain like the crook of an arm, is smaller than Thoreau's at Walden. The threshold faces due east; looking out, one can see the sun rise. Southward, the eye travels almost to Mexico—out across a vast blue stretch of valley floor, the shadows shifting as clouds build and drift; past Kitt Peak, with its observatories like polished white stones; and beyond to the beautiful humpbacked mountain Baboquivari, center of the Tohono O'odham universe.

It is a place of beauty and turbulence, the sort of landscape that seems most fitting for Mary del Villar. She has always been happiest in the midst of elemental forces and untamed spaces, following the ways of the earth. "This is an old business," writes Barry Lopez in *Arctic Dreams*, "walking slowly over the land with an appreciation of its immediacy to the senses and an anticipation of what lies hidden in it." Entering Mary del Villar's narrative, we are invited to join her slow walk over the land, to participate in that appreciation and anticipation. In its way, her account is as remarkable as the journey that inspired it. Writing with wit, humor, and casual eloquence, del Villar vividly conveys the land's immediacy—its distinctive sights and smells, its sounds and textures, and the character of the people who precariously inhabited it, following life-ways hundreds of years old. In reading her book, you share that adventure—wandering with her, for a while, down the strange roads she tells about so well.

SUSAN HARDY AIKEN

Introductory Note

WHILE THIS BOOK CARRIES BOTH MY WIFE'S AND MY own by-lines, and is the product of our joint efforts, the story had to be told by one or the other of us. Mary was, from my viewpoint, the obvious choice for the job, because she "spicks da English," because without her the expedition would have collapsed midway, and because otherwise the book would probably never have been written. With this last point she agreed. My share of the effort has therefore been limited largely to blue-penciling, with the dubious authority conferred to me by age, experience, and marital status, the disparaging remarks she made about me. Some of them slipped by, but I subscribe to them, as I subscribe to the rest of the book.

We have tried to give a true picture of what we saw and did in the course of our three-month walk. Every fact reported is true. People and places are referred to by their real names. Any similarity between the names of our burros and those of famous persons is not a mere coincidence.

To help the reader follow our tracks, we have drawn a map of the territory we covered. Sketchy as it is, we believe it to be by far the best available.

FRED DEL VILLAR

BROOKLYN, NEW YORK
September, 1952

Contents

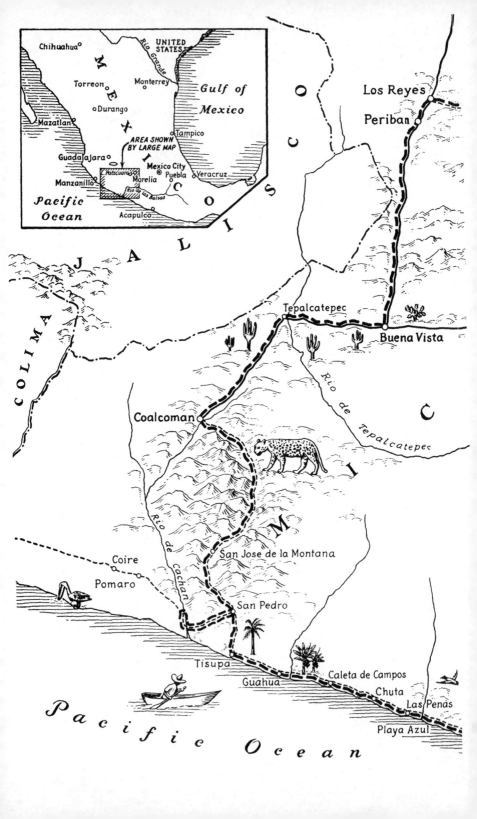

TO GUADALAJARA

TO MEXICO CITY →

Morelia

Cheran

Paracho

Charapan

PARICUTIN
VOLCANO

Erongaricuaro

Arocutin

Lake
Patzcuaro

Lake Zirahuen

Patzcuaro

M I C H O A C A N

Uruapan

Unexplored

Region

Ario de Rosales

Puente Alto

Rancho Nuevo

El Limon

Apatzingan

Agua Blanca

Las Anonas

Rio del Marques

Reparo de Luna

Cueramo

La Luz

Organal

Los Nopales

Rio de las Balsas

Pinzandaran

La Pitirera

G U E R R E R O

La Garita

La Barranca

San Diego

Melchor
campo

Cofradia

Surucua

WHERE THE STRANGE
ROADS GO DOWN

═══ Paved Roads
──── Dirt Roads
----- Trails
▬▬▬ Our Route

Scale 1:1,000,000 or 1 inch = 16 miles
(As the crow flies, but allow twice
the distance as the donkey walks)

1 The Road South

THE ROAD THAT GOES DOWN FROM ARIO DE ROSALES INTO
the hot country is deeply rutted and carpeted with fine red dust that
rises in clouds when a troop of donkeys or a truck or a herd of
cattle passes. A tourist can drive his car a mile or so along it and
eat a picnic lunch under the somnolent pine trees, watching the men
and animals that go by, journeying to the mysterious south.

This is what we did three years ago when, on a visit to Ario, we
happened to drive to the southern end of the town, where all at
once the houses stop and you see a landscape of gradually descending hills with a winding road that loses itself in the distance.

"What road is this?" we asked a sombreroed donkey driver.

"This is the road that goes to *tierra caliente*, señor," the man replied, "to the Rio de las Balsas and the sea."

And what was tierra caliente? Why, it was the south, the hot lands,
where all the fruit comes from, and tiger skins and rare woods and
gold, where there are snakes and scorpions and fever, palm trees,
parrots, buried treasure.

"And the Rio de las Balsas, have you seen it?"

"Not I, señor. It is far off, and who knows if a Christian would
get back alive? They say it is a great river, a *rio bravo*, dangerous
and full of alligators."

The road is nothing but a wheel track in the dirt, passable only
for animals, trucks, or jeeps, but we pushed our car down for a few
cautious miles until Ario was out of sight and we were alone in the
hot silence of early afternoon. We sat on the pine needles at the

1

roadside and watched the travelers going and coming. From Ario caravans of burros or mules trotted down the road, heavily loaded with the commodities of civilization—cloth and needles, knives, shoes, jewelry. The animals were directed by hoarse shouts from their *arrieros*, who walked behind carrying, as their total equipment for a hundred-mile trip, a serape and a little shoulder bag containing a bottle of water, a few tortillas, and perhaps a piece of cheese.

"Bur-r-o-o! Ur-r-o-o!" Their shouts faded in the distance. Standing up, we could see the troops appear and disappear in the curves of the road that stretched out below us. In a week's time, perhaps, they would be standing on the shores of the Balsas.

What is there about the Rio de las Balsas that captures the imagination? Before that day in Ario we had never even heard of it, but immediately we wanted to go there. Sitting on the roadside next to our bright new car, we wished that we could exchange it on the spot for a couple of horses and follow the arrieros to their fabulous country, but our holiday in Mexico was running out—and so was our money.

At the time we were living in a tent on the shores of Lake Pátzcuaro, in the cool uplands of the state of Michoacán, forty miles north of Ario. Our camping place was right under the Tarascan Indian village of Arócutin, which perches on a high bluff over the lake, so baked in sunlight that its adobe houses are bleached white. From Arócutin, you get a splendid view of the lake with its islands and its ring of mountains. If you remark on the beauty of the view to a Tarascan, he will not say, "Yes, it is lovely, isn't it?" but, "Thank you very much," as though you were paying him a personal compliment. It is his lake, and he is gratified if you like it.

We had become sort of honorary Tarascans just by giving people rides in our car and inviting them to share coffee or beer around our campfire. In return they took us out in their dugout canoes, invited us to their homes for dinner, brought us fish and duck from the lake, and consulted us about their problems. We were the *grands seigneurs* of the place, and were known to everybody as Don Federico and Doña Mariquita.

When we got back to the United States, however, we found we

were just nonentities and nobody would dream of asking our advice about anything—in fact, everybody tried to *give* us advice about hard work, discipline, security, and things like that.

We did not pay much attention, but made a dollar here and a dollar there and talked about going back to Mexico. We put an empty Chianti bottle on the mantel in our Brooklyn apartment and started dropping dimes in it "for our trip." Usually, however, a birthday would come along, and the level in the bottle would drop. We estimated that it would cost us at least a thousand dollars to go to Mexico and take a three-month trip into tierra caliente—what with horses and pack animals and supplies and guides and the like.

The thousand dollars did not seem to materialize, because we are essentially lazy people, and our idea of being free-lance writers was to sit around our apartment reading and playing chess, waiting for the telephone to ring and for somebody to ask us to write something. Since this scarcely ever happened, we had a lot of time to talk and make plans and study maps for the trip we were going to take "next year." But next year came and another year, and the cost of living went up. We sat with the bums under Brooklyn Bridge and watched ships sailing to far places and agreed with Thoreau that "the mass of men lead lives of quiet desperation."

In the end it was quite simple. We just decided to go. We estimated that we could borrow $600 or so on life insurance (a practice much frowned upon by serious-minded folk), and that instead of buying horses and expensive equipment we would just take what we had and walk, with a donkey to carry the pack for us. We would be broke when we got back, but we would have seen the Rio de las Balsas.

The fact that we had never walked any farther than from our apartment to the Brooklyn Central Library did not worry us, for we planned to take it slowly and rest whenever we felt like it. We ransacked the apartment and the houses of our friends and relatives and discovered that there was really very little equipment that we needed to buy. We had blankets, hammocks, cooking equipment, and plenty of old clothes.

This decision was made in midsummer of 1951, and we planned to

3

leave in December, in order to take our trip into the hot country during the (relatively) coldest months and complete it before the start of the rainy season. We looked high and low in New York in search of people who might have even a scrap of information or advice, but nobody knew a thing about the Rio Balsas or the Pacific coast of Michoacán. With the aid of two fairly recent Mexican maps, we traced our itinerary: we would leave from Arócutin (where we intended to buy our donkey or donkeys), cross the mountains south of Lake Pátzcuaro to Lake Zirahuen, and from there go down to Ario de Rosales and pick up our road to the Balsas. Once arrived at the river, we would try to follow it to the sea, and then head northwest up the coast. We allowed three months for the trip, and estimated roughly that we should reach the Pacific in a month, walk up the coast for a month (possibly as far as Manzanillo), and then turn east and find our way across the Sierra Madre del Sur back to Lake Pátzcuaro. Measuring distances against the scale of kilometers on the map, we judged that we would walk about five hundred miles.

Our friends groaned at the thought of such a lot of walking, but we explained that we had it very reasonably planned to walk ten miles a day for five days and rest two days—an average of about fifty miles a week. It was a fine program, except that we had not calculated the ups and downs and hardships of the trail when we proposed it.

Medical problems worried us some, for we kept thinking about snakes and scorpions, not to mention fever-bearing mosquitoes, amoebic dysentery, and all the other perils of tropical travel. Fred tracked down a snake expert in one of the city museums who advised us not to bother with serums but simply to take snake-bite kits containing little suction pumps and, if we were bitten, to cut across the fang holes with a razor, apply the pump, and pray. "Of course, if you are bitten by a coral snake there's very little hope in any case," he said encouragingly.

The rest of our medical kit was assembled with the assistance of a doctor friend, and by the time we had it all collected we decided that we had better get two donkeys instead of one, but at least we

4

felt reasonably well equipped to deal with whatever disasters might befall us. We had terramycin and sulfa for fevers or infections, paregoric for digestive upsets, and plenty of antiseptic, bandages, and packs of gauze, as well as a big wide roll of adhesive.

For firearms we intended to take a .32 caliber revolver, a .22 rifle, and a shotgun, but the Mexican consulate informed us that no firearms could be brought across the border. With considerable regret, we left the .22 and the shotgun behind and took only the little pistol, which we could easily smuggle in without incident. Our arsenal also included a big Marine hunting knife for Fred, a little sheath knife for me, a machete and a hatchet.

Among the few things we bought especially for the trip were two canteens, one holding a quart and the other a gallon, a pedometer, and a Primus stove (which worked beautifully for a couple of days and then stubbornly refused to function).

We took a bunch of old shirts, blue jeans, shorts, and a cotton wrap-around skirt for me in case I should want to look like a lady. We also took bathing suits, underwear, and six pairs of cheap half-wool socks apiece. The cheap socks were a mistake, for they never fit properly and probably caused us more blisters than we would have had otherwise.

There was a big difference of opinion between us about boots, and after many arguments each of us stuck stubbornly to his opinion. I took some twelve-inch lace boots that I had bought over fifteen years ago but had not used a great deal, and Fred got himself a pair of so-called engineer boots, which are like riding boots, with a strap across the instep and rather high heels. He had more foot trouble than I did, but he still thinks his engineer boots are wonderful. We took a couple of trial runs in our boots around Brooklyn, and decided that we ought to be able to make ten miles a day without too much difficulty.

As to the commissary department, I picked out a few pots, pans, and cups, some steel cutlery, and a couple of aluminum pie plates from the kitchenette, bought a few jars of instant cocoa, and at the last minute threw in all the dry groceries that were on the

5

shelf—rice, salt, peas, and so on. The dried peas furnished us a meal in a God-forsaken place called Guahua, and we wished there had been more of them.

As photographers, we are rank amateurs, but we took two good cameras with which we had had several months of practice in New York, a 35-millimeter and a reflex, with twenty-five rolls of film for each, and planned to take so many pictures that by the law of averages at least a few should turn out to be good.

Of course, we intended to keep a daily journal, a task to which we were both going to dedicate ourselves faithfully. Fred managed to write the account of one day's travel, as I remember, and I had to do the rest. He pretended that he had written with a typewriter so long that he could not use a pen any more, and considered that he was doing his share when he bawled me out for forgetting something.

Perhaps at this point it might be well to introduce Fred and myself a little more formally, so that the reader can see what kind of people were starting on this somewhat half-cocked expedition. Fred was born in Italy and lived in Latin America for more years than he cares to be explicit about, so that he speaks Spanish fluently. He has always been strongly opposed to physical exertion, and his favorite form of entertainment is drinking little cups of coffee in cafés, reading in an easy chair, and listening to music. But he once was a cavalry officer before Mussolini threw him out of Italy, and he still has impressive muscles in his legs. He was to need them, too. I was born and raised in New England and spent a fairly athletic childhood sailing boats and going on camping trips, but those days are very ancient history and my most strenuous exercise in recent years had been taking the dog around the block. All in all, if you had picked any two New Yorkers blindfold you probably would have found people better equipped than we to take a 500-mile walking trip. The difference is, we wanted to do it. Nobody else in New York did, or at least we did not meet any of them in our travels.

In Mexico many people asked us why we journeyed so far on foot and suffered so many hardships, and this question was sometimes difficult to answer when we were hungry and exhausted and eaten alive by insects. We went on foot because we were poor and wanted to travel, and it seemed to us that if we just put one foot after another we would eventually get where we wanted to go and incidentally see a lot of things that swifter travelers miss. Furthermore, we were fed up with present-day civilization, with war scares and radio commercials and children in Hopalong Cassidy suits, and we wanted to talk to simple people, face elemental problems, and find out if the red stuff in our veins was blood or not.

It was a bright winter day, December 21, 1951, when our car, crammed to the roof with camping gear, rolled over Brooklyn Bridge and into the Holland Tunnel to the strains of a triumphant harmonica tune.

We had solved all our last-minute problems with what we considered great judgment, including subletting our dog with the apartment (he was too old to make the trip with us) and making such complex arrangements to be sure of getting our mail that we promptly forgot what the arrangements were. We successfully evaded our landlord, who claimed we owed him a month's rent, and persuaded the income-tax people not to bother us until our return from Mexico.

We made the trip from New York to Morelia (the capital of the state of Michoacán) in six days, sleeping most of the time in the car, eating crackers and cheese and chocolate bars to save money. On the last day the car began to fall apart, and after nightfall we entered the sedate city of Morelia going backwards instead of forward, because the brakes took a notion to lock every time they were used and would unlock only if we backed for some distance. Somehow we persuaded the shuddering vehicle up to the doors of the elegant Hotel Virrey de Mendoza, one of the most beautiful hotels in Mexico, said, "Damn the expense," and collapsed in a four-poster bed.

The way they fix cars in Mexico is something wonderful. The whole insides of our buggy were spread all over the ground while a mechanic, respectfully known as "maestro" to his assistants, kept assuring us that everything would be as good as new in an hour, and children from the age of four to ten dashed to and fro with

7

vital pieces of our machinery in their grubby fingers. This was a painful sight to watch, so instead we busied ourselves with seeking out a photographer to whom we could send our rolls of exposed film from whatever post offices we might find in our travels. (He turned out to be an affable old gentleman called Lucas Lopez Z., whose tiny shop on the Avenida de la Corregidora was no index to his professional standing. He charged us very little, and his work was as good as any we had found in New York.)

We also visited the Bank of Mexico. The question of how much money to carry bothered us, for we had heard a lot about bandits in the Mexican hinterland and did not fancy being robbed of our all at the start of the expedition. On the other hand, we were told at the bank that it would probably be impossible to get traveler's checks cashed in the country we were heading for. We finally decided to take 2,500 pesos in cash to cover the expenses of the trip, and to leave another 500 pesos with a friend so that we could call for it in case of trouble. With the peso at 8.60 to the dollar, this meant that we had about $300 for the trip, including the expenses of fitting out and the developing of our film, which we paid for in advance. We estimated that once on the road we could live on one dollar a day apiece, or sixteen pesos in all, and in fact we could easily have done so except for such luxuries as beer at two pesos a bottle.

This business was transacted between visits to the maestro, who infallibly replied "*Ahorita*" to our questions about when the car would be ready. "*Ahorita*" is a useful expression meaning "Right away," but anyone who takes it literally is likely to go crazy. What the maestro meant was that he was doing his best and that we should be patient.

When at last we drove away, the setting sun was gilding the spires of Morelia's magnificent old cathedral and shadows were lengthening across the pillared arcades that line the main street. Once out of town, we flew across the high plateau of which Morelia is the center, and in half an hour we were climbing the mountains that mark the northeastern boundary of Lake Pátzcuaro. The sun had gone down, but as we descended the winding road we caught glimpses through the dusk of the broad and tranquil surface of the lake still faintly tinged with colors. Just opposite us, and not ten miles away as the crow flies, was the little Tarascan town of Erongarícuaro, where we planned to make our headquarters while fitting out for the trip.

The big city of the lake is Pátzcuaro, whose cobbled streets and wide-eaved adobe houses look much the same as they did three hundred years ago when the Spaniards were building churches and palaces and trying to civilize the already highly civilized Tarascans.

The Tarascans, in the days before the Conquest, were the only Indian nation to resist successfully the empire-building efforts of the Aztecs. In the old days the Tarascan kings lived in the town of Tzintzuntzan on the eastern shore of Lake Pátzcuaro (their tombs can still be seen there today) and ruled a domain which extended all the way to the Pacific, including some territory which is now in the state of Guerrero. When the Spaniards came, the Tarascans allied themselves with the white invaders against their old enemies, the Aztecs. They realized too late that they had exchanged one tyrant for another, crueler one.

But although the Tarascans have had to live with the conquistadors and their descendants for centuries, they have put up a continuing passive resistance to outside influences. They still speak their own language, a difficult idiom full of harsh consonants, go fishing in dugout canoes, and hunt ducks with spears. Their towns and villages are dotted along the entire shore of Lake Pátzcuaro—one of the best known to tourists is the fishermen's island village of Janitzio—and are scattered through the mountains and valleys for fifty miles around. Although in ancient times there were Tarascan Indians throughout the hot country of Michoacán and Guerrero, today they are seldom seen in the south.

Erongarícuaro is a sizable town and the market center for the southwestern end of the lake. It was dark when we left the good paved road that takes tourists to Pátzcuaro. Some day the authorities are going to extend the road around the whole perimeter of the

9

lake—about thirty-five miles—but at present it stops abruptly a mile beyond Pátzcuaro at the gate of a wealthy general's farm, and the rest is a nightmare of ruts, stones, and dust.

As we bounded along through the six villages that precede Erongarícuaro, our headlights picked up groups of sombreroed men chatting in doorways, wrapped to the eyes in their warm serapes, and barefooted women in bright wool skirts and embroidered belts carrying their babies slung in shawls over their shoulders. Now and then we had to swerve to avoid a pig or a bull or a staggering Indian still celebrating the Christmas Eve fiesta of two days before.

We passed in the dark our camping place of three years ago, and another ten minutes of driving brought us into the plaza of Erongarícuaro, where music was still blaring from the cantinas, *tiendas* (booths) were open for business, and the usual throng of men, women, and children were waiting their turn to dip water from the public fountain.

We tumbled out of the car and drew in deep breaths of the frosty air, pungent with the smell of pine needles, wood smoke, and hot Mexican food. The trip with which, waking and sleeping, we had been obsessed for three years was at last really going to begin.

2 Tarascan Friends

THERE ARE NO HOTELS IN ERONGARÍCUARO, BUT THERE IS Cholita who rents her big front room to travelers and feeds them in her kitchen. Her house is right on the plaza under the arcades, and when she is not cooking she is always to be found sitting in front of the door watching what goes on—a fat old lady with beady bright eyes and a tongue that never stops wagging. Because of a gouty leg, she does not get around much, but everybody stops to pass the time of day with her. If you tell something to Cholita, the whole town will know about it in half an hour.

We became the star boarders at Cholita's while we readied our expedition for the road, getting our bed and board—the two of us —for sixteen pesos a day, or less than two dollars. We estimated that it would take us at least a week to get our donkeys and supplies, but in fact we were on our way in four days, thanks to the assistance of our Indian friends in Arócutin.

The people in Erongarícuaro remembered us from our previous visit and were politely glad to see us again—but the people of Arócutin welcomed us like long-lost brothers. It was midday when we climbed the steep bluff to the village in search of Don Salud Ascencio. Everything was unusually quiet—no people in the streets, just white adobe houses sleeping in the sun. It was two days after Christmas, and Arócutin was recovering from the holiday fiestas.

Mexican Indians certainly drink less per annum than the average New Yorker, but when they do drink they drink in earnest. The comic cartoon Mexican who sleeps in the sun all day with his sombrero over his eyes is just a myth. Indians work hard for a living, going out to their fields every day to cultivate, plant, and harvest without the aid of any machinery, and often watering their crops by hand with two five-gallon tins slung from a yoke over their shoulders.

When they celebrate with a fiesta, they have earned it. Tequila, mescal, or just plain alcohol brings them a few days of blessed oblivion when they can forget that their crops are poor, their diet slim, their children in rags. The village band plays tirelessly, the women in holiday finery stew up the chickens they have been saving for the great occasion and serve them with hot *mole* sauce. There is dancing and singing from morning to night, and this goes on two days, three days, four—until one morning the master of the house wakes up with a splitting head and accepts his wife's decree: back to work, hombre, the fiesta is over.

Arócutin was in this final stage—sleeping it off—when we arrived and knocked at the street door of Don Salud's house. Nobody answered, so we pushed open the door and crossed the sun-baked courtyard to the porch of the two-room house where we found our friend dead to the world on his *petate*, or straw mat. We called out to him and shook him by the arm until he opened his eyes, then scrambled unsteadily to his feet.

"Don Federico! Doña Mariquita!" He embraced us both in turn, Indian-fashion. He is a little man, shorter even than the average Tarascan, with a gentle face scarred by pockmarks and a thatch of unruly black hair. Salud had been *jefe de tenencia*, or selectman of the village, at the time of our previous visit, and now, although no longer in office, he was still the head man—the man people went to with their troubles. With education and opportunity, Salud might have been a lawyer or a doctor or a senator. As it is, he cannot go further than Arócutin nor expect more reward than the thanks of his fellow villagers. His life has been a singlehanded battle with the authorities, a continuous fight to get the things that Arócutin needs. Generally he fails, but he keeps on trying.

We had exchanged a few letters with Salud over the past three years, but we had not let him know that we were coming to see him.

12

He couldn't believe his eyes at first, and just stood there shaking his head and exclaiming, "*Que carai!*" Before we knew it, the fiesta which had supposedly ended the night before was being renewed in our honor.

Salud's wife, Doña Eufrasia, appeared with refreshments. The yard began to fill with people, all of them wanting to shake our hands and welcome us back. The village *musicos*, with guitars, violins, and trumpets, struck up the song we remembered so well, "Que Lindo Es Michoacán."

We sat on the porch with Salud and the other notables of the village, while small boys scrambled on the railings to have a look at us and the rest of the people stood smiling in the sun. We felt as though we had never left, for the party might just as well have been a continuation of the big farewell fiesta which the village gave us the night before we left three years ago.

Pretty soon somebody shouted, "Que baile la guera!" (Let's see the blonde dance!) Everybody in Mexico who is not black-haired is a blond, and my nickname in years past had been La Guera. Not to disappoint them, I went out into the yard with an elderly Tarascan as my partner and did my best to dance the "hat dance." Tarascan dancing is a fast shuffle in which the partners never touch but simply clasp their hands behind their backs, gaze seriously at the ground, and prance up to or around each other. For me, in heavy boots and dungarees, still unacclimated to 7,000 feet of altitude, it was more of an endurance contest than a dance. Fred then did a turn with a pretty girl of fifteen, after which we were able to retire and watch people who really knew how to dance.

Between songs and dances we told Salud and his friends about our plans for a trip to the hot country and asked them if they could sell us burros.

"You don't need to buy burros here," said Salud with great dignity, as though we had offered to buy coal from a friend in Newcastle. "Just borrow the animals you want from the pueblo and bring them back when you have finished with them."

When we pointed out that it was to be a long hard trip of three months, and that one of the animals might easily be injured

13

or die, Salud merely remarked that burros could be replaced, after all. It was decided that, since we were greenhorns in matters of donkeys, he would select two animals for us and show us how to pack them.

"Be sure they have ears," I added as an afterthought, for you occasionally see crop-eared donkeys in Mexico—beasts who robbed a cornfield once too often and lost their ears by a machete stroke to teach them a lesson. The punishment is drastic, but corn is life itself in rural Mexico.

Salud promised that they would have ears and everything else that pertains to a burro.

Mexico is supposed to be the land of mañana where nobody ever gets anything done properly or on time, but that is another myth. We entrusted Salud with the whole problem of our animals and pack equipment—a job which took a lot of his time and brought him no profit whatever—and both he and his wife threw themselves into the project with as much energy as though it were their own trip and not ours that they were arranging. The four of us went into Pátzcuaro together on several occasions to buy boxes, *reatas*, and other gear for the burros. This we offered to do ourselves, but Salud said No: he could buy the things more cheaply than if we gringos had attempted to bargain for them.

Although Erongarícuaro was our headquarters, the business of the donkeys caused us to spend a good deal of time with Salud and Eufrasia and to know them better. They are children of the Revolution and, unlike most Indians, think of themselves as Mexicans first and Tarascans second. You do not hear Tarascan spoken in their house because they reason that Spanish is the language of their country, and they want their children to grow up free of the racial pride that has kept the Tarascans isolated from the rest of Mexico for so many centuries.

Although the majority of Indians are intensely, sometimes fanatically, religious, the Ascencios do not have holy pictures on the walls and they have not baptized their children. "No somos muy católicos" (We are not very Catholic) was the way Salud put it.

Promises of a better life in heaven did not interest him; he wanted it now.

The land that Salud works, and that is his under the *ejido* (communal) system, is the same land that his father and grandfather worked as peons, earning a few cents a day. Perhaps the land does not materially support him much better than it did his ancestors, but he is free to plant what he likes, to sell at his own price and, above all, to say what he thinks. He doesn't forget this, and he knows that he owes it to the Revolution. At the same time, the Revolution has not progressed far enough to suit Salud. All politicians in Mexico today call themselves "revolutionaries"; but the word does not mean very much any more, and to Salud and many others it seems as though efforts to assist the poor farmer had gradually lost all momentum in favor of the city trade unionists.

The schools were a sore point with Salud. During the presidency of Lázaro Cárdenas, the last of Mexico's really revolutionary presidents, there was a great burst of school building all over the country. Every tiny pueblo has its school—generally the prettiest building in town—but if you inquire you will often discover that the school is not running. No teacher. The building is all ready for the pupils, but the pay of a teacher is so ridiculously low that few people take or keep village teaching jobs. Since the emancipation of women is far from a reality in Mexico, there is a strong bias in favor of men teachers, especially in rural districts. Salud, who does not share the general feeling that women cannot be as intelligent as men, solved the problem for Arócutin by getting a woman teacher, a *profesora* who is less likely to be tempted by a better job. She makes barely enough to clothe and feed herself; but, being a Tarascan, she is used to poverty.

Another problem in Arócutin, and one which so far has not been solved, is the question of water. The village stands five hundred feet above the lake, and from time immemorial the women have had to carry water on their heads up from the lake every day. Salud has been trying for years to get the state or federal government to help with the installation of a pump, but without success. There are thousands of villages with the same problem all over Mexico. The women have always carried water, the authorities say, and if the people of Arócutin choose to make things harder for themselves by living on top of a cliff that is their own worry, not the government's.

One recent clash with the authorities landed Salud in the Pátzcuaro jail, where he had to stay for three months until a lawyer was hired at the cost of the family's entire savings to extricate him. The trouble came over new land that emerged from the lake. Like many of the lakes in Mexico, Pátzcuaro is gradually drying out, and pueblos that were once on the shore are now a mile or more from the water's edge. Below Arócutin the lake is very shallow, and every year it sinks a little further, uncovering new strips of fertile bottom land. Salud and his friends logically decided that the new land belonged to the village, and they began to cultivate it as part of Arócutin's ejido. Orders from the government told them to get off the land. The powers-that-be apparently had not decided the legal rights of the matter and, until a decision was made, they did not want squatters on the territory. Federal troops were finally sent to enforce the order, and before the people of Arócutin were evicted from the land there were some lively clashes between farmers and soldiers. Salud, the ringleader, was thrown in jail, and held without trial until the authorities decided that he must have learned a lesson.

One day when we had eaten dinner at Salud's, he brought himself to ask our advice about a matter that had obviously been troubling him and Eufrasia for some time: Was it true that Americans had ways to avoid having children and, if so, could we tell them about it? They had three boys, a grown, married son, a thirteen-year-old, and a baby of some three years. Tarascans, fortunately for them, do not seem to be as prolific as the mestizo population of Mexico. Around Lake Pátzcuaro most families have three or four children, whereas among the rural mestizos you find six, eight, or even twelve children.

There is no law in Mexico against contraceptives, and in big cities they are openly sold, but the country folk, who need such information worst, do not know where to go for it; most of them do not even realize that there is such a thing as birth control. It is curious that, although the Mexican government is theoretically anticlerical, it seems to work hand in hand with the Church in keeping such information away from the people.

The Ascencios were not the only friends with whom we renewed our acquaintance of three years ago. Down on the shore below Arócutin there was young Juan Gabriel, who used to be our nearest neighbor when we were camping on the lake. He too had his problems. Three years ago he had been a fisherman, paddling out in his canoe every day with the long-handled butterfly net which graces so many picture postcards of Lake Pátzcuaro. Today Juan has sold his nets and fishes no longer, for the lake is running out of its famous *pescado blanco,* the delicate transparent fish which used to be served in every restaurant around the lake.

The government was to blame, Juan said. Fisheries authorities, thinking to do the Indians a favor, introduced a new species of fish to the lake, and the new fish promptly ate up the white fish and then died out themselves for lack of anything more to eat. There are still a few pescados blancos which escaped the general disaster, and the Indians are hoping, now that the predators are gone, that the white fish will again grow fat and plentiful. Meanwhile, fishing is bad.

Juan now confines himself to duck hunting, for the lake is still black with ducks, mostly redheads that grow plump and tame feeding on grain along the shore. Like his forefathers before him, Juan hunts them from his *canoa* with a long, three-pronged spear which he throws with remarkable skill.

His mother sells the ducks at Pátzcuaro on market days, along with eggs which the chickens have produced. This way Juan, with his mother, his wife, and two children, manages to make a fair living by Tarascan standards, but Juan is not content. Since we last saw him, he had made two attempts to enter the United States illegally as a "wetback" and each time had been caught by the border authorities and sent home again, poorer than before.

Juan, though he is twenty-five years old and the breadwinner

17

of the family, is not really the master of his own house. Perhaps that is one reason why he is discontented. His mother, a grand old lady with a will of iron, keeps him on a tight rein. In theory, men are the lords of a Mexican household and women are meekly obedient, but as a woman grows older she gains authority, and upon her husband's death she often steps into his shoes as the head of the family, even though her sons may be grown and married. Many a Mexican home is ruled by an indomitable old matriarch, like Juan's mother, whose sons humbly do her bidding.

We had a good example of this authority when we asked Juan if he would lend us a dog to take along on our trip, for he had half a dozen assorted mongrels and we thought that a good watchdog would be excellent insurance for us and our belongings while we slept. Juan, however, said he was sorry but he needed all his dogs to keep coyotes away from the chickens. We took the refusal philosophically, but when Juan's mother heard about it she promptly overruled her son. Of course we could have a dog, and she would pick it for us herself!

Our expedition was gradually taking shape. Up in Salud's yard our two donkeys were spending their last days of peace, munching cornstalks and adding girth to their already plump bellies. One was a light gray, almost white female, loaned by Salud's nephew Damian, the other a smaller, darker male, the property of Eufrasia's brother Domingo. Being burros of *tierra fria*, they had shaggy coats, especially the little fellow, who wore great bangs over his eyes through which he peered with an expression of sweetness which we soon enough discovered to be a fraud. Since Indians do not give names to burros, we christened ours Perón and Evita.

Salud gave us several lessons in packing the animals. First you put on a *suadera*, or sweatcloth, made of burlap, then comes the *aparejo*, a heavy pad of burlap stuffed with straw which is cinched tightly around the burro's middle. The pack consisted of two wooden boxes per donkey, yoked together with ropes. These were slung over the back, loose bags and blankets were piled on top, and the whole thing was firmly roped together with a long reata, knotted by a complicated hitch. Everything had to be balanced just so, or the load would slip, necessitating an exasperating halt for repacking.

Our few supplies were bought, and our burros and our dog were ready. The day before we were to depart, Salud very diffidently asked us if we would not like to take his son Cuauhtemoc along. The boy was old enough to do a man's work, said Salud, but he preferred to run around the pueblo like a *bandido* and chase the girls. His father and mother had obviously talked this over between themselves and decided that going on a three-month walking trip might make a man of him. They were very shy about suggesting it, but it was clear that they were both keen to have us take him. He knew about burros, they said, and would help us take care of the loading and driving.

While we talked it over, Cuauhtemoc (he is named after a famous Aztec warrior-king) was scuffing the dust of the yard with his bare toes and pretending not to know that he was the subject of discussion. He was a slim, dark lad with a typical round Tarascan face. We had not planned to take anybody along with us, but we reasoned that a thirteen-year-old would not interfere in our decisions as an older man might, and that he certainly would be handy for the donkeys. At any rate, we did not have the heart to refuse, after all that Salud and Eufrasia had done for us.

"Tu Cuauhtemoc, quieres ir con nosotros?" Fred asked the boy.

"Pues—sí." He grinned broadly and kicked the dust some more in embarrassment, then ran off to tell his friends.

Cuauhtemoc came back to Erongarícuaro with us, driving the donkeys, and enjoyed a huge supper at Cholita's—probably the first meal he had ever eaten in a "restaurant." At seven o'clock of a chilly January morning we were on the road.

Perón and Evita trotted ahead, prodded by Cuauhtemoc, who strode along as proud as punch with a machete in his belt almost as big as he, and a new hat adorned with ribbons. The sun was rising over the lake, our breath was frosty in the still air, and in an hour we were under Arócutin, at the foot of the bluff.

Salud and Eufrasia were waiting for us with hot coffee and tortillas. Juan and his mother, who held the dog by a rope harness, were also there. Cuauhtemoc's parting from his parents was unemotional; there were no kisses or last-minute admonitions to keep his feet dry. Just goodbye and no turning back to wave. He knew they loved him. Didn't he have the beautiful new sombrero as proof of it?

"Adiós, que les vaya bien" (May it go well with you), they called after us. Fred and I, more sentimental than the boy, turned to wave at the little group silhouetted against the blue of the lake. Then a bend of the road cut them from our sight, and we were off for the mountains, the hot country, and the sea.

3 Christians—Mestizos and Missionaries

WE WERE ON THE ROAD TO ARIO DE ROSALES, A THREE-hour trip by car and a three-day journey on foot. When we had planned our trip, we termed this first stretch the "shake-down cruise," with the idea that anything that was at fault could be remedied in Ario, which is quite a big town and the last place of any importance we would find before striking into the unknown. A shake-down it certainly was, for we arrived in Ario with Fred lame, one donkey wounded, the dog missing, and Cuauhtemoc in tears.

It was longer than we thought. We were eventually to get used to the idea that all our journeys would be longer than we thought, but at the start we took for gospel the word of every Mexican we met en route who, smiling and anxious to please, would tell the tired voyagers that their goal was *"cerquita"* (very near). In time we came to think that the people we met on the road were not human beings but representatives of the Dark Powers sent to harry us. They would pop up anywhere—on a mountainside or in the middle of the desert—and when we asked them how far it was to such-and-such they invariably replied, "Está cerquita," with an expansive wave of the hand. "You are practically there, señor." Then we would walk three hours, four . . .

We had expected to make our first night's stop—Lake Zirahuen—by two in the afternoon, and actually arrived at four (which, had we but known it, was very good going). Zirahuen is a beautiful Tarascan pueblo, untouched as yet by *turismo* because there is no

21

paved auto road, only what is called in Mexico a *brecha*, or bad dirt road.

Our arrival was a dramatic one: as we began unloading Perón and Evita in the street outside the *hotelito*, there was a sudden blare of music from the village band and a galloping herd of bulls came tearing down the street driven by yipping, lasso-swinging vaqueros. We had walked into the middle of a fiesta, and the bulls were on their way to the ring for a *jalipeo*, the Mexican version of the rodeo.

We got the donkeys up on the sidewalk and prudently took shelter behind them: if anybody was going to be gored it would be they, not we. The bulls went by, heads swinging and mouths slavering with excitement, but our burritos stood their ground without so much as flicking an ear, and in a moment the herd was beyond us.

As in every rural community, the ring was a big stone wall with a corral annexed where the bulls were penned. Cuauhtemoc weaseled his way atop the wall in a strategic position, but Fred and I circled the enclosure for a long time without finding a place. At length a very drunk but gentlemanly Indian, recognizing a señora Americana, jumped down into the ring and called to me to take his place on the wall.

"But where will you sit?" I asked him.

"I shall stay in the ring," he replied grandly.

"That is dangerous."

"Señora," he declared, pulling his serape from his shoulder and swinging it in an unsteady veronica, "I have my cape!"

Room was made for Fred, with the result that we were all squeezed into our section of wall, unable to move. The wall was only six feet high, and our legs were dangling inside the ring, well within reach of the bulls' horns. This definitely added a thrill to the jalipeo—audience participation, as it were.

Jalipeos are the same all over Mexico. The bulls are let into the ring one at a time, lassoed and thrown by mounted cowboys, and a rope is tied around their middles. They are then mounted and ridden by daring youths while any number of would-be *toreros* sport about with their serapes and try to get the animals to charge them.

The beasts often turn out to be Ferdinands who simply run to the corral door and stand there bawling to be let out, but occasionally one sees a *toro bravo* who puts on a good performance. The show is very casually organized. When the bull is down and ready to be mounted, it turns out that nobody knows who is going to ride him, necessitating long palavers among the various aspirants. When finally the rider is picked, he has to borrow a pair of shoes from a friend, then the man who rode last has to take off his spurs (there never seems to be more than one pair of spurs available), and the candidate kneels down like a knight to have them affixed to the borrowed footgear. Usually the straps of the spurs will be broken in the process and there will be another wait while a piece of string is procured. Meantime the bull, tired of sprawling spread-eagled with his nose to the dust, manages to break loose and has to be caught again. The prospective rider decides that it is a good opportunity to have a quick one and wanders out of the ring in search of a friend with a bottle. . . . But that is part of Mexico.

Zirahuen, with its little, very blue lake, its wooded mountain peaks and Alpine climate, is a place we could happily have stayed for the rest of our lives. We could have rented a huge two-story house overlooking the lake for the equivalent of three dollars a month and eaten filet mignon every day for less than the cost of a can of dog food in Brooklyn.

The lake has an odd reputation. According to local tradition, no woman has ever drowned in it, although quite a few men have. The natives say the lake "does not like women," but loves men, and loves them to their death. I therefore went for a swim in the ice-cold water, and Fred had a good excuse to remain prudently on shore. After the swim I scrubbed our socks and underwear, using a rock for a washboard after the fashion of the Indian women, while a little way down the shore two of the participants in the jalipeo were bathing their horses with mighty splashings and loud cries.

Our dog followed us around the pueblo like a shadow. On the long, hot climb up to Zirahuen he had had to be pulled along on a rope, whimpering all the way and collapsing in every tiny bit of shade we came to. He was only a pup, and useless as a watchdog, but we had got fond of him, and he acted as though he were beginning to get fond of us. But much to our surprise, when we loaded up in the gray dawn to continue our journey on the following day, he was nowhere to be found. He had run home to his master.

It was all Robert Louis Stevenson's fault that Evita was injured. Our only previous information on the subject of donkey driving had come from reading *Travels with a Donkey;* in fact, we borrowed the idea of walking with burros from Stevenson. Readers of that classic will recall that R. L. S. had a great deal of trouble at first in persuading Modestine to do his bidding, no matter how much he beat her, and that a peasant finally taught him that a donkey can be miraculously stimulated by the use of a sharp-pointed goad.

Donkeys are creatures of habit entirely, and hate like the devil to do anything new. It so happens that there are no bridges around Lake Pátzcuaro; therefore, when we came to a wooden bridge over a rather deep stream, Perón and Evita stopped, sniffed it, and said No. We beat them furiously, feeling very guilty, but, after all, we had to cross the bridge. Cuauhtemoc, the supposed burro expert, was no more successful than we. He had never had to cross bridges before, either.

By dint of much labor the three of us managed to get Perón across, he being the smaller and less able to put up a successful resistance. Evita continued to balk, and it was then that Fred bethought himself of Robert Louis Stevenson, whipped out his sheath knife, and touched the point to Evita's stern. Instead of plunging forward, as one would expect, she plunged backward and impaled herself on the knife. Blood flowed fast, dripped down her hock and into the dust. By this time we were almost in tears from remorse and exasperation.

Giving up the bridge, we found a side path and managed to get

Evita across the stream. Cuauhtemoc simply giggled at our difficulties and said the wound was nothing. Before we could stop him, he swept up a handful of dust and rubbed it over the cut.

"No es nada," he said, and a passing Indian whose advice we sought also agreed that it was nothing. Probably we should have shaved the hair, and applied disinfectant and a bandage, but we trusted to the advice of experts and let nature take its course. As a consequence the wound festered, and it was a month before Evita's shapely rear end could be looked at without disgust. It did not bother her, however, and most fortunately it did not lame her.

This was the beginning of a series of burro ailments which convinced us we should have taken a veterinarian's course before embarking on our trip. Whenever we had such trouble we were deluged with advice and assistance, but most of it was worthless. Rural Mexicans seem to think that any ailment can be cured with pork fat, lemon juice, urine, or cut-up bits of cow intestines, and one self-appointed vet packed a wound with plaster of Paris!

In Zirahuen we were at an altitude of about 8,000 feet, and had to climb still higher before we descended. The ground was white with hoar frost in the early morning, and the road took us up through dark pine woods until the lake was a little blue postage stamp below us.

Our informants in Zirahuen had estimated that we might make Ario in one day walking *recio*, or fast, but this was an absurdity. Almost no Mexicans in the country have watches, and their estimates of time and distance are thus entirely relative. Furthermore, they walk fast, especially the Indians, whom you see hurrying along a trail almost at a trot, taking small, rapid steps and never stopping for a rest. Also, of course, the natives do not get lost, whereas we were continually taking the wrong branch of the road, or waiting at a fork until someone came to direct us. Since it is disheartening to turn back on a trail, we often walked two sides of a triangle rather than retrace our footsteps.

Our intention had been to reach Ario by a back way, without touching the paved highway that runs from Pátzcuaro; but somehow we missed the turn-off for the route, and late afternoon found

25

us trudging along an interminable dusty road in the wrong direction, lured on by reports that there was a big hacienda ahead where we would certainly get a bed for the night and a good dinner.

Our tongues were sticking to the roofs of our mouths. Dust was in our noses, eyes, and ears, and blisters were beginning to form on heels and soles. Mexican dust is like talcum powder, sticking to everything. It does not rain in this part of the country from early November to May, and along country roads one literally wades in the dust. It is no use washing, for you get dust-coated again in a moment.

The hacienda turned out to be squarely on the paved road along which cars, including those of our countrymen, zipped gaily toward Ario, with only a passing glance at the three dusty peons who glowered at them from the roadside.

It was a hacienda, all right, but the *dueños* were not in residence and the major-domo had just killed a man with his car and was trying to think up a good story for the police. Clearly we were not going to get the comfortable bed and good dinner of which we had been dreaming for the past three hours. Instead we begged hospitality from a poor mestizo family, where we were treated with such touching kindness that our discomfort did not matter. This was the first of many nights we were to pass in the houses of poor folk, and it was generally true that the poorer they were, the more hospitably they received us. They did not have much, but what they had was ours.

These people were called Tzintzun, and their dwelling was a collection of wooden hutments—a sleeping shack, a shack for the corn, and a kitchen shack. The latter had benches around the walls and an open fireplace, the smoke from which simply drifted out through gaps between the roof and the walls. Illumination was provided by flaring slivers of resinous pinewood. This was the center of their home, their hearth where, though they often went hungry, they could at least be warm, for wood was free for the cutting in the hills.

There was María Concepción and her husband, their two daughters and three sons, and María's old deaf grandmother, Mariana

26

Magellán. They had beans and tortillas which we supplemented with a can of turtle meat from our "iron rations," and later we broke out our instant cocoa and served it to everybody.

Our conversation with the Tzintzuns followed a pattern which was to become very familiar, and revolved around the chances of employment for a Mexican in the United States.

The United States of America, "El Norte," is the promised land for most Mexicans. So many *braceros* (day laborers) went from Mexico during the war to work on American farms that there are few settlements, however small, where somebody will not hail you with an " 'Allo, meester," and tell you that he knows your country and wishes he could go back there.

Some contracting for Mexican labor is still going on, but on a very small scale compared to the vast wartime migrations. The Mexicans who went to the United States during the war made more money than they had ever made in their lives, and for the most part they lived frugally and sent their savings home to their wives —or brought them home in the shape of cars, trucks, new clothes, sewing machines.

We met one man who invested his dollars in a car, started a taxi service in Pátzcuaro, and in five years was the proprietor of a bus line. Others put their savings into land and animals. Of course there were some who returned broke to their native pueblos, with nothing to show for their good wages but a few snappy shirts and hand-painted ties, but I believe these were the minority. A few did not come back at all, but married (sometimes bigamously) Mexican girls born in the United States and became United States citizens.

The thing María Tzintzun's eldest son wanted to know was whether he should wait, perhaps a long time, for a chance to go to El Norte under contract, or just go as a wetback, "*de contrabando*," as they put it. It is the easiest thing in the world for a Mexican to cross the frontier illegally at a dozen different places. At Reynosa, for instance, there is a man running a regular contraband ferry service across the Rio Grande, and the charge is five pesos a head to be delivered on the United States side. The border patrol cannot keep track of thousands of miles of frontier, and instead concentrate

27

on catching the illegal immigrants once they have crossed, picking them up on the roads, in buses, and so on. When they are caught, they are flown back to the interior of Mexico—Guadalajara or San Luis Potosí—to discourage them from returning. Formerly they were simply dumped on the other side of the border and reentered the next day.

Farmers in Texas appreciate this flow of cheap labor, and the Mexican soon discovers that being in El Norte *de contrabando* is a very different cup of tea from working there under a contract. He gets paid far below the legal minimum, and if he complains the farmer turns him over to the immigration service for deportation. Those who do not find the protection of a farmer are generally shipped back within a week or two, like our friend Juan Gabriel. But they keep doing it.

We slept on the first of many makeshift beds at the Tzintzuns'. They fixed it up for us in the kitchen with three wide boards on top of packing boxes, covered with a petate. It was hard as a rock, and we spent most of the night throwing wood on the fire, for it was very cold, and drinking coffee.

Cuauhtemoc, who was used to the cold nights, had elected to curl up with the Tzintzun boys on the porch of the corn hut, where he made himself into a neat little package in his serape, head, feet, and all. The burros crunched their cornstalks in the frosty moonlight.

The town of Ario de Rosales, which is the gateway to the hot country, has something of the atmosphere of a seaport, for there the people of tierra fria and tierra caliente meet and generate a great bustle of commercial activity. It is an ancient city, not often visited by tourists despite the excellent motor road, for once you get there there is nowhere to go but back again. No tourist car could brave the brecha—that infinitely romantic road of ours—that leads to the Rio de las Balsas.

The central plaza of Ario is a humming market square lined by prosperous shops and canvas booths where ranchers from the south can buy cloth and shoes and cooking pots, knives, saddles, sombreros, and baby chicks. Where they come from there is nothing to buy, and their eyes shine at the wonderful display of goods.

The shopkeeper in rural Mexico is a much more important man than the casual visitor might realize. Looking about one of these general stores, you would not say that it is worth very much, but appearances are deceiving. The individual sales are often very tiny —a few cents' worth of coffee wrapped in a scrap of paper, one aspirin tablet, cigarettes at a nickel a pack—but the volume is tremendous. Besides his shopkeeping activities, the proprietor probably buys and sells corn and seed, acts as agent for a Mexico City bank, and makes a few pesos lending money at a profitable rate of interest. He has a shiny new truck with his name written on the door, and he takes his wife and children to Acapulco, Cuernavaca, and Mexico City for a vacation every year.

In Ario, contributing to its "seaport" flavor, you find not only Mexican merchants, but a scattering of tradesmen from places so distant that you wonder how they ever found their way into this remote hive of commerce. We saw the names of Arabs, Jews, Greeks, and Italians over shop doors in Ario, and the best restaurant in town is run by a Chinese. As to Americans, we met only two, and they were not business people but missionaries. The story of how they received us is worth telling.

We had an acquaintance in Ario, a young fellow called Raul Villanueva, whom we had met in Morelia while both he and we were waiting to have our cars repaired. "Look me up when you pass through Ario," he had told us, and we did.

Our "expedition" came into town very much at the end of its tether. It had been a long, long walk for tenderfeet (eighteen miles), and both Fred and I were exhausted from our sleepless night at the Tzintzuns'. Fred, in addition, had worked up some very painful blisters with his new boots. We thought we would go straight to Villanueva to see if he had any suggestions about the best place to spend the night, for we were longing for civilized comforts.

Our friend was bubbling over with helpful ideas. He was a

Mexican of the modern, cosmopolitan type, well dressed, well informed, traveled, and very keen on things American, such as cars and mechanical gadgets.

"Look here," said he, "there are some American evangelists outside town who will certainly be very glad to see you, *verdad?* They have a farm—it was my father who sold them the land—and they can put you up for the night. It will be nice for them, and for you, too."

"How far outside town?" we wondered, but Villanueva told us not to worry, some friends of his were right across the street with their car and would drive us up. Later the boy could bring up the animals, verdad?

The "car" was a terrifying old jalopy which had to be pushed before it would start and, once started, would not stop, for it had no brakes. The three crazy men who seemed to be its joint owners laughed and yipped like cowboys as the machine hurtled over the cobblestones, narrowly missing burros, children, and trees. When we finally reached the farm, about two miles out, we were instructed to bail out, and the car continued on down the road, to return for us later.

The farm was recognizably American, for it had two cottages such as you might see anywhere from Maine to California, with windows, screened porches, and other non-Mexican touches. I had visions of a kindly lady who would serve us iced tea on the porch, draw hot baths for us, and perhaps miraculously produce an apple pie such as Grandma used to make.

The houses and fields were surrounded by barbed wire. We stood in our dusty sombreros and blue jeans outside this barrier waiting for somebody to see us, while trying to keep our knees from buckling from fatigue.

"Ah," said Villanueva, "someone is looking out the window. They will let us in in a moment." Sure enough, a window curtain had stirred. We went on waiting. Hope turned to puzzlement as fifteen minutes passed. At long last a young woman languidly came down the steps of one of the houses and strolled in our direction.

Her face and figure were bony, and her hair needed a new permanent. We introduced ourselves.

"Y'all must excuse me for keepin' you waitin'," she said, "but I thought you were Mexicans." She said the word "Mexicans" in the same tone which she had doubtless used in her native state speaking of "nigras."

She apparently did not think of the effect this remark might have on Villanueva (who understood English), but merely glanced over him as though he were part of the landscape. We should have left right away, but the porch still looked inviting, and perhaps there might be others in the missionary band who were less benighted.

As, in response to questions, we told the lady about our proposed trip, a lanky young man of the muscular Christian type joined us. He had a Bible in his shirt pocket. He too ignored our Mexican friend, but pumped our hands enthusiastically and wanted to know all about our expedition. Nobody mentioned adjourning the conversation to the house or offering us even a drink of water. It was very hot in the sun, even in the late afternoon, and they were perfectly aware that we had walked eighteen miles; but they kept us standing there outside the barbed-wire fence, and when they had finished exclaiming over our projects they began to tell us about theirs.

It seemed that there were two families of these self-styled evangelists, and we gathered that they endeavored to support themselves and their "work" by farming. They ran a Sunday school, they told us, and also there were a few "Christians" who attended their Sunday services. It was slow work, but they were confident of spreading the Gospel in this manner.

I had never heard anyone, no matter how anti-Catholic, refer to members of the Roman Church as non-Christians, but apparently these good folk felt that their own brand of Protestantism was the only creed that deserved to be associated with the Saviour's name.

In an effort to discover if in practice they lived up to this special and elect position as super-Christians, we asked them pointblank if they would take us in for the night. They were so sorry, but they just did not have room. They simply would not know where to put us. And there were hotels in town, of course.

In a Mexican home there is always room for a guest, even if somebody in the family sleeps on the floor. And these were our own countrymen—or to be more precise, my countrymen, for Fred was born in Italy, after all.

What sect these missionaries belonged to we did not stop to find out. It is to be hoped that pious folk somewhere back in the Bible Belt are not shelling out a weekly contribution to support the "good work" of these gentry.

When Villanueva saw that we were angry, he made it plain that he did not approve of the presence of these missionaries in Ario and had only taken us there because he assumed that they would receive us hospitably. He said that as far as he was concerned, Protestants were decent God-fearing folk, but the presence of their missionaries only stirred up trouble.

"What happens?" he said. "People like this come to a little town. They don't make many converts—maybe just two or three, but these two or three begin arguing with everybody else and create dissension. Pretty soon feelings are aroused which were never known in that town before." He added that he would not be surprised if the people of Ario threw the evangelists out. There had been incidents already.

The antique car of Villanueva's friends, meantime, had wobbled off into a ditch somewhere, and we had to walk back to Ario on our burning feet. Poor Cuauhtemoc was sitting in tears under the arcades of the plaza with the burros' lead ropes in his hand, while the animals themselves stood with their packs on, noses hanging down to the cobblestones. We made a resolve then and there always to unload the donkeys before doing anything else, and *never* to go looking for any more Americans. Those who were worth knowing would come and look for us. And in fact, they did.

4 Traveling with Two Donkeys

Do the great moments which people anticipate for years ever live up to expectations? We had gone to sleep every night in Brooklyn imagining the glory of the moment when we would leave Ario de Rosales and set our feet upon the road to tierra caliente with our hearts high, our burros stepping along briskly, and triumphant strains of imaginary music sounding in the background like a fade-out in the movies. Actually, the whole party was out of sorts.

Cuauhtemoc was again in tears, having been reprimanded severely by Fred for not seeing that the burros were properly fed in Ario. The animals had spent the night in a *mesón*, or donkey hotel, where we had paid through the nose to procure them a good feed of cornstalks. In the morning, however, they were listless and stopped to pull at every shrub on the roadside. Clearly they had not been fed. Our burro expert had thrown the fodder down and gone off to amuse himself with the local urchins, whereupon some arriero had come along and stolen our burritos' dinner to feed his own animals. We felt that we could take care of the donkeys ourselves better than that, and save money in the bargain, for Cuauhtemoc's maintenance was eating into our finances faster than we liked. Should we send him home while there was still an opportunity? Half a mile out of town we called a halt and argued out the question, while Cuauhtemoc snuffled at the roadside, hands in pockets and sombrero ribbons fluttering dejectedly.

Soon we were surrounded by a group of curious spectators, for the sight of two gringos setting out for the hot country on foot with a weeping Tarascan youth and two tired burritos is not to be seen every day. What was the trouble? they wanted to know. So we laid the case before them as a jury.

"You mean you were planning to take this *niño* [child] to the Rio de las Balsas?" said one of them. "Pero si no sirve para nada!" (He is no use for anything).

We replied that we knew he was no use but that his parents wanted him to come with us. Send him back, was the unanimous advice. He was too young for the expedition and would give us nothing but trouble. Besides, there were many *pestilencias* (pests) in the hot country. What if the child should get sick and die? The responsibility was too great. One fatherly-looking señor said that he himself was taking the bus to Pátzcuaro that afternoon and would take the boy along.

Cuauhtemoc's weeping had stopped by this time, and it was clear that the idea of going home to Arócutin was not at all repugnant. After all, he had been to Ario, and none of the boys in Arócutin could say as much. We folded a few pesos in his brown fist to pay for the bus and a good dinner, with a little over for candy, and gave him a pat on the back. He was grinning from ear to ear as he went off up the road with the elderly señor.

Perón and Evita were grazing by the roadside. From now on we were to be the arrieros. We hitched up our pants, squared our sombreros and, after shaking hands all around, gave the donkeys a slap on the stern and started them down the road: "Anda, burritos!"

Now we were really off. Never mind if we had no dog to protect us and no Indian boy to run after the donkeys. We felt that we were masters of our fate at last, and ready for anything. The sun was high in the sky, and the long-needled pines along the road gave off a sweet resinous perfume, while before us stretched a vista of ever diminishing hills and a red road winding into the hot country.

Back in Ario we had spread out our maps before a group of gentlemen who knew something of the route ahead of us, and discovered to our dismay that the maps left a great deal to be desired. They

34

were the best that could be obtained, having been issued less than ten years ago by the Secretaria de Agricultura y Fomento, but the farther along we went, the more certain we were that the men in charge of the survey had simply settled in some convenient town and filled in the names and locations of the villages and ranches from information supplied by the local señoritas: the names were mostly wrong, the locations were quite haphazard, ranches were designated which had ceased to exist twenty years ago, while several important towns of fairly recent origin were omitted completely. The maps, in short, like Cuauhtemoc, "no servian para nada."

With the help of the men in Ario, however, we had penciled in a number of corrections, and by now had a fairly good idea of what was to come, at least for the next week or so. We were to travel about twenty miles due south on the truck road until we hit a place called Rancho Nuevo, where the route divides and you have a choice either of continuing southwest on the brecha that goes to the town of Huacana and thence circles back through the desert to the Balsas, or of following the rough trail *para bestia* (for animals) which continues straight south. Of course we elected the trail. Where trucks could go, what reason to walk with donkeys?

To be sure, there were not many trucks. During a whole day on the brecha only two or three would pass, jolting along in low gear at snail's pace, jammed with passengers, mostly men, who stood up in the back or, if there was room, sprawled on bags and crates of merchandise. The bulk of traffic still came on foot or *en bestia*, and one reason we did not get along the road very fast was that it is obligatory to stop and pass the time of day with every traveler one meets.

"Buenos dias, de donde vienen?" was always the salute. We explained where we had come from and where we were going, and the other fellow would do the same. Cigarettes were offered, and perhaps it would appear more convenient to continue the conversation sitting at the roadside, while our two southbound burritos exchanged greetings with the northbound donkeys or mules or horses. We would take the opportunity to ask about the road ahead and

35

what kind of hospitality we might expect at the next settlement. Our acquaintance in turn inquired where we had last spent the night and how had we found business. Had we sold a lot? It was then necessary to explain that we were not itinerant merchants but just people on vacation—a statement few of them believed.

When a Mexican peasant travels without a *carga*—that is, without a load of stuff he is going to sell, or has just bought—he does not need a donkey, much less two. He simply throws his serape, which is also his bed, over his shoulder, and a little cotton bag over the other where he carries his few pesos, some cold tortillas, a bit of cheese, and a bottle of water. In this manner he travels hundreds of miles.

At points where we unloaded our animals, people used to stand around with expressions of combined wonder and delight as we revealed our cooking pots, hammocks, lantern, cameras, and medical supplies. When we made it clear to them that the stuff was for our own use and not for sale, the next assumption would be that we were looking for gold or silver or to buy land or cattle or *something*. Nobody would make such a long trip with burros without good reason. Boys would disappear into their houses and come back with a fistful of rocks.

"*Mire*, señor, look how they sparkle. There must be minerals in them, verdad? And I can show you . . ." We would patiently explain that we knew nothing of minerals, whereupon the boys would sigh and put away their pebbles. Clearly the señores were very cagey and did not want to share their knowledge with anyone else.

We often wished that we *were* selling something, for we could easily have paid for our trip if we had taken another burro loaded with needles, scissors, knives, ribbons, and mirrors. Of course, we were in Mexico on tourist permits, which do not allow one to engage in business, but in tierra caliente nobody cares about details like that, and the people are hungry for things to buy. The door is never closed to a salesman in the Mexican hinterland; quite the reverse: he is a welcome guest. The women, especially, were always disappointed to discover that we had nothing for sale, and it was with difficulty that we prevented them from buying the cooking pots we needed and the clothes off our backs. If we had kept track of all the offers we received, I think our equipment would have ranked in popularity like this: the revolver, Fred's knife, my knife, the lantern, the hatchet, the frying pan, and the enamel coffee cups. Occasionally, when I had used some lady's kitchen to make coffee, she would set the little enamel cups on a shelf, hoping that I would forget them. She would never steal and she would not hide the cups, for that would be dishonest. But if I were to forget them . . .

In these first days of our trip we quickly learned not to tell the passing traveler how far we really intended to journey, for those to whom we confided our plan of going down the Balsas, up the coast and back through the mountains simply thought we were *locos*. Instead, in reply to the inevitable "De donde vienen?" we learned to give the name of the settlement where we had spent the night, and in answer to "A donde van?" the next ranch on the trail. It speeded up the conversations and generally satisfied the questioner. Of course, when we met someone who was really *simpático* we would get out our maps, ask questions, and spread the whole story before him. But why not take a truck or a plane? would be the inevitable question. Look, by taking a truck the señores could have eliminated all this tiresome stretch of desert and mountains and arrived at the banks of the Balsas in a day. "But going by truck we would never have met you, señor," we would explain. He would laugh at this, for though it was the true explanation he thought it was merely a compliment, and would never believe it.

We were well out of Tarascan country by this time, and even in Ario, forty miles from Lake Pátzcuaro, Cuauhtemoc had attracted a certain attention from passers-by because of his typical round Tarascan face, which is not seen much in those parts. In the hot country for some time to come we were to see only mestizos, who varied from dark, small Indian-like folk to strapping blonds with big mustaches. Among city folk and cultured people there is a strong feeling of appreciation and affection toward Mexico's Indian groups—*inditos*, as they are fondly termed by those who love them. But you occasionally find prejudice against Indians in backward rural districts, often expressed by people who look very In-

37

dian themselves and live almost exactly as the Indians do. It is amusing to hear such folk, especially the women, refer to themselves in the old Spanish colonial term as *gente de razón,* or reasonable people, and to the Indians as *naturales.*

We met scores of people coming up from the hot country. They would be announced in advance by a cloud of dust, in the midst of which presently the shapes of men and animals would be discernible, and we would find ourselves engulfed in a sea of cattle, or else would be forced, with shouts and much running up and down, to disentangle our burros from the other fellow's and prevent Perón and Evita from turning around and following some fascinating new friends back to Ario.

The road went down gradually, and walking was easy. This was fortunate, for Fred had a newly broken blister on one heel and a consequent tendency frequently to find excuses for sitting on the roadside and smoking a cigarette. As we descended, the pine trees occasionally gave place to tiny settlements where banana and papaya trees grew in the dooryards of thatched huts. Wherever there were fruit trees, of course, there was water, and where there was water there were bridges to cross. Thus we began to learn the technique of persuading donkeys over places they do not want to go.

We discovered early in the trip that Perón had a little more courage about things new and different than Evita did. It was the only point in which he was superior to his female companion, and probably it was not courage at all, but simply lack of intelligence. When a bridge hove in sight, our technique was to get Perón in the lead, whistle unconcernedly as though everything was absolutely routine, and try to get the burro across before he realized that there was anything to be afraid of. Evita then would generally follow, sniffing each plank and blowing hard.

If this strategy failed, we would try to get Perón across by persuasion or, failing that, by main force. It does no good at all to beat them or to lose one's temper, for they will simply stand (as we had learned after Zirahuen), put back their ears, and endure anything rather than move forward. The trick is to inspire a sense of confidence, which we endeavored to do by encouraging cries and firm pushes from behind. Fortunately, our donkeys were not kickers.

When the bridge had gaps in it, however, as many of them did, there was nothing for it but to get help. If we were in luck, somebody driving animals in the same direction we were going would appear, and our balky pair would consent to follow, once it was demonstrated that an animal could pass. Without other beasts to lead the way, the burritos had to be virtually carried, a feat which cannot be performed by less than three people. One man pulls at the donkey's halter in front, while two join hands behind and lift the animal's stern off the ground. You then push him forward, wheelbarrow fashion, and if he does not want to fall down he has to make his front legs go.

People were always glad to help us in such difficulties. Otherwise, we would have left our bones on the near side of some bridge in tierra caliente as testimony to the stubbornness of asses.

In the first few hours after Cuauhtemoc's departure, we learned a great deal about our donkeys. Anybody who is choosing donkeys for a trip will save himself the most horrible difficulties if he selects animals which stop when they are told to stop. That, apart from health and strength, is the main quality that distinguishes a good burro from a bad one. In Mexico donkeys are always driven and never led. They trot along in front of their arriero, occasionally pausing to chew on a bush by the roadside, but usually starting again of their own accord before the arriero overtakes them. When a fork appears in the road, the driver of good burros can simply order them to halt until he catches up and sets them in the right path. The driver of badly trained burros has to run ahead and steer them, or, if he is too late for that, pursue them down the wrong road, turn them around, and drive them back to the fork. In the process of being stopped and turned, the bad burro will take it into his head to wander off the road into a thicket where the most fragile objects in his pack will be in danger of breaking as he crashes about in the underbrush. Calls to halt will have no effect upon the damnable animal, who by this time is afraid of being beaten and stops only when his pack is firmly wedged between two trees. While the driver fetches him, it frequently happens that the other burro will decide that wandering in the bushes is the order of the day, and will go crashing off in the opposite direction.

There is a legend about the breeding of the four original strains of Arabian horses, according to which an Arab king had the hundred best mares in his land enclosed in a corral without food or water and within sight of a beautiful fountain. When the animals were crazy with thirst, the doors were opened and they plunged toward the fountain. At this point the king ordered his trumpeter to sound the call for a halt. Out of the entire herd, four mares halted, and these were selected to be the founders of the new breed. Our burritos would have been the first to reach the fountain.

Evita, in fact, was a good animal at heart, and generally tried to do what was expected, but Perón had a bad influence on her. Upon the command to halt (which in Mexico is "Cho-o-o-oh!" or sometimes "Ch-ch-ch-o-oh!"), Evita would stop but Perón would keep going and pass her, whereupon, tossing her head, she would follow him. Eventually they would stop, but often not until they had rounded a bend of the road and wandered off into somebody's cornfield.

My husband was not naturally endowed with the philosophy essential to being a good arriero, and never attained it. His experience in the Italian cavalry might be supposed to have taught him something about animals, but there is a great difference between commanding troops astride a thoroughbred and trudging on blistered feet behind two wayward donkeys. I, on the other hand, appeared to have something of the burro in me—certain qualities of patience, stubbornness, and occasional wrongheadedness—which enabled me to get along with the little beasts. However, the two of us frequently were working at cross-purposes, and while Fred was beating one end of an animal I was patting the other. So Perón and Evita never knew what to expect.

The burros were not wicked all the time, by any means. There were hours on end when they trotted along quietly without giving us any trouble. All in all, they were far more biddable than I had expected; apart from their stubbornness (which, of course, is a quality of the whole donkey tribe), they did not give us any of the troubles which Stevenson seems to have had with his Modestine.

Perón very quickly showed himself to be the weaker of the two. Like Cuauhtemoc, he was really too young for the trip, and most of his faults could be attributed to his tender years. As time went on, Evita had to carry more and more of his load, but she did not seem to mind. Her attitude toward him was affectionate and protective, whereas with full-grown males she was scornful and stand-offish. She was a very maternal burra. The one distraction which could be counted upon to lure Evita from the path of duty was the sight of a baby burro; she could not resist them any more than some ladies can resist crossing the street to peek into a baby carriage.

Our first day's journey from Ario was a short one because of our late start, Fred's blister, and the fact that the animals were tired from lack of nourishment. At a little group of houses which called itself Puente Alto (High Bridge), Perón dramatically announced his fatigue by dropping in his tracks. We had paused at a roadside tiendita, a tiny open stand where drinks, cigarettes, and a few other commodities were sold, when, happening to turn around, I beheld Perón lying down with his pack and endeavoring to roll over. When a donkey lies down with his load, he is not just fooling; he is worn out. So we spent the night at Puente Alto, eight miles from Ario.

The people who ran the tiendita had a little adobe house and a pleasant yard full of shade trees, where a horse, and presently a cow, were tied up. They owned a sewing machine and other possessions which made it clear that they were people of substance, as it is reckoned in rural Mexico. The household was dominated by a delightful old lady whose word was law for a troop of little girls of all ages. The sewing machine was evidently kept very busy, for the children were all beautifully dressed in home-made frocks of pretty colors and designs (clean, furthermore, which is not so common in ranch families), while the men who showed up later were wearing hand-made shirts.

Their kitchen shack had a fine adobe stove and shelves of bright china and pottery, as well as a little porch with tables where the family could take its meals al fresco. We were served a supper of eggs ranchero (fried eggs with a spicy sauce of chile, tomato, and onion) and a substantial plate of beans and tortillas, after which we amused ourselves sitting on the stone wall which separated the house from the road and watching people pass.

Men and animals continued to go up and down until the sun sank behind the hills. The road, with its busy flow of loaded donkeys, mules, cattle, pigs, riders, and walkers, somehow brought to my mind the stories I used to read about England's Great North Road, in the days before the automobile. I had only to find my hero embarking on the Great North Road to be perfectly sure that he would meet with the most wonderful adventures. And now I was journeying myself on one of the few such roads left in the world. Even highwaymen were not missing from the picture, for we had been warned in Ario that there was a *gavila de ladrones*, an armed band of robbers, operating on the road. On no account were we to sleep in the open or travel at night, lest the bandidos spring from the underbrush and make off with our money—and perhaps our lives.

The rumor of the gavila accompanied us for some days as we went southward, until at length we reached an army outpost where we learned that the robbers were safely behind us. The sergeant of the garrison told us that his soldiers had been looking for the miscreants, but that it was not really a soldier's job and that a professional bandit hunter had been deputized for the assignment, a man called Huerta who was reputed to have been successful on several previous occasions. He was a rancher who hunted gavilas as a sideline. And brought them to trial? we asked. The sergeant said No, he usually shot them.

Our hosts at Puente Alto did not seem unduly preoccupied about the bandits, but stayed within their high walls at night and had a couple of very efficient watchdogs to give warning. The old lady told us that this road into the hot country had seen much history, and she herself remembered watching various revolutionary armies pass on their way to triumph or defeat, including the troops of Pancho Villa and Zapata. Like most old people, she had a tendency to think that things were better in the old days. Of course, people had less money, but they had enough to live on and they were not constantly faced with higher and higher prices. Maybe your man only earned a couple of pesos a day, but you always knew how many beans or ears of corn those pesos would buy, while today a peso is worth nothing and the price of beans and corn goes up all the time.

By the next night we were in tierra caliente. The hot country really begins after Rancho Nuevo, where, as I have said, the truck road branches off westward and the trail continues south. The truck road has to branch because there is a descent after Rancho Nuevo which takes you straight down the side of a mountain, over a jumbled mass of rocks where even a burro has a hard time keeping its balance. By the time you are at the bottom, with aching knees, you are in hot country.

Rancho Nuevo is a village lined up along the roadside in groves of dusty hot pine trees, and apparently it is a regular stop on the truck route, for in front of every shack is a table and a couple of benches where the traveler can sit down and drink a home-made *refresco* (soft drink). But by the time we arrived, which was rather late in the day, there seemed to be nothing left to eat or drink. We felt, no doubt unreasonably, that in a place like this there should be *something* to eat, but the ladies said, "Pues mire, señor, no hay nada" (There isn't anything), and so we pushed on.

This business of "No hay nada" began at Ranch Nuevo and continued off and on for the rest of the trip. The statement was not made the way an American housewife would say it. My mother, for instance, frequently says she doesn't know what she is going to give us for supper, but it always develops that there is a can of hash or a dozen eggs, not to mention potatoes, onions, and so forth. But the Mexican ranchero's wife who tells you she hasn't got anything to eat means exactly that. Eggs? No hay. Beans? Pues no hay. Maybe a cold tortilla? Tampoco. They are not holding out on you,

43

as you may see for yourself by looking around the bare kitchen. Of course, there is always corn, but it cannot be eaten raw. If you wait until tomorrow, the corn will be cooked overnight. At dawn the women will get up and make tortillas for the day, grinding the kernels on a flat stone with a long narrow stone for a pestle, then regrinding them and kneading and making the dough into flat cakes which they roast on a very hot, ungreased griddle. This corn bread is not just the basis of the ranchero's diet; often it is all he gets to eat. He seasons it by chewing on a little raw chile dipped in salt. If beans are grown locally, he will eat beans, too, but at the time we passed through the country there had been a poor bean crop and the price was considered very high. Some people simply could not afford them. Almost everybody had chickens and thus got a few eggs, but only on a festive occasion was a chicken killed. Everybody kept pigs, too, big fat ones which were regularly fed on precious corn, but for the most part they could not afford to eat the animals, and simply fattened them in order to sell them.

The traveler in Mexico's back country has to depend upon the people along the trail to feed him. No Mexican rancher would dream of refusing food to a guest, even if it means that his family must go on short rations, for he knows how hard the trail is and how hungry a traveler gets on a long day's march. In our case, we always paid for our food in the humble homes that took us in, but I believe our welcome would have been just as cordial in most places even if we had not had a peso in our pockets.

Most people who walk the back trails, however, are accustomed to a slim diet, whereas we had just come from American abundance, and the tortillas and eggs that would satisfy an arriero barely sufficed to take the edge off our appetites. Judging from the relative plenty among the people around Lake Pátzcuaro, we had assumed, when we planned the trip, that we would always be able to buy food from housewives along the way. In fact, I remember responding airily to questions on the subject, "The people must eat down there, and we shall eat what they eat." A more correct reply would have been, "If they starve, we shall starve along with them."

With a few notable exceptions, we were to be hungry most of

44

the time that we spent in tierra caliente, and the problem of finding food was more difficult than any other we encountered. What we found we accepted gratefully, and when we found nothing we did our best to be philosophical. The ranchers gave us all they had, and if it was not enough, well, *paciencia*, perhaps tomorrow would bring better luck.

At least we had our iron rations, such as they were. We managed always to carry a good supply of coffee and sugar and rice, and we left Ario with half a dozen cans of meat and fish. In addition, I usually had a can of *manteca* (lard) and an onion or two. When our hosts proved to have nothing to offer, we would resort to the pack boxes and throw together some kind of meal—always based on rice—and would invite them to share it with us. It was coffee that kept us going, however, for we had plenty of it, and we brewed it strong and sweet. We often set out in the morning with nothing but coffee, and walked for hours on it.

The descent from Rancho Nuevo into the valley below was a good introduction to Mexican trails. While the brechas have to be constructed to take slopes in a gradual way, the trails just go straight up and straight down, except in a few cases where the climb would be too steep even for a mountain goat. This trail was like a stairway for giants hewn out of the rock and then dynamited. For some time I scrambled ahead of the burros in an effort to pick the way for them, but it soon developed that Evita was better than I at that sort of thing. Several times we had to call a halt and rerope Perón's pack, which kept slipping up to his shoulders and threatening to upset him. Why it was always Perón's pack I don't know, for the two animals were loaded in exactly the same way. Perón was just that kind of donkey.

At Rancho Nuevo we left the pine trees behind and came down into fertile, semitropical vegetation, among which we distinguished the fronds of banana and coconut trees. The valley was rimmed by mountains on all sides, so that it was difficult to see how we were to get out of it, and beyond the immediate mountains peaks bulked to the southward as far as the eye could see.

A half-hour's walk across the floor of the valley brought us to El

Limón (The Lemon), a tiny village well watered by mountain streams which flowed beside the trail and into which our donkeys gratefully dipped their noses. At El Limón we and the burros passed the night together in a mesón. The accommodations for Perón and Evita were excellent—a nice little stall under a tile roof— but there seemed to be nowhere for us to lay our heads but the stone floor. The mesón had been a flourishing caravanserai in the days when all the traffic to and from the south had to pass over the mountain trail, but now, by-passed by the brecha, it seldom housed guests.

A swiftly flowing brook ran right through the center of the courtyard, and it was with great relief that we pulled off our sweaty boots and bathed our feet. Both of us had a number of blisters by that time and, although by keeping them well bandaged they did not cause too much trouble, it was always good to get out of our boots and to put on moccasins and clean socks in the evening.

The people of the mesón were celebrating somebody's birthday or some saint's day, and the place was bustling with guests and racket. We ought to have stretched our hammocks in a corner of the yard and endured the noise, but there was a magnificent full moon and we were tempted to take our serapes out into a nearby pasture and sleep in the soft grass.

When we headed for the pasture with our blankets, one of the girls of the mesón called after us that we had better not sleep there, the place was alive with *niguas*. We supposed that niguas were some sort of biting insect, and did not pay much attention. If we got bitten too much, we would return to the mesón. As it turned out, we did not feel a single bite of any kind and passed quite a restful night. It was several weeks before we discovered that niguas are indeed insects, not the kind that sting but the kind that bore.

We had come to the hot country prepared to face snakes, scorpions, tarantulas, and the other sinister poisonous creatures that are generally thought of in connection with the tropics. No one had told us about niguas. They are a flea-like insect, the female of which eats her way under the skin of your feet and there lays her eggs. If left to themselves, the niguas will grow and multiply in your foot until you have a very painful and dangerous ulcer.

It was perhaps a week after leaving El Limón that I noticed what I thought was a broken blister on the sole of my foot, but yet it was not quite like a blister, for there seemed to be something inside and, when squeezed, black watery liquid oozed out. Still innocent about niguas, I assumed that it was an infected blister, doused it with disinfectant, and hoped for the best. After a day or two Fred complained of a curious blister on *his* foot. Ignorant that we were acting as hosts to growing colonies of parasites, we walked on the niguas with increasing discomfort for about three weeks, until finally somebody happened again to mention the peril of niguas and we discovered what our "blisters" were. They had to be cut out, leaving impressive holes where the tissue had been eaten away.

5 The Son of the Crocodile

How hot is the hot country? when it becomes a physical impossibility to be out under the sun after eleven o'clock in the morning, then you know you are in tierra caliente. What degree of heat is reached in the midday sun we never found out, but in the shade it often hits 100 and hovers around 95 until the sun goes down.

From El Limón until after crossing the Rio de las Balsas we found ourselves traveling in one of the hottest regions of Mexico. The animals suffered even more than we did, for they were donkeys of tierra fria, accustomed to the cool breezes of the high central plateau. We expected them to shed their long coats eventually, but they did not, and indeed became an object of curiosity for the people we met, many of whom had never seen a shaggy burro before. In tierra caliente burros are used less than in the north, and anybody who can afford to do so keeps mules instead, which are stronger and bear the heat better. We ourselves had considered taking mules but were horrified at the price we were asked. Around Pátzcuaro mules were selling at 800 pesos—almost $100—and they cost twice that much in tierra caliente, while a good burro could be bought for 80 pesos.

Our little animals stepped along briskly in the hours before sunrise. But when the sun had been up an hour their energy began to flag, and by ten o'clock they would be plodding along with their noses an inch from the ground. We ourselves were not doing much better.

48

The desert in the part of Mexico we were now entering is not the flat, monotonous land that you find in the north, but a mountainous rocky waste overgrown with cactus and shrubs which at this time of year were leafless and dry as a bone. From a distance many of the desert hills appeared to be verdant, but upon close inspection the greenery turned out to be only the fleshy, plate-like branches of cactus trees.

The desert began after we had climbed out of the valley of El Limón and down another precipitous rocky incline which brought us about noontime to a pretty village on the shores of a little green river. It was called La Playa (The Beach), and we stopped there largely because Evita needed some veterinarian attention. The wound on her stern was at its most unsightly stage, exuding pus and occasionally bleeding afresh, and we were afraid of flies getting into it. The local gentry at La Playa advised *unto de puerco* (pork fat) as a remedy, and thought we might obtain it at a house on the riverbank to which they directed us.

It was in this manner that we met our first Pinto. In the old days people believed that the Pintos were a distinct race of Indians, and legend even held that they were the result of a mating between a Mexican demigod and a female crocodile. They are distinguished by their skin, which is mottled dark brown and vivid pink. It has now been ascertained that this disfigurement, which can be hereditary as well as acquired, comes from the bite of a tiny fly which is prevalent in these parts. Strangely enough, only people with Indian blood seem to be affected by the disease. At any rate, the Pintos, because of their grotesque appearance, have a reputation for being fierce and wild. Even in Ario, where people should know better, we had been warned about them. "Look out for the Pintos," our advisers said, "*son bravos.*"

There was nothing *bravo* about our first Pinto—nor any other Pinto we met, for that matter. He was an old, whitehaired gentleman, with a very sweet smile upon his brown and pink countenance, who urged us to unload our burros and come to his porch for a siesta. When we spoke vaguely of journeying on, he advised us against it.

"You are in tierra caliente, señores," he said drawing up chairs for us, "and you cannot travel in the midday sun here. Nobody does. Besides, the road ahead is *muy pesado* [very difficult]: black volcanic sand without shade or water."

As he spoke, another group of travelers came down the trail into La Playa, a family with half a dozen loaded burros and innumerable children. They promptly unloaded their animals, built a fire, and prepared to have dinner under the shade of a big tree. In fact, it was getting hotter by the minute, and we were very glad of the Pinto's invitation to stay and eat with him.

As well as meeting our first Pinto in La Playa, we ate our first *carne seca*, or jerky. In the hot country, obviously, fresh meat cannot be kept for more than a day, and therefore when an animal is slaughtered most of the meat is cut into thin strips and dried in the sun. It is then heavily salted and lasts for months, getting harder and harder as time passes. Jerky is never very appetizing, but it is meat, and a good cook, with much trouble, can make it edible.

The Pinto's wife first washed the meat several times, shredded it into bits, and then softened it by rubbing it on her *metate* (corn-grinding stone). After this preliminary process, she made a sauce of tomatoes and chile in which she stewed the bits of meat and into which she stirred a couple of eggs. It was served to us on rice (our contribution to the meal) and tasted quite decent. Careless cooks, however, simply fry or roast the jerky, and in that case it is unpalatable. The sight of a line of meat drying in the sun was always welcome to us, for it meant that an animal had just been slaughtered and that we were still in time to get a meal of fresh, or almost fresh, meat.

As the heat increased, we were gripped by a feeling of deadly lethargy and could scarcely make intelligible answers to our host's questions. The traveling family under the tree had finished eating and were all asleep, their heads propped against their carga, which they had stacked up carefully in the shade. Our donkeys had stopped nibbling their cornstalks and were lying down with their eyes closed, their noses drooping in the dust.

The only bed in the Pinto's house was on the porch and was occupied by a grown son of the household who was laid up with an infected foot. Observing our drowsiness, the old man told his son to find himself another place and urged us to take the bed for a siesta. With muttered apologies, we stumbled across the porch and flung ourselves down, sleeping heavily for an hour or more.

Beds in the hot country are very intelligently made. They are nothing but a big square wood frame with legs, upon which strips of rawhide are laced. Upon this "spring" you throw a petate or two, and thus have a comfortable and hygienic sleeping place. These beds are called *catres*. In homes nearer to civilization they are sometimes made with burlap or canvas, rather than with rawhide, and occasionally are built to fold, like camp cots. In the poorest ranch homes they are not movable but "built in": four pieces of wood with crotches are sunk in the ground to support the frame, and if there is no rawhide or cloth handy the springs are made of slim saplings, about half an inch in diameter and carefully chosen for straightness and uniformity. Even these are not too uncomfortable if padded by a couple of straw mats.

We soon discovered that any bed was preferable to a hammock. Taking a nap in a hammock for an hour or two is very fine, but spending the night in one is far from restful, especially if it is cold—and to our surprise it was cold at night even in tierra caliente. On our whole trip we slept only one night without a blanket, and very often wished we had more than the one serape apiece we had allowed ourselves.

Our hammocks were probably not the best that could be designed. Like the rest of our equipment, they had not been bought expressly for the trip, but had already served a long and useful life supporting devotees of hammock reading under the apple trees in Maine. Incidentally, they were impregnated with salt from their service on the seacoast and thus absorbed any trace of moisture out of the air. One was an old navy hammock of canvas, and the other was a slightly larger model which boasted a fringe and a trace of what must once have been bright colors. Fred, being slightly taller, had the latter, and I got the navy job. Each of us thought the other fellow had the best of the bargain.

51

We endeavored to sling the hammocks carefully so that they would have an even curve; but it generally turned out that the lashings would slip a little, and we would discover either that our heels were higher than our heads or that we were constantly slipping downhill, getting our feet entangled in the ropes.

It takes about fifteen minutes to get comfortably settled in a hammock, and we always tried to have everything at hand that we might possibly need during the night—generally piled in our sombreros on the ground under us. We slept in our clothes, so that undressing was unnecessary, although if clean underwear and shirts were indicated we generally put them on at night, after our hosts had retired, rather than in the morning when, with the whole household assembled to watch our departure, there would be no private place to dress.

Since it was almost always chilly, we put on sweaters to sleep in, and usually socks and neckerchiefs as well. The technique is to roll up in the serape so as to make a long neat bundle with feet, shoulders, and everything tucked inside. After sleeping this way on your back for an hour or so, you generally wake up with a sense that your spine is about to snap; it then becomes necessary to turn over on one side, a process which of course disrupts the neat bundle and requires a new wrapping. By this time you are thoroughly awake and discover that you need to go to the bathroom, that is, the yard, which means beginning the whole packaging procedure all over again.

Pigs are another bother. Everybody keeps pigs in Mexico, and the animals roam around loose, scavenging for food even on the porches of the houses. We were frequently awakened by a soft bump from below, which meant that a pig was passing under us. Occasionally they did not merely pass under, but stood there and scratched their backs against ours. And the little pigs would run off with our moccasins to try out their teeth.

But all these discoveries were before us as we entered the hot country, and we were quite eager at the start to try our hammocks. We got the opportunity at a settlement called Agua Blanca (White Water), where we arrived at sunset and begged hospitality of a little old woman. She lived in a tiny thatched hut without even a porch and had another tinier hut for a kitchen, the two being surrounded by a fence of rails.

We had left our Pinto friend at about four o'clock and had walked for three hours through very fine black sand interspersed with bits of lava, the product of some fairly recent volcanic eruption. The sand was hot, and hard to walk in and, as the Pinto had warned us, there was no shade at all on the trail, just organ-pipe cactus and thorny desert bushes.

The old lady at Agua Blanca gave us an unexpected treat for dessert—honey. Of all things which we might have brought with us but did not, sweets were what we missed the most. We both have a sweet tooth, and at home we used to eat quantities of French pastry and ice cream, but somehow we had set off on this trip without thinking to bring even a jar of jam. In rural Mexico people simply do not eat sweet stuff, except sugar cane if it is grown nearby, so the old señora's honey was a very welcome surprise.

But we were firm about refusing the old lady's bed. Two weeks later we probably would have accepted the offer and let her sleep on the floor, as she was perfectly prepared to do. But at the start we were chivalrous. The kitchen hut was just wide enough to sling our two hammocks from the crossbeams at either side, but as I was preparing to pass the ropes around the beam the señora took them from my hand.

"Oh, no, not that way," she said. "Don't put your hands up in the thatch; there may be *alacranes*" (scorpions). She herself managed to throw the ropes over the beam without touching the roof or side walls.

"Are there many scorpions around here?" we wanted to know. She said that there were plenty and that they stung fiercely. Generally one did not die, but it was very painful and made a person sick for several days.

All that night the thatch rustled over our heads, and at each rustle we pictured scorpions scuttling about and preparing to drop on our faces. I believe that the noises in the thatch were largely caused by the strain of our hammock ropes on the beams, for every time we moved there was a new set of noises from above. We both pretended to accept this explanation, at any rate; but whenever a new rustle came I would hold myself rigid for a moment, waiting for something to drop on me, and I could sense that Fred was doing the same. Occasionally we lighted cigarettes and exchanged remarks, such as that there was no use being afraid—there probably weren't scorpions at all. Secretly, we knew there were.

At length we slept, as tired people will, and in the morning there was not a sign of scorpions, though we carefully shook out our blankets and emptied our boots before putting them on. Like all unpleasant conditions, we soon got used to the idea of scorpions and seldom gave them a thought, beyond never putting our hands into a place where we could not see.

People in the hot country seem to have a sort of pride in all the discomforts and pests of their land, and even the kindest of them take a certain perverse pleasure in observing the suffering of a stranger—just as sailors will enjoy the sight of a landlubber hanging green-faced over the rail. We actually saw very few of tierra caliente's famous poisonous creatures, but we heard enough hair-raising stories about them.

The night after Agua Blanca we spent at a ranch called Las Anonas where our host, a very talkative old gent, kept us awake late into the night with blood-curdling tales of snakes and scorpions. Oh, yes, he had been stung by alacranes several times, but, *gracias á Dios,* he was strong and had survived. Children, however, generally died from the effects of a scorpion sting; his own brother, down the road there, lost a niña a few months ago.

This man had heard vaguely of injections to counteract the scorpion's poison, but it had never occurred to him to look into the matter. He said the only thing to do was to rest and, if possible, to drink a concoction of *hojas de mango* (mango leaves) which was reputed to be very helpful. As to cutting the wound and sucking out the poison, he said that some people used this method for snake bites, although he did not fancy it himself, but that it did not work with scorpions.

This apathy toward a menace which can strike down the healthiest child and even bring an adult close to death's door was not universal in tierra caliente, for we later encountered more progressive settlements—equally far away from civilization—where a supply of the antidote (I believe it was a calcium preparation) was always kept on hand for community use and several señoras were trained in the art of injecting it.

In this entire desolate region, from Ario de Rosales downward, there are no doctors. So far as we could see, in rural Mexico there are no federal or state programs to bring medical aid to the remote and poverty-stricken hinterland. The people are woefully ignorant of how to treat sickness and injuries and often employ remedies which are at best useless and at worst actually harmful. They take aspirin for anything and everything, because this is one *remedio* that is cheap and available at any tiendita, and they drink infusions of various leaves—such as mango, orange, lemon—to which they attribute wonderful powers.

Everywhere we went, the first thing ranch families wanted to know was whether we carried any remedios. "Remedios for what?" we inquired. Oh, anything, so long as it was medicine. They felt weak, had pains here and aches there, and could the señores give them something to make them feel better? Often it was just plain malnutrition from which they were suffering, but sometimes it was worse than that.

At one ranchito we were asked for a tonic to build up the strength of a child who was *débil* (weak). Upon our inquiring just what sort of weakness the child had, we were informed that he had been very sick with fever some months ago, a fever which had raged through all the nearby ranches and killed several children. Now it seemed that some of the children who had recovered were unable to walk.

"But apart from being crippled, the boy is healthy, eats well?" we asked.

"Oh, si, señor. He eats everything and feels good, but when he tries to stand up he fall over—like this." The father made his knees buckle to show how it was.

It was clearly a case of infantile paralysis. We told the man there

55

was no use giving his boy remedios; the only thing to do was to massage the boy's legs and take him to swim every day in the arroyo where he could build up his muscles. To cheer the poor man, we told him that one of the greatest *presidentes* of our land had the same disease and yet had become a leader of men. Although the advice we gave him was probably all that could be suggested, we felt sure that the despondent father would have been much happier had we given him a bottle of some evil-smelling remedio.

At another ranch on the Balsas a man with badly inflamed eyes begged us for something to cure him. He carried a bowl of some yellow liquid in which he was constantly dipping a very dirty rag and bathing his eyes.

"What is that you are using?" we inquired.

"Urine," he said. "It is supposed to be very good, but for some reason it doesn't help."

We gave him a tube of mercuric oxide and told him for heaven's sake to keep that filthy rag out of his eyes.

In Mexican cities there are usually too many doctors, all competing and few making a very good living, yet in the country there are not enough, for fees cannot be collected and doctors are called in by poor folk only in desperate cases. Even Erongarícuaro, which is a fair-sized town, has no doctor. A young fellow came for a couple of years to try to set up a practice there, but he could not make a living and had to move away.

It is ironical that millions of dollars are being spent in a joint effort to wipe out hoof-and-mouth disease among Mexican cattle while nobody cares about disease in the people. If a rural health service could be based upon the same organizational set-up as the foot-and-mouth-disease campaign, it would work wonders at relatively low cost. The cattle inspectors ride out on fixed circuits which cover all the ranch country and, when there is a suspicion of disease, send for veterinarians at headquarters strategically located throughout every state. The same system could be used with teams of visiting nurses (and I believe many could be found willing to devote a few years to such an adventurous career) who could report back to physicians stationed at clinics in various small towns.

56

This is the kind of program which "Point Four" ought to finance, and which would do more good in international friendship than millions spent upon propaganda and the entertainment of politicians.

Apart from such mysterious epidemics as the outbreak of polio which I mentioned, the prevalent trouble in the hot country is *paludismo* (malaria). Almost everybody seems to get it, and it is accepted as an affliction sent by the good God for his own inscrutable purposes, and one about which nothing can be done. People do not realize that it is borne by mosquitoes, and if they did know it the knowledge would not do them much good. In the rainy season the whole country is deluged, and stagnant water collects in every hollow. Insects of every kind, which are bad enough in the dry season, multiply furiously during the rains. Some people put up mosquito bars to keep the pests from bothering them while they sleep, but of course they are bitten while they work around their homes or in the fields.

The dry season is relatively mosquito-less, but there are plenty of other insects. Coming down through the desert from Ario, it was the stinging flies that bothered us most—the same tiny black flies which supposedly give the Pinto his mottled skin. Their bite is sharp and painful, and itches afterward very much like a mosquito's but instead of raising a welt the fly leaves a little crimson fleck, and the mark lasts for weeks.

Occasionally we found entire settlements infested with fleas which dwelt mostly in the dust on the ground and attacked our legs about as far up as the knee. But the pests that we met in the desert and around the Balsas River were nothing compared with what the coast had in store for us.

When we were five days and fifty miles out of Ario, the expedition began to feel in need of a rest. We had not had a day off since Zirahuen. What had happened to our nice idea of walking five days and resting two days? The chief trouble with the plan was that it presupposed our reaching a place where we would like to spend two days, and the desert had not thus far provided the kind of creature comforts that we felt were indicated for a rest stop.

57

So on we trudged on our nigua-riddled feet while the pedometer which I carried in my belt ticked off the miles. The donkeys were as tired as their arrieros, especially Perón, who obviously was carrying too much weight and could not do so much longer. We had left Las Anonas very early in the morning, packing up by moonlight in order to travel as far as possible before the heat began. Our trail took us across a wide desert plain which was crossed and recrossed by a broad arroyo. We had to go through the arroyo at least six times, and it was generally too deep for us to pass by jumping from rock to rock. At every crossing we had to sit down and take off our boots, wade across, dry our feet, and replace the boots. The burros balked a little about crossing, but it was only a token objection and with some persuasion they went ahead: they did not really object to crossing water so long as it did not come up very high on their legs or flow very fast. Incidentally, whenever they came to water it would remind them that they needed to relieve their bladders, so that if we wanted to drink we would have to run ahead of the burros, or make a detour upstream.

Arroyo water tastes the same all over Mexico—chemical and brackish. If you bathe in it, it leaves traces of white salts on your skin, just as it encrusts with salts the rocks in its streambed. The difference between an arroyo and a river is that arroyos often dry up completely toward the end of the dry season, while rivers, having more distant sources, do not. We crossed some dry arroyos a quarter of a mile broad—jumbles of glaring white stones, with perhaps in the very middle a tiny trickle of water which even the animals would not touch.

I do not know whether all burros are as fussy about their drinking water as ours were, but we soon came to look upon them as water testers for us. If they drank (and especially if Evita drank, for she was the most particular), the water was probably all right for us. More than once I can remember filling our canteens at some little stream, only to have the donkeys sniff the water disgustedly and move on. In that case I would throw two or three chlorine pills in the canteens and hope for the best.

We had plenty of chlorine pills and ought to have used them

regularly, but we just didn't bother. The main reason was that the directions on the bottle said you had to wait half an hour in order to give the pills time to kill the bugs. Thirsty people can't wait half an hour, not when they have been out in the desert sun for three or four hours. We used the pills for a few days, then one day said the hell with it and threw ourselves down to drink at a stream. Before long we were doing what every other traveler did—drinking from arroyos and stopping at each ranch we passed to ask for a little "agüita," which we would drink gratefully from a community cup and think nothing of it. The pills were used only when we were forced to drink water that appeared stagnant or otherwise highly suspicious.

I would not advise anybody else to follow our practice, for I think it was bad and thought so at the time. However, it can be said in defense of our water-drinking habits that there is a far less danger of amoebae, typhoid, and so forth, in the country than in small towns where people live in congestion with privies often too close to the source of their water. Yet it is in towns that most people consider themselves safe, just because the water is presented in a nice carafe with a plate over the top, as though jealously preserved from all possibility of contamination.

In addition to water, of course, it was sometimes possible to get beer and soft drinks at the tienditas along the main trails. I have never cared for warm beer, so I generally bought the refrescos, which were not bad if put out by a big firm, but usually awful if they came from "amateur" bottlers. The latter operate in all the little towns in Mexico, and their technique is to make up a batch of some sickish sweet substance, slightly carbonated, and put it in old beer bottles with apocryphal labels, such as lime, lemon, or orange. As to where the water comes from, or whether the bottles are washed—well, a drink of arroyo water is probably much safer.

As we progressed southward, the price of beer, refrescos, and cigarettes went up in the tienditas, for freight rates were high, especially where everything had to come by donkey- or mule-back. We often paid more for two tiny half-pints of beer than for our dinner.

We stumbled across the arroyo for the sixth and last time at about eleven in the morning—time to take shelter for the siesta. Rounding the curve of a hill, we saw, shimmering in the heat ahead of us, a little cluster of shacks made of twigs and grass, where a great number of burros and mules were tethered.

This unprepossessing place, sprawling in a bowl of the intensest heat and cut off from any possibility of cool breezes by a ring of desert hills, this little hell, as it appeared, was known as Reparo de Luna (Moon Haven). It turned out to be one of the most delightful places we visited.

6 Moon Haven

To begin with, there was iced beer at Reparo de Luna. A fat señora sold it out of a gasoline refrigerator at two pesos per bottle. We thought that she was a mirage and that the frosty, sweating bottles she held out to us would disappear or turn into cactus before we got them to our mouths. But they were real, and it was good beer from Mexico City.

There is no use trying to describe what it is like to find an iced drink in the middle of the desert, but no Bedouin ever greeted an oasis with more joy than that with which we settled down for the week end at Reparo de Luna.

Reparo is frankly dedicated to the needs of the flesh, serving as a market for all the tiny hill and desert ranches for miles around, as well as a center of repose and rehabilitation for travelers. The brecha which we left at Rancho Nuevo here finds its way back across the western hills to rejoin the trail, so that truck passengers as well as arrieros stopped at Reparo for meals and cold beer.

The settlement actually is no larger than most of the tiny villages we passed, but instead of being spread out over half a mile of trail the houses are built in a compact square, and every house is a restaurant, a tienda, or a cantina. The area in the center, known as the *placita*, or little plaza, is a broiling hot stretch of sand where itinerant merchants spread canvas awnings to provide a little shade where they may display their wares, thus giving the placita something of the flavor of an Oriental bazaar.

Reparo also boasts a gold and silver mine which has been closed for some years but now is about to be reopened. The mine shaft is in the mountains behind the village, and the administration buildings and engineers' cottages are perched on a steep hillside ten minutes' climb from the placita.

After downing three or four beers and unloading our burros, we marched up the hill to see if we might find an engineer who would offer to put us up in one of the comfortable-looking cottages, but we were out of luck. The two engineers had hopped off to Mexico City in their private plane for the week end, leaving in charge a very crusty old major-domo who would not even give us the time of day. It was evident that he believed we were prospectors seeking information about the mineral wealth of the district. Our story of being journalists was clearly a blind to cover our search for gold or silver or uranium, and he was determined not to tell us a thing. As for spending the night on the mine property, we did not even ask but faced about and started down the hill.

Just below the mine buildings was a big spreading stone house with a wide veranda, which we had assumed to be the residence of some big shot in the mine, but upon passing it again we saw that it was a barracks. A soldier with unbuttoned shirt was sprawling in a chair dandling a child on his knees, his rifle propped against the wall behind him. Deciding to pay our respects to the military, we mounted the veranda and asked for the officer in charge.

He turned out to be a sergeant, a short, stocky fellow who looked trim and efficient in the dark green cotton uniform of the Mexican army. The life of troops in remote outposts such as this is informal and leisurely. Their sole purpose is to preserve order and protect property—in this case the mine—and they seem to feel in general that their mere presence is sufficient to carry out this mission. If one man were to shoot another in the placita of Reparo, the soldiers, if they happened to be around, would make an effort to catch the culprit; but if someone were to come and report a shooting which had taken place some hours before, the military would probably point out that by now the murderer must have fled to the mountains, and that, as everyone knows, it is no use chasing fugitives once they are loose in the hills.

In posts such as the one at Reparo, the married soldiers have their wives and children with them, and all live happily together in the barracks. If it is necessary to march on foot in order to reach some remote post, the women, who are known as *soldaderas*, march right along with their husbands, carrying their babies on their backs. We met one outfit on the coast which had marched in this fashion fifty miles in two days—a distance we had covered in four.

The sergeant at Reparo invited us to stay in the barracks, declaring that he could easily find us a room and an extra bed, but we refused his courtesy. We could not think of inconveniencing the military nor of trespassing upon their kindness. In short, we had no intention of spending our week end in a barracks; it was not our idea of a rest. We were preparing to take our leave when the sergeant, glancing at Fred's pocket, said in his most polite accents:

"Incidentally, señor, do you have a permit for that pistol?"

Fred was carrying the little .32 wrapped in a bandana in his front pocket, where it made a bulge which we had assumed was not noticeable. In fact, we had quite forgotten that permits are necessary for pistols in Mexico and that soldiers are required to confiscate any unlicensed arms. Fred heaved a sigh and placed the revolver in the sergeant's hand, admitting that we had no permit.

"But look, Sergeant, it is such a little gun," he said. "I carry it only to defend my mujer [woman] from bandits and wild beasts. You would not want to travel these trails alone with your wife without protection, would you? Besides, if I were planning to commit any mischief I certainly would have chosen a bigger pistol than this, don't you think?"

"Mire, señor," replied the sergeant, returning the .32. "We are supposed to confiscate all unlicensed pistols, but in your case . . . Well, just don't let me see it again. Hide it in your carga until you are out of town." And he looked the other way as Fred slipped the revolver back into his pocket.

Having subsisted largely on eggs and beans for the past week, we were intoxicated by the amount of meat we found in Reparo de Luna and the bustle of butchering activity in the placita. Pigs were being dragged off to slaughter squealing at the top of their lungs, squawking chickens were pursued by women with cleavers, beef carcasses were strung up and carved before audiences of hungry dogs that now and then exploded into snarling combat over a discarded scrap.

The placita boasted two *fondas*, shacks of interlaced twigs with grass thatches where a table and a few chairs were the only advertisement of the fact that meals could be purchased there. One of these became our headquarters, where we ate four or five times a day, chatted in the evening over bottles of beer, and, when the last customer had left, slung our hammocks from wall to wall and slept.

The proprietor of the place was an energetic little woman called Doña Cirila, who rejoiced both professionally and maternally to entertain guests who ate so much and relished her food so enthusiastically. She gave us meat for breakfast, meat for dinner, and meat for supper, and between times sent her handmaidens out to buy us cold beers without number.

It was a wonderful thing how much beer we could consume. Our budget was shot, but in the country ahead we knew there would be no more oases like Reparo until we hit the coast, so we spent our pesos freely. The beer did not seem to affect us in the least. It was so hot that the stuff just evaporated in our stomachs without either intoxicating us or making us seek the nearest bathroom. This latter point was a convenience, for the bathroom at Reparo was the desert, and it was an especially bare and treeless expanse where one had to walk a long way before reaching the relative privacy of a cactus or a dry streambed.

Mornings in Reparo were lively and energetic, but when the sun got up toward its zenith the hubbub began to ebb, people sought out shade and, after *comida*, took long siestas during which the placita was peopled only by scavenging pigs and dogs. To go forth in the desert in the early afternoon was to be hit by a sledgehammer of heat which brought on giddiness and spread a sense of unreality over everything. The mountains, the houses, and the cactus trees undulated in waves of heat. For some reason, when it is so hot, you feel odd little "cold" shivers, particularly up and down your legs. You do not sweat in such dry heat, for all the body's juices seem to dry up.

While we took our repose at Doña Cirila's, the burros rested in the shade of a thatched pavilion, along with a number of other transient animals, restoring the plump curves of their bellies on corn and *rastrojo* (cornstalks). To water them, we had to drive them almost half a mile away to the arroyo, where, tethering them to a tree on the bank, we took the opportunity to bathe and wash our clothes.

This arroyo—the same one which we had crossed six times in coming to Reparo—was the settlement's only source of water. Since the stream was hot and rushed over the rocks with considerable force, the ladies of Reparo found it more convenient to bring their dishes to wash there, rather than to bring washing water to their houses. There was always a quaint procession of señoritas wending their way from the village in the late afternoon, carrying upon their heads zinc tubs full of plates and cups. They would deposit the china in a suitable spot where the current was rapid, but not too rapid, wait until the water had done its job, then stack the dishes into the tub and start back. By the time they were home, the sun would have accomplished the drying. Toward the end of the *seca* (drought), we were told, the arroyo dries up almost completely and the women have to dig holes in the streambed and painfully dip their water by the cupful as it oozes out.

The half-mile walk to and from the arroyo was tiring, especially after bathing in the warm, enervating water, and it was at Reparo that I made my first experiment in bareback burro riding. Fred never cared for this form of equitation (possibly because the elegant young lieutenant of cavalry that is dormant in him recoiled at the thought of such a mount), but I found it quite useful to hop aboard Evita when it was necessary to drive the animals a long way to drink or pasture.

The trick of riding a burro is to sit as far astern as possible so as to avoid the sharp backbone in favor of the better upholstered rump. Without a bridle I found it difficult to steer the animal,

65

but managed to direct her by waving a stick on one side of her head or the other. She trotted along briskly and saved me considerable walking, though I would not have wanted to travel very far in that manner. Perón was no good to ride; being so small, the padded area of his stern was practically nonexistent.

Evita's wound was still causing trouble, and we found a very personable young man who guaranteed to fix up the sore with various secret and special remedies of his own. He was a boy of about twenty, who seemed to take quite a fancy to us, and to repay him for his services we invited him to a roast-pork dinner. So intrigued did he become with us that he proposed to accompany us to the Rio de las Balsas, declaring that he was going the same way and would enjoy having our company.

As we were preparing for bed, Doña Cirila came to us with an expression of concern on her kindly face.

"You must not let that boy go with you," she said excitedly. "He will kill you on the road and take your money." She explained that our friendly young man had a very bad reputation; he had killed and robbed a man when he was fifteen, and was suspected of various other unsolved murders. "He thinks you are very rich," she went on, "and if he wants to come with you it is only to put his knife in your backs in the middle of the night."

We were a little worried about this development and wondered how to evade the youth in a diplomatic manner, but Doña Cirila solved the problem. The next day we did not see our young friend around Reparo.

"He took a truck north," Doña Cirila told us with satisfaction. "This morning he came to me and started asking questions about you, how much money you had and what you were doing here. I told him you were *bien cargados* (well loaded), but not with money, with *balas* (bullets)." She had terrified the poor fellow with an account of our prowess as pistol shots, claiming that we both went armed to the teeth and had won numerous prizes for our skill as marksmen. The would-be robber, she said, turned green and slunk off to take the first truck in any direction.

Apart from Doña Cirila, our best friend in Reparo was Don Genaro, the proprietor of a small general store across the placita. We met him in the afternoon at siesta time when we were circling the marketplace in search of diversion. He had brought his catre out and placed it under the awning in front of his shop, where he could doze and still be prepared to wait on customers, if any turned up. Our first impression of Don Genaro was of a very round and brown stomach, smooth as a baby's; he was lying on his back with his shirttails out and his magnificent belly exposed to the possibility of a breeze. He lifted the brim of his sombrero half an inch—it was tilted over his eyes—and, seeing us, waved a plump brown hand languidly.

"Sit down; rest yourselves," he said. "It is too warm to be about." He made room for us on the catre, and the three of us sprawled together and talked away the hot hours.

Don Genaro was fascinated and horrified to hear about the long trip we were taking—and on foot, too, *que carai!* He was full of chivalrous concern about me. What was the señor thinking of to take the señora on such an expedition. The poor lady, how unhappy she must be! Did she think when she married the señor that he would drag her across the desert and the mountains on foot?

Fred and I both protested that it had been as much my idea as his, and that I was enjoying myself. Don Genaro did not believe it, and declared that Fred must have deceived me.

"I can see how it happened," he said. "You told the señora: 'Come, we are going to Mexico; we will take a marvelous trip in the tierra caliente. Don't be afraid, there are airplanes and buses and trucks to take us where we want to go.' And when you got her down here you made her walk, promising all the time that there were airplanes and buses and nice hotels to come. Every day she looks around and asks, 'Is this where we get the airplane?' And you keep saying: 'Not yet, *querida*. Now get busy and load those burros.' The poor señora."

He told this version of our story with great dramatic emphasis, imitating a woman's voice and then a man's voice and making gestures with his hands. At every pause he would look at me and ask, "No es verdad, señora?" (Isn't that so?)

Our plump friend thought that we ought to settle down in Reparo to make our fortune, and for a few hours, while we talked with him and with other men who gathered around, we almost considered it seriously. We could get hold of land for nothing, Don Genaro said, good land where we could plant *ajonjolí* (sesame seed). This was a great crop around Reparo, and people were making good money out of it. Naturally, señores like ourselves would not want to work the land; we would go shares with a poor man who would put in his labor for a half-interest in the crop.

Fred wanted to know whether we could breed mules in Reparo— an idea which he had been mulling over in his mind for some time, and which was becoming increasingly interesting, since the farther south we went, the higher the price of mules became. Don Genaro replied that we certainly could raise mules; there was pasture land for the asking, and one had but to buy some mares and a good burro and wait a few years. In the meantime, one could plant ajonjolí and live on that, verdad?

How had Don Genaro himself come to settle in Reparo? Well, it seems he had run off with another man's wife twelve years ago, and the two of them had set out for the hot country to find a place where they could live in peace. The reason he knew how Fred had lured me on with promises of airplanes was that this was exactly what he had done to get his stolen bride to follow him.

"I was penniless," he said. "I arrived here on a market day with nothing but a bag of green chile over my shoulder. So I sat down and sold them in the market, and that way we made a beginning. Today I have my store and my woman behind the counter and my *chamacos* [kids] growing up and learning the business."

Fred pointed out that there were strict laws in Mexico regarding immigration, and that we might get in trouble with the government if we settled down in Reparo; but Don Genaro shook his head vigorously.

"Here there is no trouble with the government," he said firmly. "You are our friend. That is all that counts."

We made another acquaintance in Reparo who struck us as a man of mystery, and although he eventually took us into his confidence to a certain extent we still felt that we would have liked to know much more about him. He was an itinerant merchant of cloth, Don Miguel, who was also taking his meals with Doña Cirila.

Fred and I were having a discussion about the road ahead and wondering at what point we should come out on the Rio Balsas, when Don Miguel suddenly spoke up in perfect English to answer some of our questions.

"But I didn't realize you spoke English!" Fred exclaimed. Most Mexicans who speak even a word of English make it known to you immediately.

Don Miguel smiled and said that he had been in the States a good deal. He was a tall, good looking man of about forty, almost white of complexion but with the high cheekbones and broad, low forehead of an Indian. He looked more like an American Indian than like a Mexican. He had a great deal of dignity and reserve and was obviously far better educated than the average traveling merchant. His English was not only perfect, but his accent suggested that he had learned it by being born and brought up in the United States, probably in Texas or Arizona.

Don Miguel was able to straighten us out about the trail ahead, for he had traveled it often himself. He said it was his custom to go as far as possible by truck, then hire donkeys and continue into the isolated countryside. After we got to know him better, he told us that every year he spent the winter in Mexico and the summer in the States. Knowing English as he did, his immigration status was never questioned. He simply crossed the border *de contrabando* and quickly moved northward to find a job in states where the immigration service is not active. No one would have suspected that he was not a native American; in fact, we had a persistent idea that he *was* and that he did not want it to be known.

There was something about the man which suggested a mystery in his past. He was aloof and spoke little, and the expression of his face, always composed and serious, set him apart from the rest of the gay, vigorous life of Reparo. He might have committed some crime, but we did not think so; he struck us more as the victim of some terrible tragedy or bitterness.

We hoped to meet him again, for he planned to cover some of the territory we were heading for, but he departed the night before we left and our paths never crossed.

Like all market villages, Reparo was the scene of some heavy drinking on Saturday night. The ranchers, after making their purchases, hung about the placita drinking tequila or alcohol, quarreling and singing and boasting, as drunks will. One young fellow was showing off his horse to the others, and in order to display the animal's speed he went careering off into the desert in the direction of the arroyo. Nobody thought anything about it when he failed to return, but long after the village had gone to bed there was a sudden burst of talk and excitement in the placita. Someone on his way to the arroyo had found the horseman dead under a tree. What had happened was obvious. He had ridden under a low-hanging branch which had taken him right in the forehead and killed him instantly.

The next day the offending branch was cut down, and a little cross of sticks was erected to mark the scene of the tragedy. Wherever anyone dies in the open in Mexico, a cross is put up, usually unmarked, so that people passing may ask a blessing for the poor devil, whoever he may be, who died there. Some of the dangerous mountain highways are lined with these somber monuments.

The body was housed in one of the shacks on the placita for the night, and next day the boy's mother came and took him away. Everybody felt sorry for her; but then, as Don Genaro observed, we all have to die some time, and he was happy when he died, at any rate.

Before setting out on the trail again, we decided to see if we could not lighten the animals' carga. To this end we unpacked everything from our boxes and bags, while an inquisitive audience of about twenty men and boys stood around admiring our possessions and wondering what they were worth. One man fell in love with our hatchet and, since it seemed unlikely that we would ever need it, we sold it to him for fifteen pesos—a couple of dollars. We gave Doña Cirila a big frying pan which was heavy and took up more room than it was worth, and jettisoned a few other items for the same reason.

In this manner we were able to eliminate the two boxes which Perón had been laboring under and to replace them with two bags. Perón thus carried the clothing, hammocks, and serapes, while Evita, in her boxes, took the heavy equipment—rolls of film, medicine kit, food, and the like. This was tough luck for Evita, but she was a strong burra and would carry anything we piled on her back. Having completed our reorganization, we were ready to pull out of Reparo on Monday morning.

We hated to leave, not just because of the iced beer and meat, but because we had made warm friends there whom we knew we probably would never see again, and the thought of "never" is always a sad one.

7 Under the Southern Cross

To TRAVEL IN THE DESERT BY MOONLIGHT IS A WEIRD and enchanting experience. Except for the distant bark of a coyote, there is absolute stillness; the donkeys' feet make no sound as they trot along over the sandy soil; the towering cactus trees cast odd shadows, and every bush at the roadside looks as though it might be a crouching bandit. The cold illumination of the moon gives plenty of light to see the way, but it has no depth, so that occasionally the walker stumbles over a stone that did not appear so large as it was, or takes an exaggerated step to pass over an imaginary obstacle that turns out to be only the shadow of a clump of grass.

South of Reparo we found that the only way to make time was to travel with the moon. If we waited for sunrise and for the señora of the house to prepare breakfast, the heat would already be upon us at the start of the day's walk, and in a couple of hours we would have to seek shelter until late afternoon.

The moon, which had been almost full that night at El Limón in the field with the niguas, was now on the wane, but for another week it would still provide enough light to walk by in the early hours of the morning. Since we never slept very soundly in our hammocks, we needed no alarm clock to tumble out at two or three o'clock in the morning. At that time the air was deliciously cool, almost cold. Getting dressed was a matter of pulling on our boots, buckling our belts, and making sure that knives, first-aid kit, pistol, pedometer, wallet, and cigarettes were all in their proper places.

Trying not to awaken our hosts, we would tiptoe about, collecting and repacking our gear, unslinging the hammocks, whispering maledictions at the night-prowling pigs. Fred would then go off to fetch the burros, which were generally tied nearby, dozing over their pile of fodder, and while he cinched them into their working harness I would make coffee—usually our only breakfast.

The Primus stove which we brought with us especially for coffee making had worked beautifully in the first days of the trip, but, like all such gadgets, it refused to function when we really needed it. We still had a pint of gasoline, however, and I discovered that a few corncobs sprinkled with gas produced a fine fire almost instantaneously, and there are always corncobs scattered around the yard of a Mexican ranch. Our coffee was finely powdered and very black, and we used to boil the sugar along with it and then clear the grounds by throwing a burning ember into the pot. Two or three cups of this brew gave us strength to face the day's march. Sometimes we would reheat a couple of cold tortillas on the embers, but they were hard to choke down and generally, after a bite or two, we would feed the remainder to Perón and Evita, for whom they were a great luxury.

Breakfast over, Evita would be loaded with her boxes and Perón with his bags, reatas would be cinched around the loads, lead ropes wrapped about the animals' necks, and the party would move off silently down the trail.

At eleven o'clock of the morning we left Reparo, we were forced to stop for siesta, hanging our hammocks in the porch of a rancho and sleeping for two hours a drugged sleep that left us feeling just as tired as before. At sunset we were in a settlement called Cueramo, the last stop before the Rio de las Balsas, where we were warned that a long stretch without shade or water lay ahead. They gave us a bad supper at Cueramo, nothing but *frijoles de la olla* (cold boiled beans) and tortillas, so that when we departed at three in the morning, with only coffee in our stomachs, the eerie feeling produced by moonlight in the desert was augmented by the lightheadedness of hunger.

We traveled at a good pace, speaking very little, even the animals seeming to be bemused like sleepwalkers. Just before dawn we noticed for the first time a new group of stars that hung on the horizon ahead of us. It was the Southern Cross, and we set our course by it for many days. More than anything else, the discovery of the famous constellation of southern latitudes made us realize that we had come a long way. We were to know the night sky well before the end of our trip, to learn when the various constellations rose and set, to judge without consulting a watch when it was time to get up.

Even though walking by moonlight was infinitely preferable to walking by sunlight, we unreasonably looked forward to the sunrise. We knew that the sun, an hour after its sudden appearance over the desert hills, would cause us nothing but misery, yet, walking in the night, we were always glad to see the morning star and to watch the eastern sky grow pale. There is something sad about being abroad before dawn, and we thought of the sun as a friend, although it was not.

Mexico's sunsets are usually more spectacular than its sunrises, for by evening the western sky is full of piled-up cumulus clouds for the colors to play upon; whereas at dawn there is clear pale blue from horizon to horizon, which turns to fiery red for a few minutes and then, suddenly, the sun appears over a mountaintop, casting long shadows across the desert and warming your cheek even with its first rays.

By the time the light came, on that walk from Cueramo, we felt the need of a rest and, tying the donkeys at the side of the trail, set about making coffee. I always kept the coffee-making equipment at the top of one of Evita's boxes, so that we could reach in and get it without unloading; the water came from the gallon canteen, which Perón carried dangling from one side of his load. We badly needed food, but we did not dare take the time to unload and cook rice and jerky for fear the sun would get up too high before we found shelter for the siesta. The desert is always amply provided with dry sticks, and we quickly had our pan of coffee boiling over the fire. For greater nourishment, I remember, I laced it with the last of our instant cocoa.

We were just preparing to drink the concoction when we saw two figures coming up the trail from the south. They were an elderly man and a boy, driving a herd of cattle from the Balsas to Morelia. They had allowed the cattle to spread out on either side of the trail and were coming along slowly, so that the beasts might have an opportunity to feed. We invited them to stop and have coffee with us, apologizing that we had nothing more to offer them, not even tortillas.

The old man thanked us graciously and remarked that he had passed a house a little way back on the trail, and that perhaps the señora would have some tortillas. He would send his nephew back to ask. The boy obediently turned and went off at a fast trot, while his uncle sat down on a rock and gratefully accepted a cup of our coffee and chocolate brew.

It was just before sunrise, and there was a great serenity on the desert. We were all three tired, and it was a luxury to sit there and watch the growing light and talk quietly about who we were and where we had come from. José López, for that was his name, had one of the noblest faces I have ever seen. He was an unusually tall man for a Mexican, dressed in overalls and a broad-brimmed sombrero, and he carried a staff to prod his animals. Driving cattle over the desert country on foot must have been an exhausting and infuriating job, but his expression was one of complete tranquillity. So intelligent were his dark eyes and so gentle his smile that one felt he would know the answer to any problem, even one completely outside his range of experience, and would be able to offer wise counsel.

It was almost an hour before the nephew came back empty-handed, reporting that the señora had not yet made tortillas. Since there was nothing else, we all drank some more coffee and then, as the sun appeared over the hills, went our separate ways.

The lone shack in the desert where the boy had sought tortillas was about three miles away from our resting place. He must have run all the way and back to have returned so quickly, yet he had not expressed any reluctance when his uncle asked him to go, nor any irritation at not having been able to get food. The country man in Mexico is endowed with almost incredible patience, because he is not used to having things made easy for him and accepts hardship and disappointment as perfectly natural developments. We more "civilized" folk, on the other hand, seethe with rage when we miss a bus or get an overcooked egg in a restaurant. Perhaps our exasperation is really an expression of fury because we are forced to live so far from the natural world.

The Rio de las Balsas rises in the state of Guerrero and flows some three hundred miles in an east-to-west direction, forming the boundary between the states of Michoacán and Guerrero, until, south of Ario de Rosales, it turns toward the Pacific. The tourist who drives to Acapulco on the *camino nacional* crosses the Balsas on a bridge at Mezcala and probably does not give it more than a glance, little realizing that it is one of Mexico's major waterways, flowing for hundreds of miles through territory which is still marked on the maps as *Región Inexplorada*. This unexplored country, both on the Michoacán and on the Guerrero sides, is mainly a jumble of mountains where so far only a few trails and settlements have been tentatively traced by airplane surveys. It extends south almost to the Pacific Coast and north nearly to the main highway that runs from Mexico City to Morelia across the wild Sierra de Ozumatlán. There is a point on that highway called Mil Cumbres (Thousand Peaks), where everybody stops to look at the breathtaking view of mountain spires that stretch southward as far as the eye can see. Here the tourist is actually looking at the Región Inexplorada which, except for a few known areas, stretches all the way to the Pacific.

The Balsas, in its meandering course across the mysterious unexplored land, is fed by several smaller rivers and numerous arroyos and streams which pour southward from the mountains and the high central plains. Some of its waters come from the snows of Popocatepetl and Iztaccihuatl—the mighty volcanoes which tower over Mexico City—and some from the northwest where the new volcano, Parícutin, suddenly exploded into life in the middle of a cornfield ten years ago.

The word *balsas* means both "pools" and "rafts," and nobody is quite sure what the conquistador who named the river had in mind. Some say the name refers to the primitive rafts which the Indians of the region used in the old days, while others contend that it applies to the deep stretches of calm water which might be compared to pools.

Up to the point where it turns toward the Pacific, the river is navigable and was once one of the main arteries for travel and commerce between the hot lands and the north. Today the brecha to Ario takes much of this traffic, and on the Guerrero side another brecha has been pushed about halfway down the shore of the river. Today you seldom see the big flat-bottomed river *barcas*, propelled by oarsmen with huge sweeps, which used to come down merrily with the current and return laboriously against it. When the river turns south, there begins a series of rapids that make it impractical for the large clumsy craft to continue on to the sea, but I imagine that skilled canoeists could run the rapids all the way without making a portage.

We joined the river at the point where it curves southward toward the sea, at a cattle ranch called Hacienda de la Luz. In eleven days we had come about 125 miles, not as the crow flies but as the donkey walks, and since we had taken three days off (at Zirahuen and Reparo), our average was about fifteen miles per day.

It was noon when we stood on a high parched bluff and looked down at the Balsas, which at this point was broad, deep, and as blue as the sky, flowing silently, without rocks or sandbars, between high banks lined with a fringe of shade trees. Had it not been a stiff climb down to the shore, we would have plunged in, clothes and all, for it was suffocatingly and unbearably hot at La Luz.

I almost did not see the river at all that day, for it was a walk of a hundred yards or so to the top of the bluff and I had flung myself down on the porch of a shack in a state of total collapse.

"Come and see the river," Fred called to me.

"Later," I grumbled. "I just can't move."

"Listen," said he, "you have walked over a hundred miles just to

see this river. You can walk a few more steps now and look at it."
And so I struggled out into the sun on my burning feet, and we
looked at the Rio de las Balsas. I was glad that I did.

It is a noble river that, like all broad streams, makes you long
to have a boat and float down its current idly, watching the
shoreline drift past and at night camping on some sandy beach. To
travelers who had slogged mile after exhausting mile through the
broiling desert, this was an especially pleasing idea. Perón and Evita
were doing their job, but if someone had offered us a canoe at La
Luz we would have bade our burros goodbye without a shadow of
regret.

La Luz was not a settlement of independent ranchers, such as
we had seen on our trip south, but a large property owned by an
absentee landlord. In the more populated parts of Mexico, most of
the haciendas have been expropriated from their owners and divided among the villages into ejidos. In some cases the original
owners have been left with a small fraction of their great holdings,
but often the entire property went to the peons and the splendid houses crumbled into ruins. Along the Rio Balsas, however,
much of the land is still owned by wealthy families, who live in
Morelia or Mexico City and only pay an occasional visit to their
ranches, leaving the management in the hands of major-domos. Except for the little corn patches which are planted by the peons
for their own consumption, there is no farming—it is all open range,
arid, rocky, and mountainous. The best grazing season, of course, is
between June and November, when the rains make the desert land
spring to life and water runs in countless little rivulets which
later will be dry as a bone. At the end of the rainy season the
cattle which are ready for sale are rounded up and driven north,
fat, sleek, powerful beasts that bring good prices.

It was our impression, however, that the people of the haciendas
did not fare so well as the cattle. We found that there was less to
eat in the house of an hacienda laborer than in that of an independent rancher, that the people were more poorly dressed, more
apt to be sick, and in general seemed to take less joy in life. Some
of the ranchitos we visited certainly were poor, but the man who

78

works for himself always has hope, while the peon knows that his life will be the same from year to year until he dies.

At La Luz there were five or six families living in typical hot-country houses, which are mostly roof. They are built by sinking into the ground a number of tree trunks with crotches at the top, stretching crossbeams over the crotches, and then roofing it over with grass, or tile if the family can afford it. How big a thatched roof is depends entirely on the energy of the builder, for it does not cost him anything but his labor. Under the roof there is generally one room with walls of adobe or interlaced branches, where the mother and father sleep and where clothing and other precious possessions are kept. The kitchen, of course, is always a separate shack, to minimize the danger of fire.

Our practice in coming to a settlement was to select the biggest roof and ask for shelter there, but it often turned out that the largest house had the least food, so that after unloading our burros we would go from house to house, buying an egg here and a couple of tortillas there until we had enough to assemble a meal. This was the way it was at La Luz, for our hosts had nothing to offer, and we made a half-hour tour of the hacienda before returning triumphantly with three eggs.

The lady of the house didn't look like a Mexican at all, but had exactly the appearance of an Irish washerwoman—round and jovial with a typical Irish grin and a figure like a sack of potatoes. Her husband, Don Antonino, on the other hand, was dark as an Indian, skinny, sad, and had ears like jug handles.

As we ate our lunch of eggs and rice, we consulted with Don Antonino about the next stage of our journey, for we did not know which side of the river to travel on from that point and supposed, from indications on the map, that we might have to cross immediately into Guerrero. Don Antonino advised us to stay on the Michoacán side and follow the river down for about fifty miles to a place called La Garita, where we could take a barca to the other side and continue our trip to the coast by way of the mountains of Guerrero. Was there no trail downriver after La Garita? we asked. He said No, there was not, and that to follow the windings of the Balsas all the way to the coast would be a tremendous detour, not to mention the heat of the riverbank, which was something *espantoso* (fearful).

Our next step, we were informed, would be to ford the Rio del Marqués, which was described as a very tricky undertaking. If you missed the exact spot for the crossing, you would get in over your depth and perhaps drown, for the current was very swift.

We had already come fifteen miles from Cueramo, starting at three in the morning, and should have had sense enough to call it a day, but Don Antonino told us that there was a fine hacienda on the far bank of the Rio del Marqués, and that the dueños were in residence and would certainly welcome us hospitably. We were still hungry, and we knew we could not buy food at La Luz, and it was this more than any other consideration that impelled us to push on to the Hacienda del Organal with Don Antonino as our guide. The river was only an hour's walk, he said, and the hacienda was right on the opposite bank.

We waked up our burritos, who were lying down dozing in the heat, loaded up once more, and at four o'clock set out westward across the baking hills accompanied by our host on horseback. Of course, it was no one-hour walk, though a horse might have made it in that time at a canter. Don Antonino had no better conception of time than the rest of his compatriots. At the top of each hill we expected to see the Rio del Marqués before us, only to be told that it was cerquita, and that we had but to climb "that hill there" (accompanied by a vague gesture that might have taken in the whole range of distant mountains). To make amends for the length of the journey, our guide offered us his horse, which we at first firmly refused; but as hill after hill was passed, we gave in and allowed Don Antonino to walk while we took turns on the horse. Otherwise we would have simply fallen in our tracks there among the rocks.

It was sundown when at last we reached the Rio del Marqués, and slid down a steep sandy bank to the water. It seemed to be flowing very fast, and in the near dark it looked black and forbidding. It required almost half an hour to rearrange our packs, for if the donkeys had crossed as they were all our equipment, including our precious rolls of film, would have been in danger of a wetting. We therefore put Evita's boxes across the saddle of the horse and reroped Perón's bags so that they sat right on top of his back. It would not matter too much if the bags got wet, as they only contained clothes. We removed our boots and put on moccasins, and Fred and our guide took off their pants. Not to shock Don Antonino, I crossed in my jeans, which were in need of a washing anyhow. Since I am usually more sure-footed than Fred, I was elected to carry the knapsack containing our journal, exposed film, and various other important items.

When we stepped into the water there was only a faint glow left in the sky to see by. Don Antonino went ahead, leading his horse; I followed with Perón, and Fred brought up the rear with Evita, who of course began behaving badly at once, despite the fact that her companion was marching into the water like a grenadier.

"For God's sake, can't you help me with this animal?" came Fred's voice, with an edge of hysteria. Looking back, I saw him far behind, waist-deep in the black water, pulling helplessly at the burra's lead rope, while she simply stretched her neck and flattened her ears. I turned Perón over to Don Antonino and struggled back across the slippery round stones to give Evita a heave from behind. This did the trick and started her moving, but in the process I stepped on a stone which rolled under me and down I went with a great splash. Almost before I was in, I was out again, but the knapsack with our most treasured possessions was dripping.

"Now look what you've done," cried Fred in despair. "All the pictures we have taken—ruined. . . ." and his voice trailed off in imprecations about females, both of the human and donkey species.

"If you knew how to manage a donkey, you idiot," I spluttered, pushing my dripping braids out of my eyes, "this never would have happened."

And so we bickered back and forth, shouting at the top of our lungs to make ourselves heard above the roar of the current. When we reached the middle of the river, we had to walk downstream for some distance before continuing across; then the bottom shoaled, and we were able to move along easily in water only up to our knees.

Ten minutes of this curious midriver promenade brought us to the point on the far shore where we again had to enter the deep water. This time it was even deeper and the current much swifter. Don Antonino's horse, accustomed to the ford, went imperturbably forward, and when the time came for Perón to follow it was not hard for me to lift up his hindquarters and force him to go ahead or be swept downstream. Fighting my way back with the water boiling around my chest, I managed to grab Fred's hand just as I was about to lose my footing again, and together we shoved Evita into the stream and followed, holding to her pack for assistance. The excitement of the last part of the ford made us forget our quarrel, and by the time our feet struck dry land we were friends again.

Examination of the knapsack revealed that our films had not been damaged; a double layer of waterproof canvas had kept the inside of the bag dry. If the film had been ruined, I would really have been in the soup, for Fred has a way of being implacable about what he refers to as my carelessness. This time the good waterproof canvas saved me; at another time I was saved by the amount of calcium that chickens eat in Mexico. We had, by dint of much trouble, procured four precious eggs which I put in my shirt pocket to carry back to the house where we were stopping. Fred observed that if I left them there, I would forget about them and they would fall out and break. Oh, no, of course I wouldn't forget. But I did. In the act of leaning over to pick up a vessel in which to put the eggs, I lost them all—one, two, three, four. The miracle was that they did not break, not even one of them! I said nothing, but after that I never carried eggs in my shirt pocket. I never fell down in a stream again either, come to think of it. One miracle is all that can be expected.

Don Antonino, still without pants, walked a few steps up the bank with us until we saw a bright light ahead, then he and his horse turned back into the now pitch-black river. He had asked us five pesos for his services, and seemed very pleased to get an extra peso as a tip.

We heaved the boxes back aboard Evita, Fred pulled on his jeans over dripping shorts, and we hurried toward the lighted hacienda, as though fearful that it would disappear before our eyes.

As we stumbled out of the darkness, wet, muddy, and disheveled, we were greeted by a pretty young woman with a flower in her neatly combed black curls, a figured silk dress, and high-heeled shoes. With the manners of a grande dame, she invited us to come in, using the time-honored Spanish expression which to me seems the most gracious way of receiving a guest: "Aquí tiene Usted su casa" (This is your house).

Her name was Señorita Cabrera, and she was keeping house for her two brothers while they spent their college vacations riding the range and checking up on the state of their father's property. The family lived in Morelia and spent no more than a few weeks every year at El Organal. Already, the señorita admitted, she was getting bored with the heat and the insects and longed for the comfort of the city. Lady that she was, she could not help bending down occasionally to scratch her legs, which were cruelly bitten by the little black fly of the Balsas. Pants would have been more comfortable, but girls in Mexico are seldom seen in trousers.

The hacienda was a fine stone building with a broad porch which ran the whole length of the front and off which the various rooms opened in the usual Mexican country-house style. The señorita took me into her room to change my dripping clothes; it had a ceiling so high that it was almost lost in the obscurity, and big ponderous Victorian furniture which had come all that way the Lord knows how—by truck, perhaps, from Morelia to the river and down the river in boats? I felt strange looking at my disreputable self across a mahogany bureau with a huge framed mirror on top. I was not accustomed to civilized life any more, and wondered if I would be able to stop myself from blowing my nose with my fingers and other arriero practices we had picked up on the trail.

When I had donned my rumpled wrap-around skirt and a clean shirt, I was informed that supper was ready. It was served at a table on the veranda with real china and silver and a white cloth. A well trained maid in a neat cap and apron handed the plates around with silent efficiency. It was all most unreal.

In addition to the señorita, there was her twenty-year-old brother José, and the major-domo of the hacienda, a dark and silent older man who probably would be happy when the gentry went home and left him in peace. The other brother, who was a medical student, was off on a trip to some distant quarter of the hacienda.

Supper included beans served *refritos* (fried), which is the only really satisfactory way to eat them, meat, cheese, hot chocolate, and all the milk we could drink. We gorged, and between mouthfuls told the Cabreras about our trip and our intention to see as much as possible of their state of Michoacán. They all expressed polite interest, but we could see that these people, like the ranchers and the arrieros we met on the trail, could not understand why anyone would want to endure such hardships simply *para conocer tierra* (to know the country). It had probably never occurred to them that the Rio Balsas was interesting; it was just a place where they came once a year and endured the heat in order to please Papá. They were amused at us and our burritos, but such expeditions as ours were for crazy gringos and not for *gente de razón*.

8 Hungry Haciendas

We left el organal with a glowing impression of the hospitality of hot-country hacendados, and we were cheered to learn that there was another hacienda situated at a convenient spot for our next night's halt.

Our stops at haciendas, among other advantages, helped to balance the budget, which we had put so far out of joint at Reparo, for gentlefolk on their country estates would not dream of accepting payment from guests, even uninvited ones, and of course we did not insist. There were many poor ranchitos, too, where our offers of payment were refused, but in those cases we always pressed the point until our hosts would shyly admit that perhaps a couple of pesos for ourselves and a few centavos for the donkeys would not come in amiss. Fred had a magnificent speech which he always used on these occasions. Sweeping off his sombrero at the moment of parting, he would address our hosts as follows:

"There are things that can never be repaid, such as your hospitality and kindness, señores, but I should like to be allowed to recompense you at least for the expense and *molestia* [trouble] which our visit has caused you." The lady of the house would then figure up the number of eggs we had eaten and how many *manojos* (armfuls) of cornstalks had been put down for our burros, tally against this the fact that they had shared some of our coffee and rice, and finally, very timidly, inquire whether two or three pesos would be too much.

85

At the haciendas, however, we would piously express the hope that God would repay them (Que Dios se lo pague), and they would reply with equal piety that they hoped God would go with us (Que Dios les acompañe), an interchange which left everybody happy, especially if Fred, with his caballero manners, accompanied it by kissing the hand of the señora or señorita.

We had been told at El Organal that the Hacienda Los Nopales was cerquita, but being no longer greenhorns, we estimated that it would probably take us all day to get there—a guess which proved to be correct. In order to visit the hacienda, we had to leave the main trail and follow a side path which took us about two miles out of our way—two miles which we would painfully have to retrace on the following day. We found a cluster of ranchitos near the branch of the trail and considered stopping at one of them, instead of going on to Los Napales, but visions of a supper as good as that of the night before lured us on.

We were following a will-o'-the-wisp, however, for Los Nopales turned out to be a sad disappointment, a catastrophe. We approached the house at sunset. Although not as elaborate a manor as Organal, it too was built of stone and had a wide veranda, occupied at the moment of our arrival by a fat old lady. While I held the donkeys, Fred went forward to pay his respects. We always managed it this way because it did not look well to tie up the burros without asking permission, and if we left them loose they generally strayed into a cornfield or misbehaved in some other manner.

Hailing the aged señora, who turned out to be deaf, Fred asked if we might spend the night. Her husband was away from the house and she did not seem very pleased to receive visitors, but she grudgingly agreed that we might stop.

"My wife is with me," Fred yelled at her.

She replied, "Oh."

As I was tying up the donkeys, she inquired, "And where is your wife?"

"There with the donkeys."

"Oh."

We unloaded the animals, piling up our carga on the edge of the porch, and I approached the old lady to shake hands.

"But where is your wife?" the señora asked Fred again, ignoring me. He explained hastily that I was wearing *traje de hombre* (men's clothes) for comfort on the trail.

"Oh," she commented.

In order to convince her that I was really a woman, I took shelter around a bend of the veranda and hastily changed into my skirt; but she was still unsatisfied and, after inspecting me for several minutes, once more turned to Fred:

"Su señora no tiene pelo" (Your wife hasn't any hair).

"For God's sake," Fred said, "take down your braids and show them to her."

I unfurled my pigtails from the top of my head where I had pinned them and displayed them in front of the señora's eyes.

"Oh," she said, and apparently was at last convinced that we were all right, for she told us to sit down.

This was the only occasion on the whole trip when we had difficulties over my masculine costume. I knew, of course, that pants are not worn by Mexican women except by a few brash young moderns in tourist centers, but the notion of an expedition of this sort in a skirt was impossible. When we stopped somewhere to rest for a day or two, I would get out my wrap-around, but the rest of the time I wore jeans or shorts (knee-length for the sake of modesty) and a man's sombrero. Except for the old woman, no one we met ever questioned my attire, and indeed a few of the women remarked wistfully that it must be a convenient costume for going about *en el campo*, although of course had they tried themselves their menfolk would have thought they were out of their minds.

The señora at Los Nopales was not a conversationalist. In reply to our inquiry about food, she told us that she had already eaten, but that her husband, Don Rutilio Flores, would soon be home and that we might have supper with him. This topic having been dealt with, she sat in her straight-backed chair and blinked at us, while we, reposing in our hammocks, blinked back.

After a couple of hours of this, there was a sound of galloping hoofs in the distance, and presently Don Rutilio drew rein in front of the veranda with a great jingling of spurs. He was a ruddy-faced old man with a plump waistline which bespoke plenty of good food, and he wore the tight-fitting, fringed trousers of the Mexican vaquero and a big sombrero studded with silver. Unlike most of the hacendados around the Rio de las Balsas, Don Rutilio made his home on the ranch and seldom left except for short vacations.

He greeted us with great cordiality and urged us to sit down and talk to him, saying that it had been a long time since he had had a chance to hear about the outside world. The señora, meantime, shuffled off to the kitchen shack, and our hopes rose. She placed a pitcher and a few glasses on the table and then sat down again.

"You must excuse me for not offering you more to eat," said Don Rutilio, "but the fact is, I never take anything at night but a drop of milk."

So saying he led the way to the table where, sure enough, there was nothing but a pitcher of milk and a few cold tortillas. I took two glasses of milk, which was a lot better than nothing, but Fred went supperless for he cannot abide milk—especially the warmish boiled milk which one always gets in Mexico.

"Now," said Don Rutilio genially when the miserable meal was over, "sit down and talk to me."

As it turned out, he did most of the talking himself, chiefly on the subject of how tired he was of ranch life and how he would like to have a million pesos and retire to Acapulco or Cuernavaca, to dress in fine clothes and eat elegant food with the proper wine accompanying each course. That would be the life! We felt really sorry for the poor man living alone with his old lady who would not even bestir herself to get him a decent meal.

After an hour of this conversation, our host informed us that it was his habit to go hunting on moonlight nights and, fetching his rifle, he bade us good night and was off again at a gallop.

We spent a grim night on the porch in our hammocks while the señora made the air ring with her snores from an inner chamber and the pangs of hunger chased themselves around our stomachs. Some time in the wee small hours Don Rutilio clattered in once more and flung himself down to sleep on a catre, soon vying with his wife in what sounded like a snoring contest.

In the gray dawn we loaded up and got out of there, without breakfast, of course, for by now we knew enough not to have any hopes about that. The two miles back to the trail exhausted us, and we decided to stop at one of the ranchitos we had noticed the day before and beseech them for the love of God to feed us.

When we told the story of our reception at Los Nopales to the people at the ranch of El Charco (The Pool), everybody laughed fit to kill. What was so funny?

"Mire, señor," said one of the boys, "nobody ever gets fed at Los Nopales. The señora is *un poco rara* [a little odd], you must have noticed, and as for Don Rutilio, he has an *amiguita* [girl friend] in a little house not far from the hacienda. He spends all his time and eats all his meals with her. And what meals! No wonder he is not hungry when he goes home!"

"He said he was going hunting last night. . . ." Fred remarked, and that set them off into new gales of laughter.

"Oh, he loves to hunt at night, does Don Rutilio, but the game he hunts is not of the kind you shoot at. And he doesn't take it home for his señora to see, either!"

They were kind to us at El Charco, and Doña Juana López, the lady of the rancho, soon had a meal of rice and beans and eggs laid out for our breakfast. Since it was eleven o'clock by the time we finished eating, we decided to call a halt for the entire day and to set out for the next stage of our trip by moonlight in the early hours of the morning. Everybody agreed that this was the best plan, and to celebrate our holiday we persuaded the señora to kill a chicken for our dinner.

The ranch was half a mile from the river, and after a long siesta through the hot hours of noontime we went down for a swim. The Balsas near El Charco runs wide and shallow over a bed of stones and black sand so fine that it is scarcely distinguishable from mud. The Guerrero bank goes up steeply, but on our side there was a wide margin of sandy lowlands, probably flooded over in the summer rains, where willows and other water-loving trees provided a cool resting place for burros, pigs, horses, and cows.

The current, augmented a few miles back by the torrent of the Rio del Marqués, flowed at a racing speed, as though eager to have done with its long journey and find rest in the broad surges of the Pacific. Wading in above waist depth, I cautiously tried my strength against the rush of the water and found that even my most strenuous efforts did not suffice to keep me swimming abreast of the spot where Fred stood soaping himself on the bank.

The fact is, Fred does not know how to swim. I look upon this as a shameful secret, but he is quite blasé about it and is perfectly happy to lounge in shallow water, observing with an air of amused tolerance the rude antics of those who swim and dive.

Returning from the river clean and hungry, we found Doña Juana's family engaged in the pursuit of our dinner, an athletic chicken with a talent for getting into cactus thickets and other places where it could not be followed. After half an hour, when it seemed as though we were not going to have chicken for dinner after all, one of the boys set his dog after the bird, and in a moment, with a flurry of feathers and much squawking, the bird was firmly grasped in the jaws of the big mongrel. He relinquished his prize resignedly to Doña Juana, for Mexican dogs know better than even to dream that a chicken could be for them.

In Mexico the number of ribs to be seen on a dog is a good index of the economic status of his master, and around the Rio Balsas we saw some of the thinnest, most pitiful canine specimens in the country. Mexicans are fond of their dogs, and every ranch has a number of them to act as guardians and keep the coyotes away, but if there is not enough to eat for the children it goes without saying that there is nothing for the dogs. They must forage for themselves, and if they get a tortilla or two every day they are lucky.

Perhaps it was the pathetic condition of the dogs that made us hate the pigs so much. There were always pigs, and except in the most elegant houses they were always underfoot. While the dogs had to compete for scraps of old tortillas, the pigs got the best of everything; the dogs were often spoken to severely, but the pigs were treated with loving tolerance. For the pigs some day would go to the market and return in the shape of dresses for the señora, ammunition for the señor, and beans for the chamacos.

In tierra caliente, they do not call pigs by the customary name of *puercos,* but instead refer to the gross animals as *cuchis*—an affectionate abbreviation of *cochinos.* These cuchis are not the round pink fellows one sees in American sausage advertisements, but rangy, long-legged scavengers with huge ears, tremendously long snouts, and rows of gleaming teeth.

We waged a constant war against these creatures, and it was a clandestine war because on the surface we had to pretend to admire them. They rubbed their filthy sides against our legs while we sat at table, scratched themselves on the undersides of our hammocks while we slept, upset our boxes of carga and raided whatever food they could find, devoured our rawhide shoelaces, tripped us up, drove us crazy. If our hosts noticed that one of their pigs was bothering us, they would call out, "Cuchi!" in accents of good-humored reprimand, the way you might speak to a child, and perhaps the pig would remove itself, only to return in a moment.

Toward the latter part of the trip, as the donkeys grew thinner and more tired, we tried to buy corn for them every day, which we generally fed them at noontime. Corn was expensive, and a *medida,* or measure of four quarts, cost us two or three pesos, practically as much as our own dinners. It took the donkeys a long time to crunch down a medida, and unless there was a feeding trough (which there seldom was) we had to stand guard all the time they fed, otherwise the pigs would steal the corn from under the noses of our patient animals. Often we would set the corn in a tarpaulin on top of some raised place where we assumed it would be safe, only to return and find that the pigs had managed to upset it, and that the precious corn was all over the ground with half a dozen cuchis shoveling it in as fast as they could go, snarling savagely at our burritos when they tried to share it.

This is not all. When the time came for one of us to respond to the call of nature and seek seclusion in *el campo*, the pigs knew by unfailing instinct that this was not just an ordinary walk. They would fall in behind the unfortunate victim, grunting happily, and form an expectant circle around him when he found his bathroom site, observing the process with their little red eyes and making obscene comments to each other. It was wise to go on these expeditions armed with a staff, by waving which and shouting "Cuchis!" in savage tones, it might be possible to spare oneself the ultimate indignity of having them close in before the job was over.

Pigs!

The moon, now only a thin slice of its former self, was still high when we left El Charco for the next leg of our journey, a hacienda called Pinzandarán.

The day was marked by the loss of our pedometer. It seemed as though the few things we bought expressly for the trip either turned out to be useless, or got broken or lost, while the nondescript gear we assembled from our Brooklyn kitchen and our friends' attics served us faithfully all the way. For some 150 miles now the pedometer had been ticking off the miles from its nest in my watch pocket, attached to my belt by a metal clip. Then on the way to Pinzandarán I found that it was gone and, since I had obviously lost it by my own stupidity, there was nothing to do except agree when Fred berated me.

I am one of those people who lose things, break things, and mislay things, and I chose to marry a man who cherishes things, keeps them in good condition, and always knows where he has put them. On this expedition I was in charge of the pack, and it was supposed to be assumed that I knew where to put my hand on any required object at a moment's notice. Of course, different things were required every day, and since it was impractical to repack the entire carga continually I just reached into the jumble in Evita's boxes and Perón's bags until my sense of touch put me in contact with the item I was looking for . . . if I was lucky. If I was not, I began pouring things out on the ground, muttering under my breath that I supposed "it must be around somewhere," while Fred commented that it probably had been lost, that everything got lost, and that we might as well leave the carga behind since eventually it would all be lost—and so on.

As for the pedometer, we did not really need it any longer, for we knew by this time that on the average we walked two miles an hour, counting halts for cigarettes, chats with passing strangers, and delays caused by doubts over which trail to take. This rate we had checked time and again with the watch, and it always came out to two miles an hour, except in a few cases when we went fast over level ground without stopping.

On this particular day we certainly did not do better than two miles an hour.

South of El Charco and Los Nopales, the hills on the Michoacán side of the Balsas began to turn into mountains, rising abruptly on our right and matching in desolation the sierra on the Guerrero side at our left. Our trail now led us along the bank of the river, which, narrowing down between steep shores, ran deep and swift, hurling itself in wild turbulence over a succession of cataracts of broken rocks and sand spits.

Halfway to Pinzandarán we met a couple of natives of the region who informed us as usual that the hacienda was cerquita and that we had only to *dar la vuelta al cerro* (go around the hill) in order to get there. From long experience with this kind of information, we had come to allow at least three hours for a place described as cerquita, whereas *No está lejos* (It isn't far) probably meant five or six hours, and *Siempre está retirado* informed us that it was a devil of a long way. Similarly, if we were told we would arrive at noon, we estimated it would be sundown by the time we got there, and if they said we'd surely make it by sundown we figured we would be arriving in the middle of the night. There was another expression which particularly annoyed us—*Aquí no más está* (It's right here), which good news, coming at the end of a long trek, generally meant we still had a couple of hours to go.

After a while we learned that by subjecting our informants to

93

a careful cross-questioning we could generally find out more about the trail ahead than their first casual answers had indicated. The best way was to ask whether the distance ahead was the same as the distance we had already come, or half or twice that much—a question which, not being related to time or speed of travel, they could usually answer fairly accurately.

Pinzandarán was about a mile and a half from the riverbank, while the hacienda itself was placed in a spot entirely surrounded by desert hills from which a stifling hot wind blew continually, raising the dust but bringing no relief. It was the hottest place we struck on the Balsas or anywhere else—an oven of relentless heat which scarcely diminished even at sundown.

We struggled up to the veranda at about noon, to be greeted by a pair of young girls who informed us that they had very little to eat in the house because it was *dia de vigilia* (day of fasting). We begged them to do their best, slung our hammocks, and promptly dozed off in a stupor, not to awaken until several hours later when the sun came around to our side of the porch. The girls, who were the daughters of the foreman, had not stirred a finger to prepare us any food, but were reclining on a catre gossiping and playing with a six-month-old baby to whom one of them was singing in a high, reedy voice. Her repertoire was limited to one song which she sang over and over all day; it was a song which we were later to hear on Mexican juke boxes when we got back to civilization, and whenever it was played it took us back to Pinzandarán—a place, incidentally, where we do not want to be taken back to.

When asked about our dinner, one of the señoritas heaved herself up with a sigh and said we might eat some beans if we liked, but of course no meat, it being Friday. Fred pointed out that we were travelers and had not eaten all day, and that dispensation is granted in such cases; but the girl said there wasn't any meat anyhow, so the discussion was purely academic. Not to be worsted, we got out our faithful hunk of jerky and tore off a piece, telling her to cook it with the beans and let us worry about the question of breaking the vigilia.

94

The señorita took the meat with an expression of great distaste, as though she were committing a sin merely by touching it, and went off to the kitchen shaking her head dubiously. Fred followed her, pointing out that he himself was católico and had been born in Roma where the Pope lives, verdad? that he was a personal amigo of the Papa, and that he felt sure that the Pope would say it was quite all right for her to cook the meat for us.

In the end the señorita won out. She did, in fact, cook the meat, but she must have done so by impaling it on a stick over the embers, for it was hard as leather, charred, and impossibly salty. When she was not looking, we fed it to the dogs and supped on frijoles and warmed-over tortillas.

It was 100 degrees in the shade of the veranda. We reslung our hammocks out of the sun and went back to rest, while the girls, having put the baby to sleep, fetched a parakeet and amused themselves by feeding it bits of tortilla. It was a tiny green bird with a loud voice, and our doze was punctuated by its screechings. It knew one phrase, "*Periquito burro!*" (Stupid parakeet!) which it reiterated constantly, accompanied by the laughter of the two girls. I got up and played with it myself for lack of anything else to do, but it promptly bit me on the finger.

Late in the day, by good luck, an old lady came to call and told me that she had some eggs at her house and might sell us a few, so that when Fred awoke I was able to cheer him with the news that I had negotiated the purchase of four *blanquillos* for our supper. The proper name for eggs in Spanish is *huevos*, but, since this word is open to a double entendre, Mexican countryfolk, especially women, speak primly of "little white ones."

We ate two of our little white ones for supper, boiled and wrapped in tortillas, and prudently saved the other two for lunch on the following day, for we knew we would have a long trek to the next settlement.

Pinzandarán was the only place on the entire trip where we slept the night through without blankets or sweaters. It continued stifling half the night, and only toward the early morning did a breath of cool air enter the simmering valley. We were up at four o'clock, and I made coffee in the girls' kitchen while they slept in one of the inner rooms. Since we planned to cook out for lunch, I shamelessly swiped half an onion which I found near the stove (politely leaving the other half in case they needed it). I felt not the slightest guilt, for I was quite sure the señorita had burned our meat on purpose.

We were off well before dawn but, as so often happened, got mixed up in trying to find the trail and wandered about aimlessly for an hour, following tracks that turned out to be mere cattle paths. At one point, thrashing about in the woods, we almost tumbled down a steep bank into the Rio Balsas.

In due course the good Lord sent us a man who, like a true Samaritan, went several miles out of his way to put us on the trail. The kindness of the Mexican *campecino* was a constant source of wonder to us. We met dozens of people in the course of our wanderings who, one way or another, helped us out of difficulties and did it gladly, with no expectation of recompense. Of course, there were a few occasions where we requested the assistance of a .guide and made it clear that we intended to pay for his services (such as at the crossing of the Rio del Marqués), but in general the help we received at every hand was freely given and repaid only with thanks.

Several times we were set on the path by strangers who would walk a mile or two with us to make sure that we did not miss a turn-off, and frequently on the trail we would be overtaken by horsemen or burro riders who would suggest that we ride their animals for a stretch and rest ourselves. These people seemed to feel that we were honoring them by visiting their remote land.

Our friend of Pinzandarán bade us goodbye when he had assisted us to cross a stream, saying that from there on we could follow our noses (*derecho no mas*). We shook hands, as one always does in Mexico upon meeting or leaving people, and he took his leave of me with the words, "*Adios, joven,*" assuming, in the dim moonlight that I was a boy. Since there was no point in entering into long explanations about my sex and costume, I tipped my hat like a well brought-up muchacho.

9 Over the River

As dawn paled the sky, we turned our backs on the river and began to climb, for at this point the Michoacán side of the Balsas is too rugged for a trail, and the traveler is forced to cut around behind the mountains. It was a climb of about four hours, during which we surmounted hill after hill, only to discover that the *puerto*, or pass, was still high above us. The path led us through dry scrubby woods where there was good pasturage, and the thickets rustled constantly with the movements of grazing cattle, horses, and burros. It was a cool walk, for even after the sun rose we were generally traveling in the shadow of the mountains.

About noontime we stood at the puerto and caught our breath. A rail fence with a gate kept the Pinzandarán cattle from straying into the next valley, and near the fence grew a wild gourd vine. On the other side, the trail followed the bed of an arroyo which, while practically dry, still had moisture enough in its banks to support a vigorous growth of foliage. It was here that we saw our first lianas hanging from the trees like twisted cables—a sight that delighted us with its suggestion of exotic jungle lands to come, for in truth we had had enough of the desert and longed for green trees and flowers, for fruits and tropical abundance.

The foliage attracted a number of colorful birds—a pleasant change from the buzzards, crows, and dun-colored birds of the desert. There were blue and black ones with long tails, flashes of green that might have been parakeets, and we saw one beautiful beige fellow with a crown of spiky feathers, each one surmounted by a knob.

Even more than before, we wished that we were naturalists, able to name the creatures that we saw, to know what kind of rocks we were walking on and what were the rare trees under whose branches we passed, able in our ignorance only to admire and wonder.

Now and then, of course, an old friend would appear in this new setting, and I would be able to tell Fred with assurance, "That is a cedar waxwing," or, "Look at the downy woodpecker," occasions which gave me as much smug satisfaction as correctly naming a symphony heard on the radio. But most of the time we both stared with open mouths.

The arroyo down which we were traveling had another surprise for us: we saw our first snake. It was about three feet long, light brown in color with darker horizontal stripes, and it moved out of the path politely when it saw us coming. Fred was quite excited and thought that perhaps it was a viper, but to me it looked like an overgrown sample of what we called in my childhood "milk snakes"—harmless little things that I used to play with in preference to dolls. I suppose I shall never feel the normal fear of snakes until I am bitten by one, for they resemble my old playmates too much. As for this brown specimen, we described it later to a native of the region who declared that it most certainly *was* poisonous and asked why we had not killed it.

We did not have to worry much about snakes on the trail, however, because the burros were extremely snake-shy, and always saw them before we did. Evita was particularly scary and, after seeing her first snake, shied at any curved stick which could remotely be thought to resemble one. In the region of Pátzcuaro there are no poisonous snakes, and that the burros realized by instinct that these creatures of tierra caliente were a different breed from the Tarascan snakes and ought to be avoided at all costs seemed wonderful to us.

Rounding a bend of the arroyo, we came to a spot where a tiny trickle of water flowed amid the dry rocks, and we decided to make a halt there for lunch and a siesta. The water was brackish, but it would serve for coffee and rice.

It was pleasant for a change to be by ourselves, and able to relax without the necessity of conversing at length on such subjects as job possibilities in El Norte and the high price of frijoles. Wherever we stopped on our travels we were always surrounded by people, even when we slept. It was definitely not an expedition for honeymooners, for the only place you could be sure of privacy was the middle of a desert bare enough to be able to see, and be seen from, several miles in every direction.

While Fred reposed under the trees upon a serape, I set about the preparation of eggs and rice (which was our standard picnic lunch when we were lucky enough to have eggs). I consider myself an expert in rice cookery, and for the benefit of campers who sigh at the white sticky stuff they are called upon to eat when the potatoes are gone I am willing to reveal my professional secrets:

A cup of rice is about right for two hungry people. It should first be washed, drained, and set in the sun to dry; meantime, the cook heats a couple of spoonfuls of fat (any kind) in a saucepan and cuts up some onion into it. When the onion is lightly browned, add the rice and mix it up thoroughly, so that every grain is coated with grease, then add about a cup and three-quarters of liquid and a teaspoon of salt and let it cook over a slow fire, without stirring, for fifteen to twenty minutes. If the liquid evaporates before the rice is done, a tiny bit more can be added from time to time. The liquid can be water, water with tomato juice and pulp (better), or meat broth (wonderful). While the stuff is cooking, you can heave in meat scraps, left-over vegetables, sausages, or anything else that takes your fancy. When it's done, the rice will have absorbed every drop of liquid and each grain will be separate. But try it at home a couple of times to get the knack before serving it up at a campfire.

With fried eggs on top of our rice, and mugs of strong coffee, we were suffused by well-being and sprawled upon our couch of grass smoking and talking.

99

"Hello, there!" came a loud, hearty voice, and we sat up in astonishment, for the words were spoken in English. A big man in a Texas hat and high-heeled boots, riding a magnificent mule, was coming down the trail.

"I've been following your tracks all day," said this apparition, swinging down from the saddle. "Knew you wasn't Mexicans by the boots you wore, and when I caught sight of the burros tied up there, with halters and all, I figured they must be yours."

He was a cattle inspector from the Comisión Mexicano-Americana para la Fiebre Aftosa, called for short the Aftosa Commission, which for the past five years has been waging war on hoof-and-mouth disease throughout Mexico. It was set up with United States Government funds appropriated by Congress, when the cattle infection threatened to cross the border and devastate the herds of the American Southwest, and has been so successful that today the disease has been almost wiped out in Mexico.

The inspectors always work in pairs, one American and one Mexican, visiting every ranch in a given territory five or six times a year, and making sure that all cattle are vaccinated. At the start of the program, thousands of infected animals were killed, their owners being promised compensation from commission funds. The campecinos did not understand what it was all about. When they saw men killing some of their herds and jabbing needles into the rest, they saw red, and the inspectors had to be diplomats to get away with their lives. Some were not diplomats, and were killed by the embattled ranchers.

The Aftosa men are not allowed to carry arms for their defense, but they may take soldiers with them on trips where they expect trouble. Most of them prefer to go alone, however, because it often happens that the soldiers get tough and try to use force on people, so that bullets are more apt to fly when the military are present than when they are left behind. Eventually, priests were enlisted in the program, and told their flocks from the pulpit that the Aftosa program was a good thing and that the rancheros must not shoot the inspectors who came to help them. After that, things improved in centers where there were churches; but in re-

100

mote country, such as we were traveling in, the inspectors still feel a chill between their shoulder blades as they ride the back trails.

This chap, who joined us for a cup of coffee, squatting on his heels in cowboy style, was very friendly, giving us much good advice about the territory we were entering, but some of his observations on Mexico left us with a bad taste in our mouths. He had nothing but contempt for the country and its people.

We asked him where his partner was, having heard that they always went in twos.

"Oh, he's no partner," said the Texan; "he's just a flunky who does my work for me. I left him back yonder on the trail. Didn't want him around while I talked to you folks."

We happened to observe that we were low of smokes because we had given away so many cigarettes, and he looked at us in amazement.

"I don't give away cigarettes," he said. "Hell, I wouldn't give these people a thing, not a thing."

He was sympathetic when we spoke of the difficulties we had encountered in getting enough to eat. As for himself, he never went hungry, for he had a system for extracting food from his hosts: he threatened to fine them for various breaches of Commission rules if they did not give him meat and plenty of it.

"I can fine the governor of this state, if I want to," he boasted.

We thought this fellow was lucky not to have been found face down on the trail with a bullet in his back.

We were later to meet many other Aftosa men, and found that most of the American inspectors worked and lived with the Mexicans like brothers. When we told them of our meeting with this first very untypical member of their group, their immediate comment was that he must have been a Texan. They said the Commission had made a grave mistake in hiring a lot of men from the Lone Star State, often well qualified because of their knowledge of ranch work and familiarity with the Spanish language, but hopelessly prejudiced against everything Mexican. The Texans acted superior and tried to push the ranchers around on the assumption, bred into them from childhood, that a Mexican is no good and does not deserve to be treated like a white man.

At one ranch in Guerrero where we later stopped, we happened to ask about the American cattle inspectors and whether they were popular with the ranchers.

"Oh, we have a very nice fellow now, *muy simpático*," said our informant, "but the last one was ugly and tried to give orders to everybody."

"What happened to him?"

"Oh, we shot him."

Just like that.

Our last stop before crossing into the state of Guerrero was at a little ranch settlement called La Pitirera, up in the hills a mile or two from the riverbank. We were greeted, at the house where we chose to stop, by two young men whose first inquiry was whether we had any *vino*, by which they meant, not wine, but spirits. This was the first time such a request had been made of us, and we felt rather uneasy. There was something odd about the boys—their movements were jerky, their eyes bright and feverish. Thwarted in their desire for vino, for we never carried liquor, they then asked us for remedios, and it was obvious that the kind of medicine they desired was one of those tonics which are largely based on alcohol. They were sick, they said, felt weak and tired all the time—and indeed they did not look normal.

The boys hung around, watching us unload our carga while their mother lighted a fire to prepare some carne seca for us, and when it was obvious that we had nothing alcoholic to offer them they drifted away. An hour later they reappeared. The tension and nervousness that we had noticed before was gone, and they seemed relaxed and talkative, full of boasts and extravagant statements.

We recalled that we had been warned farther back on the trail to look out for marijuana smokers. The weed is grown in some of these remote settlements, and there is a twofold danger—both from drug-crazed people who might want to pick a fight, and from those who plant the stuff and who might fear that we would report

them to the authorities. We would not have recognized the marijuana plant if we had seen it, but we thought we recognized the
symptoms displayed by these young men.

It was not only our hosts who were queer. Upon visiting other
houses in search of eggs, we found the whole settlement to be odd.
There were two people with hairlips and one boy of twenty-odd
years who appeared to be a complete idiot, his head hanging to one
side and saliva dripping from his mouth. The rest, while more or less
normal in appearance, seemed listless, sick, and lacking in intelligence.

When time came to "retire" to the rough catre prepared for
us on the porch of the tiny twig-shack that was our hosts' home,
the boys and their mother shut themselves inside and left us to
ourselves.

Fred slipped his gun inside the waistband of his jeans: it was one
of the few times in the course of our entire trip when we felt we
had actually been in danger, and we were glad when the red dawn
colored the sky and we were able to load and move on. That we did
not have trouble either this time or on a few other occasions I attribute entirely to Fred's knowledge of how to handle people. In
this part of the world, most men carry pistols and human life is not
particularly valuable. Fred, however, has an unerring instinct for
dealing with drunks or locos, persuading them that he is their
friend, that he admires them and their country, that he agrees
with everything they say, and yet showing that there is a point
beyond which they cannot go and that they will regret it if they
do. It is a gift, and I do not know how it is done, but as long as Fred
was around, even in the most ominous situations, I never had reason
to be afraid.

La Garita (The Sentry Post), where we were to cross the Balsas,
consisted of one little house, the dwelling of the ferryman. It was
occupied at the moment of our arrival only by children who
pointed to the river and told us that we could find their papá on
the shore with his barca.

At La Garita the Balsas, running deep and green, is funneled between precipitous shores so narrow that a stone can be tossed to the opposite bank. The *barquero* had picked himself an excellent site for his ferry service, for the current sweeps across from the Michoacán to the Guerrero side and then swerves back again, so that a skillful boatman can make the round trip with a minimum of effort. On both shores there are little steep beaches of fine white sand, affording a good landing place for the barca. These beaches, only a few yards wide, seem to have been expressly designed for the ferry, for the rest of the shore at this point is a dangerous mass of tumbled rocks.

The barca was a flat-bottomed craft about twenty feet long, with a railing along the sides and a hinged gangway at either end which was dropped upon the sand when the craft touched shore. It was propelled by two long sweeps.

We waded through the sand, tugging at the lead ropes of the burros, who knew that something different was afoot and felt sure that they were not going to like it. Two other passengers were ahead of us, ranchers from Guerrero, who, as we arrived on the scene, were persuading a white horse and a handsome big mule to enter the ferry. The animals had obviously made the trip before and did not give any trouble, nor did Perón, who allowed himself to be pulled aboard without protest; but Evita planted her feet in the sand and firmly announced her intention of staying in Michoacán. She had to be lifted bodily and dumped into the barca, creating such a rumpus that the mule, which had been standing quietly, decided he was not going to risk a trip with such a violent female and went plunging out of the barca with wild backward bounds, almost upsetting us all.

The barquero decided to cross with the horse and the burros and to make a special trip for the mule, so, pulling up the stern gangway and settling to the oars, he headed the barca upriver into the racing green water and, turning with practiced skill at the right moment, let the current take us to the opposite beach.

We paid our fare of a peso fifty and stepped into Guerrero. Above our heads loomed the slopes of an immense range, the Sierra del Gallo, or Rooster Mountains, which we would have to cross to reach the Pacific coast and the mouth of the Balsas. It looked formidable and almost sky-high.

We had heard much about the hillmen of Guerrero, and none of it was reassuring. According to the desert people, the Sierra del Gallo was full of renegades and criminals, men who shot first and asked questions afterward.

In Mexico the bad people are always somewhere else, on the other side of the river or in the next town or across the mountain. The river dwellers distrust the hillmen, the hillmen are suspicious of the men who live on the coast, the *gente de razón* are afraid of the Indians, and so on. Thus we had been warned about the Pintos, who turned out to be like anybody else; we had been told to look out for robbers on the road from Ario, but we hadn't met any; and three years ago, when we first went to live among the Tarascans, we were told by friends in Mexico City that these gentlest of people were hostile to outsiders and would resent our presence among them.

Our first couple of hours in Guerrero were spent negotiating a very narrow path which proceeded downriver for about five miles before turning up into the sierra. It was a devilish trail along the foot of the mountainside where we had to walk in single file and where a misstep would have sent us plunging down the slope and into the Balsas a hundred feet below. As the river widened, the rocks gave way in places to steep beaches, where the hot wind picked up clouds of sand and flung it into our eyes.

I proposed to take a last swim in the Balsas, but Fred, observing the racing current and the steepness of the shore, thought the idea of continuing the trip without a wife was distasteful and laid down the law: I could dabble at the edge of the water, but swimming was out. This was a reasonable precaution, and I found a sort of bathtub in the rocks where, protected from being swept away, I could let the cool current sweep over me.

We had heard that there were *caimanes* (alligators), in the Rio de las Balsas, and while I was bathing Fred kept watch in the expectation of seeing a huge mouth open in readiness to engulf me. Apparently the river once was full of them, but they have been hunted a good deal. Today only a few are left, and those few **are** not very large. But at least it was a satisfaction to bathe in waters where there *might* be alligators.

The bath and the picnic lunch that followed—rice and a can of very bad corned beef from our iron rations—were our farewell to the Balsas until, on the other side of the sierra, our trail would take us down to the coast, to the point where the Balsas meets the sea.

Loading up while the sun was still high, we struggled a few more miles along the shore and at length followed the path up a high bluff where a shack was perched. Looking north from this vantage point, we saw the mountains through which we had come from Pinzandarán—imposing in their huge bulk, but mere dwarfs when compared with the towering sierra that rose above us.

10 Silent upon a Peak in Guerrero

THE FIRST MAN WE MET IN GUERRERO SEEMED TO BEAR out the warnings we had received: he carried a .45 automatic in a side holster, and it was cocked.

We were struggling up the winding mountain trail heading for a ranch which the ferryman had told us we might reach in time for spending the night. All around us the woods stretched out so thick that the path ahead was hidden from our view at every turn. Not a sound, not a sign of life broke the silence of the midafternoon. Out of this nothingness the man with the cocked .45 materialized, and Fred did not like it.

"Buenas tardes," the stranger greeted us, politely tipping his sombrero. "A donde van?"

Since it was perfectly obvious that there was only one place to go and that was up, we answered, "*Arriba*," and he fell in step with us. He too, it seemed, was going up. He was a young fellow in his early twenties, who walked on his toes like a fighter and darted keen glances at us and our equipage. Had it not been for the peculiar and suspicious way he toted his gun, we might have been glad of his company, but, as it was, I noticed that Fred maneuvered our line of march along the narrow trail so as to walk right behind our new friend.

I went ahead with the animals, and the young fellow cut a stick from a tree and helped me drive them. He seemed happy to have someone to talk to. He was a deserter from the army, it appeared,

107

and did not dare leave the mountains for fear the soldados would get him. It was a hard life, he said, always in hiding, and had it not been for the amigos he had in the sierra who provided him with food and clothing, he would not have known how to live.

This story, plus the cocked automatic, was anything but reassuring, and I began to wonder how it would all end. Fred told me later that at this point he shifted his gun from its holster to the pocket of his jeans. He never lost sight of the fellow's right hand, he said, and if that hand had gone anywhere near the cocked automatic, well, there would be nothing else to do but shoot first, would there?

The young fellow was going on with his story. He had heard that there was a commission in Morelia contracting labor for the Estados Unidos, and he had some relative who was a *licenciado* (lawyer) trying to fix him up with phony papers so that he could apply for a job.

Did I think he would be happy there? Very happy, I said, wishing he were there now.

Night was falling, and still there was nothing in sight but the woods and the rocks and the trail going up and up.

"And where are you going to spend the night?" the young man wanted to know. I mumbled something vaguely, hoping that the inadequacy of my reply might be attributed to my scanty knowledge of Spanish, and trying to hint that we, too, had amigos in the sierra who might pop up like mushrooms at every turn of the path. I suggested that, since we and our animals were going slowly, he might like to push on ahead by himself.

But it did not work. No, he said, he would conduct us to the house of some of his friends, where he himself was planning to spend the night. I stole a glance at Fred, who was walking behind us with his right thumb hooked in his belt. He said nothing, so I guessed that his decision was to wait and see.

We went on and on, and it was pitch dark when the trail finally leveled off and we came out in a clearing where two houses nested among the mist-obscured mountain peaks. The sound of our arrival brought shadowy figures to the door, *ocote* (resin wood) torches were lighted, and we found ourselves being introduced to the deserter's friends—a huge family with a flock of grown boys and girls who were individually and collectively the handsomest people we had met in our wanderings.

The cheerful way in which they made us welcome told us immediately that our fears had been unfounded and that these people were no criminals. With new warmth in our hearts, we shook hands with everybody, including our misjudged traveling companion, who had not, after all, been a romantic bandit, but just a nice boy who did not want to be a soldier. Now that we were safe, were we a little disappointed in him? Perhaps.

The Benitez family lived a gay, prosperous life in their desolate mountains. It was a different world from the haciendas of the Balsas, and seemed to be a much better one. Our hosts had a comfortable adobe house with a wide porch and a tile roof, worked their own land and raised their own cattle. There were four boys, ranging from about sixteen to twenty-five years of age, strong, tall fellows, light of skin and delicate of features, and two girls, slim and pretty and, incidentally, very good cooks, who would obviously make perfect ranch wives for some fortunate muchachos. The parents, with all this abundance of youth in the house, would not need to do a stroke of work.

All were well dressed, especially the girls, who wore fresh cotton dresses and shoes, and possessed little adornments such as necklaces, earrings, and ribbons for their hair—unlike the women of the desert and the river, who generally went barefoot and dressed in dirty and shapeless garments.

When our burros were unloaded and turned into a paddock for the night, we were invited to the kitchen, where the girls were busy patting out mountains of tortillas for us. The chief dish was a savory venison stew. There was plenty of it, and we kept coming back for more, apologizing all the time, but unable to resist the unaccustomed pleasure of stuffing ourselves with fresh meat. The tortillas, too, were especially tasty. We had become connoisseurs of tortillas in the past few weeks, and found these of the Sierra del Gallo the best we had ever come across. They were big and tender and golden in color, whereas the average tortilla is brownish and the substandard one is gray. The girls were pleased when we complimented them, and continued their kneading, patting and roasting with even greater energy. When we could not cram down another morsel, we were served steaming cups of *canela*, or cinnamon tea, a sweet, stimulating drink which was a pleasant change from strong coffee.

The boys, who sat and watched us eat, were amused at our excitement over the venison; to them eating deer meat was an everyday occurrence and they probably would have preferred pork. They told us that the mountaintops were swarming with deer and that they shot one every week or so, eating the meat and making a profit on the hides, which they dried and packed in bundles that sold for six or seven pesos a kilo.

"What do you shoot them with?" Fred wanted to know, and one of the boys went into the house and brought back his weapon, a .22 pistol. Of course, he said, some people preferred rifles, but he liked the automatic. It was light to carry and quick to shoot, especially if you carried it cocked. (This explained the cocked weapon of our deserter friend which had caused us so much worry.)

A .22 bullet seems a very small caliber to kill a deer, but these *venados* are little fellows no bigger than goats, and only sport a prong or two on their antlers. Moreover, they are plentiful and relatively tame, especially in the rainy season, when they get fat and lazy on good grazing. Still, to shoot a deer on the run with a pistol is quite a feat, and these men did it as a matter of course. Heaven help their enemies!

When the talk turned to guns, Fred had to display his little revolver, which they chuckled over and admired like children with a new toy. One of them wanted to buy it on the spot for twice what it was worth, but we did not feel like parting with it. We might just as well have sold it, for if we ever came to exchanging shots with a ranchero we would not have come away alive; if the ranchero did not kill us, his friends and relatives would have. But it was good for our morale to have the little thing at hand, and it might have served, perhaps, to frighten away a jaguar.

110

We slung our hammocks in the shelter of the porch and spent a cold night, waking now and then to draw our serapes more tightly around us. We got up at dawn, damp and chilly, to find the rancho enshrouded in fog, and made ourselves coffee on a corncob fire before the family arose. Since we were in no great rush to depart in this comfortable weather, we waited to have breakfast with our friends. The deserter told us that we had come to the parting of the ways, for he was going west to attend a wedding fiesta at the ranch of some friends, while our trail continued south. We were really sorry to see him go. In the friendly light of morning it was hard to see why he had appeared so sinister, but as he walked off upon his way we noticed that the big .45 was cocked again and ready for action.

Fetching the burros from the little enclosure where they had spent the night, we were mystified to find a wound at the base of Evita's left ear, the blood from which had run down her neck and dried there. What could have happened to her in the night? We were puzzling over it, when one of the boys approached, looked at the wound, and nodded his head.

"*Mordida de murcielago,*" he said. It was the bite of a vampire bat. He told us that these nocturnal bloodsuckers were a great pest in the mountains, and troubled the cattle, horses, and burros perpetually. They always bite around the neck, where the unfortunate animal cannot easily shake them off. I was preparing to wash the wound, but the boy restrained me, saying that the hardened blood would be the best protection against *gusanos*, the maggots which hatch out from flies' eggs. The wound in Evita's rump, now almost healed, had not developed gusanos, for we had guarded against that possibility by swabbing it with creolin (known in these parts as *mata-gusano*, or kill-worm) every time we could get hold of it. Poor Evita, everything seemed to happen to her.

Though I had announced to Fred that morning that the ordering of our laundry necessitated a stop at the first arroyo we came to, it was noon before we reached a beautiful sandy-bottomed stream with a turquoise blue pool, deep enough to swim in. The pond was waist-deep and pleasantly cold, with broad warm rocks around its rim on which to sun ourselves. I heaved our filthy dungarees into the water, and, after scrubbing socks and shirts at the water's edge, plunged in after the pants and beat them clean upon the now soapy rocks. We spread the clothes on branches where the sun would dry them in an hour or two and got into shorts and our last clean shirts. It was pleasant eating our lunch in the cool green shade, scolded at by birds and lulled by the roar of the water, which, rushing from the pool through a narrow outlet, flung itself down in a miniature waterfall to spread out over a wide sandy bed below.

Not until three o'clock, when the clothes were dry and ready to repack in Perón's bags, did we decide with regret that it was time to be getting along.

The trail did not spare us in the afternoon, but continued its sharp ascent of the stony mountainside. Because of the climb and the altitude, we were soon breathing heavily and taking frequent rests. The burros, on the other hand, invigorated by the cooler atmosphere and accustomed to high altitudes, trotted along with more vigor than they had displayed in weeks.

It was then that Fred bethought himself of a mountain-climbing technique which was to save us much labor: he remembered that in northern Italy and the Alps peasants hang to the tails of their donkeys when climbing mountains. We were a bit leery of trying it, for we imagined that a donkey might have to be trained from infancy to stand such treatment, but, looking out for kicks, we timidly closed our hands around the tassels that bobbed upon the ends of the burros' tails. They were surprised but they did not protest, and we soon found ourselves being pulled up the slopes at a good pace with very little effort.

In the course of our acquaintance with Perón and Evita, we had had many reasons to be irritated and exasperated by them, but at this moment we loved them and called endearing words of encouragement to them as they hauled us along: "Anda, Evita bonita!" and, "Vamos mi general!" After that, whenever a steep climb showed up ahead, one of us would sing out, "Tails!" and the expedition would halt so that I could run ahead and catch Evita's stern appendage, while Fred followed behind Perón.

We never saw any Mexican doing this, and those who watched

us were usually amused, although conceding that it was a good idea. Mexicans who live in the mountains and travel the trails frequently are so used to climbing that it is no trouble at all for them. They don't need any help on ascents. Many times in mountainous country, when we asked about the trail ahead, we would be told it was "*puro parejo*" (all level), only to encounter a series of extremely tiresome climbs and descents. Our informants did not intend to mislead us; they simply did not think of any climb as worth mentioning unless it was a truly terrible one. The Appalachians would be "puro parejo" to them.

The good time we had made by Fred's inspiration was wasted, however, when we managed to get ourselves lost. We had come out on a small plateau through which an arroyo ran, and found one trail crossing the stream and another running down the bank. Our usual practice when faced with a fork was to take the trail that seemed most used, but this was not always easy to determine. In this case we elected to follow a cattle track that took us over on the wrong side of the stream and, gradually narrowing, left us after half an hour or so, struggling and cursing in the middle of a thicket. There was nothing to do but go back, which involved extricating the burros from the underbrush to the accompaniment of much yelling and crashing of branches. It was a good thing we made so much noise, for somebody on the other bank of the arroyo heard us and shouted that we were on the wrong trail. Following the sound of their voices, we managed to shortcut back, crossed the arroyo, and emerge disheveled on the other side.

Our rescuers were two hunters, one afoot and one on horseback, who stood waiting for us to come up to the trail. The horseman was a big strapping fellow with one of the most luxurious curly mustaches we had ever been privileged to see. They both carried .22 rifles but said that they were low of ammunition and wondered if we had any to sell them. The only bullets we had were, of course, of the wrong caliber, so we offered them cigarettes instead and thanked them for putting us on the trail.

"*Por nada*," they said. They were glad to be of service to strangers.

As we smoked, we talked of El Norte, where the mustachioed horseman had worked as a bracero.

"Tell me," he inquired, "is the revolución still going on?"

We could not imagine what revolution he meant, and wondered vaguely if he might be talking about the Civil War.

"You know," he said, "the revolución that was happening while I was there six years ago."

Of course, he was referring to World War II. Since the only wars in Mexico have been revolutions, revolution and war are synonymous to a Mexican. We were happy to be able to inform him that it was over and that we—Mexico and the United States—had won.

"*Bien, bien*," he said, "and tell me, what happened to that man?"

"What man?"

"The bandido who started it all—with the little mustache."

"Oh, Hitler?"

He smiled and nodded. "*Exactamente*, Eetlaire, what became of him?"

"He was killed."

"Killed, eh? Que bien!"

That was all he cared to know about the revolución, for it followed a pattern perfectly familiar to him: a bandido started a revolución; he either got killed, like Pancho Villa or this fellow Eetlaire, or else he won, in which case he was no longer a bandido but *el presidente* and *mi general*. However it turned out, things went on just as before in the Sierra del Gallo. But he was pleased for our sake that we had disposed of Eetlaire. *Sic transit gloria mundi*.

The hunters were not traveling in our direction, but they had come from San Diego, the ranch where we intended to spend the night, and told us that the trail was difficult.

"Mire," said the man who was on foot, showing us the sole of his huarache. "If you look for this print it will take you right to San Diego."

The sandals were soled with rubber tire with a bold tread and made beautiful clear prints in the dust, so that we were able to go confidently forward until, near sunset, the tire prints brought us to the door of the rancho.

114

We were five days in the Sierra del Gallo before we topped the last mountain ridge and saw the blue Pacific at our feet. It was five days of cool walking with good food at every stop, except for one unfortunate occasion when we dined on an eight-year-old goat, the rancid taste of which stayed in our mouths for days. Generally we got venison with spicy gravy.

Handsome people were the rule in the mountains, we discovered. Indeed, they all seemed to be from the same mold, for we saw many who could have been the brothers and sisters of the Benitez family. No doubt there is much intermarriage among the hill folk.

Walking on from San Diego, we were able to note down another "first" in our journal for the day—the first tarantula. I do not care if I never see a second. The creature crossed our path, moving along crabwise on its furry legs with great deliberation. I almost stepped on it, for we had come to expect that the burros would warn us of danger on the trail, and in this case they didn't. It seems that burros are not scared of spiders, however large. This one was as big as a man's hand, horribly furry and colored black and orange. We did not think to exterminate it, but just stood and stared as the thing negotiated the trail and disappeared into the long grass.

There were scores of birds and flowers we did not recognize, huge hanging ants' nests where we were told parakeets laid their eggs, and groves of giant trees festooned with lianas, where the noonday sun scarcely penetrated. In many places we walked through tunnels of vines and interlaced branches which had been hacked out by the machetes of the mountain people. During the rainy season, when the creepers grow with wild energy, it must be a task to keep the trail open. Probably every man travels with his machete and strikes down encroaching vines here and there as he walks; otherwise it would soon be impassable.

We ran across Aftosa men again in Guerrero. This time, too, the American member of the team was a Texan, but he was of Mexican origin and his name was Santiago González. The cattle inspectors are easily distinguishable from rancheros by the fine animals they ride; each inspector has a string of six horses and mules furnished by the Mexican Government. Since most ranchers' mounts in Mexico are small, like cow ponies, the Aftosa men seem to tower on their huge beasts.

We met González at a ranch called El Águila (The Eagle), where we were engaged in discussing with the señora how we wanted our rice and eggs cooked, when the two Aftosa men drew rein before the house. The Mexican inspector apparently was not hungry, but González was, and we invited him to share our lunch.

"No, thanks," he said, "I'll just take a couple of eggs." The señora handed him two blanquillos which he nicked at either end with his knife and sucked down raw, with a gurgling sound and evident enjoyment. "They're nice and cool this way, and I don't waste any time."

He was a tanned, black-haired chap in his thirties, speaking English and Spanish with equal fluency, and evidently perfectly at home among the ranchers of Guerrero. He told us that he worked out of La Unión, a town on the coast about 150 miles above Acapulco. He and his partner had a route to cover in the mountains that took them about sixty days, and when they finished it they started out again almost immediately. He was a bachelor and did not mind the long absences from headquarters. In fact, his only complaint was that his job would soon fold up, for he said the disease was almost licked.

Theoretically the Mexican and American inspectors are on equal terms, but the gringos are much better off as far as pay goes. While the Mexican inspector gets thirty-three pesos a day from his government (about $4), the American gets forty pesos daily from Mexico and $10 per day from the United States Government. Most of them live on the Mexican salary and bank the American allowance.

Our lunch-time interview with González was brief, for he had many cattle to see that afternoon; but when we arrived at our overnight stop, a hacienda called Cofradía (Brotherhood), we found the two inspectors sprawled in hammocks on the veranda, while their animals ate corn which had been spread out upon saddlecloths at the edge of the porch.

The four of us had supper together, a meal of rice and carne seca

116

from our supplies, topped off by glasses of milk and hunks of cold boiled winter squash, which is considered quite a delicacy in Mexico. When we spoke laughingly of all the warnings we had received about the tough hombres in the Sierra del Gallo, González and his partner smiled, but assured us the hombres were really plenty tough. Most of their fighting, however, is among themselves. There are family feuds in the mountains, just like those of the Kentucky hill people. They start when one man shoots another in a dispute or a drunken fight. The family of the slain man takes up the quarrel and before long the two clans are taking pot shots at each other in the woods. González said quite seriously that somebody is killed almost every week in the Sierra del Gallo territory. González, incidentally, was the *muchacho muy simpático* that had replaced the unpopular inspector whom the mountain men shot.

It was on the following day that we clambered, hanging to our donkeys' tails, up the last ridge of the sierra and, emerging from the woods, stood blinking in the sunlight at the view before us.

"Oh, good Lord," said Fred despairingly. "Look at that long blue line of mountains we have to cross yet."

"Mountains, hell," I said. "That's the sea."

11 The Privy Pigs

THE PACIFIC OCEAN, EL PACIFICO, THE WINE-DARK SEA!
We had walked 250 miles to stand at last upon this mountaintop
in Guerrero. Across the level field of blue lay Hawaii and the myriad
coral atolls of the South Seas. A clean salty breeze that had come
thousands of miles unpolluted by man and his habitations dried the
sweat on our faces and ruffled the shaggy forelocks of our animals.
We felt as though the vast body of water were our own discovery
and we were the heirs of Balboa and Xenophon's ten thousand
Greeks, as though we ought to raise our red and black Tarascan
serape on a pole for a banner and march down to plant it in the
sands.

"Vamos, burritos!" we yelled, and plunged down the mountainside, out of the cool breeze and into the tropics.

It was three days, however, before we actually stood on the shore
and watched the giant swells crashing upon the sand. Between the
sierra and the coast stretched a broad green belt, luxuriant with
coconut and banana plantations and humid with ponds, swamps,
and streams, where the Balsas, nearing its goal, flows wide and
majestic through the delta land.

Surucua, at the foot of the sierra, looked like a big settlement
after the mountain ranchos, for it had a dozen houses, some of
them built of adobe. Oxen were being driven home from their day's
work in the *huertas* (plantations), cows were being milked, smoke
was issuing from kitchens, men and boys throwing down sacks
of copra and sesame seed from the backs of patient burros.

It was our thirst that led us to find a very gracious hostess for our night's stop. We were longing for a beer—we had not found any for a couple of weeks—and went from house to house asking if there was a shop where we could buy *cerveza*. At length a boy told us we might find some at the hacienda.

The hacendado was away, but Doña Adolfina, his housekeeper, invited us in, saying she had no beer to sell but that she would be glad to give us some. Why didn't we unload our donkeys and make ourselves at home?

We got bananas with our supper, the first fruit we had tasted since we left Ario de Rosales, with the exception of some seedy white cactus fruit which we had politely tasted in the desert and spat out when the back of the donor was turned. And we got *buñuelos,* paper-thin pancakes of wheat flour, fried in deep fat and served with honey.

Doña Adolfina was obviously glad to have us, for she wanted to talk about El Norte. Perhaps when we went back we would take her with us to Nueva York as housekeeper? I do not think she quite believed us when we described our one-room apartment and the kind of life we lived in it.

We set out at nine on the following morning. Our hostess would not accept a cent for her hospitality, but we pressed the point a little because, after all, she was the housekeeper, not the mistress of the place, and might be able to use a few pesos for herself. She looked at us with a puzzled expression and said she had heard that the Norte Americanos always wanted to pay for things: Was it because they did not like to accept favors or what?

"We are not like that here," she said with great dignity.

We put away our money in confusion and assured her that if she ever did come to the Estados Unidos she knew where to find friends.

We started at a brisk pace. We were now only one day's walk from Melchor Ocampo, at the mouth of the Balsas, where we planned to settle down for a bit. We were tired and dirty and running short of clean clothes and cigarettes, and the lure of a big "town" was strong. Plantations of coconuts, bananas and pineapples

119

lined our way, and we were continuously in the shade of the trees; occasionally the brecha forded shallow swampy spots where white herons stood on pipestem legs, their long beaks poised thoughtfully over the water.

Our last stop in Guerrero was at El Naranjito (The Little Orange), a drowsy village built upon the sandy soil of the delta where a few recently planted palm trees strove ineffectively to give an impression of cool shade to the barren square that was intended to be a plaza. There were houses on three sides of the square, mostly palm-leaf shacks, but including two or three more imposing adobe structures. A group of twenty-odd children sat cross-legged under one of the palm trees, being instructed in the three R's by a serious young schoolmaster in collar and tie. This was the first school we had seen since we left Ario.

One of the adobe houses turned out to be a tienda. As we drank our beer—which to our joy came out of a refrigerator—we watched a woman repairing a section of the wall which had become cracked and unsightly. She had a bucket of mud mixed with bits of straw and was carefully spreading the plaster over the wall, smoothing it down with her palms. In tierra caliente adobe houses are not made of sun-dried bricks as in the north; instead they put up walls of sticks and twigs and build up a thick mud coating upon this foundation.

The repair work was being done by a woman servant, for the owners of the tienda were prosperous folk. We had arrived on a busy day: they had just butchered a cow, and both men and women were running around with tubs of blood and assorted inner organs. The señor invited us to come in, and set up deck chairs for us in a huge room which resembled a patio except that it was roofed. The butchering was in progress on one side of the room, under the supervision of three or four huge, patient dogs, while in the kitchen a bevy of women of all ages were clustered around the big stove preparing comida. Two fighting cocks, tied in opposite corners of the room, crowed defiance back and forth. Swarms of flies, drawn by the blood, buzzed heavily round and round.

When the children came home from school, we sat down at a

long table and joined the family in an excellent meal which included rice, beans, several kinds of meat, fried eggs, cooked bananas, and pitchers of milk. Here, too, we were not allowed to pay, except for the beer which we had bought in the shop.

"Oh, no," the lady of the house told us, as she spooned bits of banana into her smallest child, "you are our guests, and if you come back this way, *tienen aquí su casa*."

It was with the warmest recollections of Guerrero that we crossed again into "our" state, Michoacán. An hour's walk from Naranjito brought us to a wide, shallow branch of the Balsas which we forded without difficulty, the water just coming up to the bellies of the donkeys, and in another hour we were standing again on the banks of *el rio grande*, waiting our turn to cross to Melchor Ocampo by one of the numerous dugout canoes which did ferry service there.

The Balsas at that point is wide and deep, flowing with solemn grandeur toward its marriage with the sea. The sun was low, and on the other shore, shaded by a high bluff, naked boys were swimming and diving. A boatman approached us, saying that if we wished to cross we must unload our carga, as the burros would have to swim. The animals, having no idea what was ahead of them, stood calmly on the sandy shore while we piled their boxes, bags, and harness into the waiting canoe.

"They can't swim, you know," Fred told the barquero. "They have never had to swim in their lives."

"No importa," the boatman replied. "They will swim, all right. But you come first with the carga, please."

The burros were left with a boy to hold them, and we were swiftly poled across to the far bank. Peering into the gathering dusk, we watched the canoe return. There was a long pause before it reembarked, and we saw the water churned white with splashes as Evita battled against the inevitable. When the canoe drew near again, we found that the barquero had two friends helping him; they were squatting toward the stern, firmly grasping Perón and Evita by their ears, while the terrified animals, with rolling eyes, lashed out with their feet seeking bottom.

121

They were the saddest and most subdued donkeys I have ever seen when they emerged dripping on the bank, their long fur plastered to their skin and their big eyes fastened upon us reproachfully. In the dusk we had to stagger up the bluff with our carga, piece by piece, for there was no room to load the burros on the steep bank. We were already in Melchor Ocampo (the town reaches to the riverbank), but it was a five-minute walk to the plaza, and there was nothing for it but to go through the whole process of repacking the animals in order to go the few last steps.

"Melchor," as it is usually called, is a typical hot-country settlement with houses of palm leaves and twigs, numbering, I would guess, no more than five hundred souls. Although most maps do not show it at all, Melchor considers itself a place of importance, for it lies in the center of a prosperous plantation country and its plaza is busy day and night with the hum of business being transacted. It has a movie house, a post office, a school, and numerous stores. There are even a few planters in Melchor who own tractors and jeeps.

In the center of town, around the plaza, the palm-leaf houses give way to adobe or brick structures with arcades which shade the streets. Being still a relatively young town, the plaza has not had time to develop much dignity, but it is trying. There is a flower garden, protected by chicken wire from wandering pigs and dogs; walks have been laid out, a bust (presumably of Melchor Ocampo, Benito Juárez' foreign minister) stands in the center, and there are a number of the cement benches which you see in every Mexican plaza, and which bear the names of the citizens or shops that donated them.

We stopped at a busy tienda run by an energetic elderly widow and her daughter, where everything from cloth and canned goods to kerosene and face powder could be purchased. As a crowning touch to its prosperity, this shop had a *paleteria*, or quick-freeze refrigerator, for making the ices on sticks which are so dear to Mexicans. The paleteria must have been a gold mine, for everybody in town seemed to be sucking at paletas all day, and the girls of the shop were constantly busy mixing new batches of sirup to pour into the little trays.

The *viuda*, when consulted about places to spend the night, replied that we could have a room in her house, if it suited us, for two pesos a day. The room was one of two simple, bare adobe chambers opening off a pretty patio bright with flowers and pungent with the odor of lemon blossoms.

For us, the simple quarters were a great luxury. There was a burlap-covered catre, a chair, a table, a kerosene lamp and, most wonderful of all, a door that could be shut. We unloaded the burros and boarded them across the street with an affable gentleman called, to our surprise, Señor Green—when asked about his name he mystified us by saying that he was of Scandinavian descent—who took the animals as a favor to us, for he was a man of position and not one who needed to make a peso boarding burros.

The viuda told us that our meals could be arranged at two pesos each for breakfast and dinner, and as for supper, which is a very light meal in Mexico, we could pick up what we liked in the plaza, or buy some bread and make coffee for ourselves. Our daily expenses, therefore, were ten pesos—about $1.25 for the two of us.

When I had donned my faithful wrap-around skirt, we set out in search of supper, for the flaring of several little lights at the opposite end of the plaza told us that women must be selling food there. Open-air restaurants are a feature of Mexican towns; usually they only operate in the evening, when the townsfolk, who have eaten huge comidas at three or four in the afternoon, come out for a stroll and stop for a cup of chocolate or a few enchiladas.

In Melchor there were only four or five tables, each lighted by its own little kerosene flame, and the food was very simple. We found sweet bread and coffee, and a macaroon confection made of shredded coconut which was wonderfully sweet and sticky.

We had just returned to our room and were preparing to go to bed when a series of shots rang out. Fred climbed back into his pants and rushed off to see what was going on, coming out on the plaza just in time to glimpse a man with a pistol in his hand

123

running off up the street. The plaza was still full of people, and buzzed with excited talk.

It seemed that the man Fred saw running off had made an unsuccessful attempt to assassinate another chap. The latter had shot back, but in the dark they had missed each other, and the assailant, having emptied his gun, had fled. The story behind it was that of a family feud. The assailant had been working in the United States when he received word from his family in Melchor that his brother had been murdered. He came straight back, got his pistol, and went after his brother's slayer. The prevailing opinion was that, although he hadn't got him this time, he would do so sooner or later, and the intended victim seemed to share the opinion, for he asked to be shut up in the jail overnight.

There was a small garrison of soldiers in Melchor, and on the morrow we saw a handful of them setting out in a halfhearted attempt to find the would-be assassin. After a few hours, when it was clear that he was no longer in town, they returned and gave up the chase. Everybody shrugged. Obviously the man had crossed the river into Guerrero and, once over a state boundary, there was no point in looking for him. The soldiers knew this perfectly well to start with, and had only gone on their little expedition to satisfy the urgent demands of the intended victim, who was scared to death and, as the people of Melchor said, *con razón* (with reason). Nobody felt sorry for him. It was a family fight, and such matters are beyond the law. If the fellow did not know how to defend himself, he had no business shooting the other chap's brother, verdad?

Señor Green, with whom we discussed the shooting, deplored the hotheadedness of Mexican youth, saying that such shooting affrays brought only trouble and sorrow to those who were involved in them.

"My own son," he said, "killed a soldier here, and now we can no longer be together."

When we expressed sympathy and asked if the boy had gone to prison, Señor Green looked offended.

"Oh, no, but he had to leave the state and now is living in

Vera Cruz. As a matter of fact, he is doing very well in business there."

Shooting a man is not regarded as a very serious crime in the back country of Mexico, any more than it was in the old American West. Robbers and cheats are universally condemned as *mala gente*, but a murderer—well, *quién sabe* what good reasons he may have had for his action?

We found the people of the coast a very different race of men from the desert ranchers of the Balsas or the mountain men of Guerrero. Deep in the interior, far from roads and communications, life goes on exactly as it has done for centuries and as it probably will continue for centuries to come; but on the coast the pace is accelerated. The *costeños* are busy planning roads and harbors, building stores, planting new huertas with which they hope to make their fortunes, speculating, gambling, looking for gold and minerals. . . . The world has not heard about them, and their villages are not on the map; but all that is going to be changed—not yet, maybe, but soon.

Most people we met in the coastal settlements were not natives of the region, but had come there seeking their fortunes. Knowing nothing of the Pacific coast, we had imagined that we would find villages of fishermen and folk who made their living from the sea, but nothing could have been further from the truth. In all the miles of seacoast that we followed, we never found one professional fisherman, and very few who even fished occasionally. They are afraid of the sea.

The Pacific, along the shores of Michoacán, is not a very friendly or useful ocean. There are no harbors. Along the entire coast of the state there is not a single sheltered cove where a boat can ride out a storm, and I could count on the fingers of one hand the spots where it would have been feasible to bring a rowboat or canoe to the shore. The southeasterly part is all open beaches, and the northwesterly section is nothing but rugged cliffs.

What little coastwise trading there is, is carried on by small boats which operate out of Manzanillo, in Colima, or Zihuatanejo, in Guerrero. The biggest of these traders is an Arab who, in a launch about thirty-five feet long, makes a run up and down the coast every couple of months, bringing merchandise to the little shops (soft drinks, groceries, and the like) and taking away passengers, copra, sesame, and pigs. Farther up the coast, where there are no roads at all, the arrival of El Árabe was eagerly anticipated every time a dot on the horizon indicated that a boat was passing by. Picking his weather carefully, the Arab would run in close to shore and launch a canoe, which would drop the freight and pick up whatever the people had to sell. Boats being so few and far between, he was able to set his own prices, and doubtless made a very good thing of it. We were told that he had consolidated his position with the authorities by marrying the daughter of the harbormaster in Zihuatanejo.

In addition to El Árabe, there was a handful of mariners who made long trips up and down the coast in frail dugout canoes with one-cylinder engines—expeditions which must have been perilous in the extreme because the craft when well loaded had only a few inches of freeboard between themselves and the Pacific surges.

The settlers on the Michoacán coast are always pleased to do business with the boatmen that come from Guerrero and Colima, but it would never occur to them to go into a business of that sort for themselves. Even the temptation of doing away with the middle-man's profit would not lure them on the sea, no thank you. Their minds are simply not oriented that way. They were drawn to the coast by the many rivers and arroyos which, widening into huge ponds, afford well watered ground for coco huertas and banana plantations; by the wooded slopes which can be cleared and sown to corn and sesame; by the money in people's pockets which can be spent at little shops that some day may develop into thriving enterprises.

In their leisure time, instead of going fishing, they go looking for gold nuggets in the arroyos, squatting with their pans in the fashion of the Forty-niners. Gold is accepted for barter in all the tiendas (at a rate substantially below the world market price), but most of the costeños prefer to use their gold for adornment. We wondered at first why so many people had gold teeth, and were surprised that they could afford such expensive dentistry. In fact, it was not from necessity, but pure show, and we were told that there are *dentistas* in this region whose entire practice consists of melting down people's nuggets to make gold caps which they then cement onto perfectly sound teeth—front teeth, of course, for more swank. The gold that did not go into teeth was made into earrings and beads for the women.

Melchor Ocampo was a metropolis to us, and its tiendas as tempting as Fifth Avenue show windows. We replenished our depleted supplies, exclaiming with joy upon the discovery of a few dusty little cans of chicken paté and Vienna sausages. We refilled our near-empty bags of rice, coffee, and sugar, and, by going from store to store, finally discovered a place which could supply us with our favorite brand of cigarettes. For the past few days we had been smoking whatever we could find in the tienditas we passed, strong black tobacco, the kind that is favored by country people. It made me dizzy, especially before breakfast.

We got out all our laundry and had it washed for a couple of pesos, Fred shaved for the first time in a week or more, the journal was caught up with, letters home were written and mailed, photographs sent back to Morelia for developing, the bedding was aired, the carga repacked, and everything put in trim for the walk up the coast. It was at this point in the trip that the presence of the niguas in our feet began to be really bothersome, and I duly noted down, for the first time: "Fred and I both have funny sores on the bottoms of our feet." But we still did not realize what was the trouble.

Melchor, our haven for two days, was a delight in all respects but one—its bathroom facilities. The settlement is so civilized that its houses have *excusados*. They more or less resemble the American backhouse, but there is one added feature—pigs. The shanties are built so that the pigs have access to them from behind, an arrangement which ensures a beautifully clean backhouse, although it did not strike us as very esthetic.

Here in the viuda's house, however, the seats were rather low and the pigs ravenous. A slat had been nailed up to keep them from biting people, but it did not seem very strong, and the pigs, straining against it, were able to bring their vicious snouts to within an inch of one's exposed underparts. This was disconcerting in the extreme. We used to try to tiptoe in very quietly, but the pigs always heard, and with grunts and squeals of joy would seem to be battering the privy to pieces as they jockeyed for position, snapping at each other.

So frustrating was this phase of our life at Melchor, that we finally gave up the attempt and, upon our departure, chewed down half a dozen milk of magnesia pills and hoped that our terrified digestions would thus recover their equilibrium.

12 Beachcombing

BEFORE TURNING UP THE COAST, WE HAD ONE IMPORTANT appointment to keep: we wanted to see for ourselves the union of the Rio de las Balsas with the Pacific, and we decided to do it in style, without our four-legged partners.

We found a boatman with a gasoline engine who would be glad to run us down to the *barra* and back, a matter of five or six miles. Our barquero was a lithe, dark-skinned fellow with muscles magnificently developed from carrying bags of copra, which, in fact, was his occupation when we came to the riverbank. A very small boy was helping him. The man would pick up a bag from the top, and the boy would assist him by pushing up the bottom until, with a mighty heave, the man would get it to his shoulder, trot over to the boat, and drop it inside. When the canoa was loaded to the gunwales, we were instructed to get aboard, Fred sitting amidships upon the copra and I in the stern, next to the barquero. The rusty one-cylinder engine responded to a couple of cranks of the wheel, and we were off with a *bang-bang-bang* that reverberated hollowly against the high bluff.

As we looked back upriver, a line of desert hills caught the morning sun, similar to the cerros we had climbed before reaching the ferry crossing at La Garita; ahead of us the shores were flat and swampy. Now and then we passed clearings where huertas had been planted and where the owners or caretakers waved to us from their open-air camps, consisting of no more than a *ramaje* (shelter) and a fireplace.

Between the clearings the delta land grew increasingly jungly as we chugged along, while the river, becoming shallower, moved more swiftly, rushing over snags and sandbars in a froth of bubbles. Our barquero, who knew every inch of the bottom, steered skillfully between half-sunken logs and jagged stumps; now and then we felt a whisper of sand under the keel as the canoa brushed across the bottom.

We had to preserve the carefulest balance, scarcely even moving our heads, for every slight motion caused a lurch that threatened to dump us all into the water. For ourselves, it would not have mattered much, but we were carrying the two cameras, our most precious possessions, and did not fancy the idea of offering them up as a sacrifice to the Balsas.

The river delta was teeming with a fascinating abundance of bird life, which increased as we left the plantations behind, until every branch along the tangled shore seemed to have its occupants. There were long-legged waders of all sizes, from giant cranes to erratic little sandpipers; egrets with long white plumes, ducks, cormorants, and pompous pelicans winging in from the sea like formations of flying boats. When the channel brought us close inshore, they all took off with raucous cries, alarmed by the hammering of the little engine.

"Allá está la barra," said the boatman, and, as we headed into midstream again, there opened before us a shining path of water which, except for the interruption of one little islet, stretched all the way to the horizon. The barra itself was a high-piled sandbar, on the left side of the riverbank, which had been thrown up by the sea to provide a most convenient sheltered landing place. We turned out of the swift current into the still water behind the bar. When the banging of the engine suddenly ceased, we heard the rush of the river as it raced through the narrow gut between the island and the bar.

Wading ashore and standing on the highest point of the bar, we watched the two waters meet. The powerful current of the river pouring out modified the incoming rollers so that, by the time they touched the bar, they were gentle waves which did not break, but just slid quietly up the sand with a little hissing sound. On the far side of the islet was another wider channel of the river, and the two streams, scouring their way around the rocky obstruction, joined and spread into a wide mouth which was both sea and river. The whole area swarmed with birds that fished in the narrow guts, nested on the island which was white with their droppings, and scurried in flocks up and down the edge of the sandbar. They were mostly ducks and sandpipers, with a few terns and gulls from the sea.

Not only birds were fishing. A man with rolled-up trousers waded into the water as we stood there and, with a graceful gesture, threw out a casting net, retrieved it, and threw it again, looking for small fish to use as bait. This was the one spot we saw on the coast where fishing was carried on more or less regularly, the river's mouth making access to the sea safe and easy.

Our barquero was unloading the copra and stacking the bags upon a large pile which he had brought on previous trips. Eventually a big *lancha* would come up from Zihuatanejo to carry the coconut meat away. Standing to leeward of the bags, we could smell the sickening sweet odor of decayed copra, which, when you have once smelled it, you can never mistake for anything else.

By following a path along the jungly shore, the boatman told us, we would come out on the beach where his family lived. He would not accompany us, for he had several more loads to fetch and would be shuttling up and down all day. The path, which was flooded in places by sea water and seepage from the swamp, took us up the shore of the river mouth for a way and then cut inland, to emerge in five minutes' time upon a broad beach of white-gold sand which stretched southeastward as far as the eye could reach, its lower edge fringed all the way with a moving border of foam.

It was a calm day, and the deep sea swells rolled in slowly and far apart, heaving themselves up as they reached shallow water until their tops curled under and they collapsed with a hollow boom and an explosion of spray. From the head of the beach we could feel the cool fog of the spray on our cheeks.

The house of the boatman's family was a ramaje with hammocks and catres underneath, an open-air fireplace, and clothes and cooking utensils hanging from the branches of trees. They seemed to be living a very carefree existence, with nothing to do but keep an eye on the copra on the other side of the point, go fishing, swim, and doze in their hammocks. Theirs was the only settlement on the beach, and all this sand and sun and ocean were their private preserve.

We had hoped to find, if not a shore dinner, at least some fish, but the ladies of the camp told us they had sent all their fish to be sold in Melchor. There was beef, however, and they began to prepare it for us, while we went for a swim, joining two naked brown boys who were standing waist-deep in the surges, playing with a toy canoe. We had our bathing suits on under our clothes, which simplified matters. I doubt if so brief a swimming costume as mine had ever been seen on a woman in those parts, where modesty requires that girls bathe in their petticoats.

The water, cool but not cold, was a delight, and we stayed for a long time, letting ourselves be buffeted by the waves. While we sunned on the sand, a cavalcade of young people, mounted on horses and burros and carrying coconuts slung from their saddles, drew up at the ramaje and, dismounting, stripped off their outer garments and came running down the sand. They were from Naranjito, and had come for a Sunday's outing at the shore. They acted just as everybody does on a Sunday at the beach, giggling, chasing one another, splashing and ducking, with shrill screams from the girls and loud laughter from the boys. Except that the boys wore their undershorts and the girls their slips, they might have been any gang of kids on any beach. When they were all exhausted, they retired to the shade of the ramaje and ate their lunch, with the cocos for dessert.

When we had eaten ours, which was not enough to satisfy appetites made ravenous by the sea air, we headed back for the barra, where we sat for an hour or more, enchanted by the birds. By remaining very still, we were able to take some fairly close pictures of the flocks of ducks, but the pelicans would not come within camera range. As we watched, a little boy of about ten strolled in sight with a .22 rifle and with two shots brought down two

132

ducks. It was not so much that he was a good shot as that he simply could not fail to hit something when he fired into the massed flock that scoured the water's edge for fish. The birds took off at the sound of the rifle, but returned again in a few moments. We examined the ducks that the boy had brought down, and I was able to identify them as blue-winged teal.

In midafternoon we heard the *put-put* of the one-cylinder engine as the barquero came down with another load of copra. Our return trip against the current was slower, and a couple of times we grounded on shallows where our boatman would have to jump out and push. The fare for the trip was fifteen pesos (about $1.80), which, considering that it was not a special trip, seemed to us rather high. The reason undoubtedly was that it was a *canoa de motor* and therefore was expected to earn more money for its owner than an ordinary canoa. Most Mexicans in the country figure their own labor as worth practically nothing, but the work of their animals and machines, because they cost something, has to be adequately compensated. A barquero who took us down paddling all the way would have charged half the price, even though it cost him much more labor.

We had been advised that Playa Azul, the next settlement up the coast, was about three hours on horseback. This meant that we should have been able to cover the distance on foot in twice the time, but of course it was soon apparent that Señor Green, who supplied the information, must have been riding a race horse.

The part of the trip from Melchor northwestward up the coast to Playa Azul had appeared to us, from the map, as the most difficult part of the whole journey, for we could see that there were several rivers, branches of the Balsas, flowing down to the sea, and we wondered how we were to cross them. No trail at all was shown on our map. The rivers, however, proved to be dry. At this time of year, when the seca is well advanced and the flow of the streams decreases, many of them do not get to the sea at all, but simply dam up behind the high beach, where they spread into broad, stagnant *esteros* (ponds), and only break out over the beach when they are swollen by the rains. Most of the rivers shown on the map were in this category, although later on there were one or two larger ones which gave us some trouble.

We had about an hour's walking to reach the sea from Melchor, not by the route we had followed to the barra, but by a trail that went straight out through coco plantations to intersect the beach some five miles west of the river mouth. We could hear the crash of the waves long before we emerged from the palm trees to the shore. Our trail stopped there, for we were to continue to Playa Azul by the beach, and since everyone who walked this way followed the hard sand close to the water, their tracks were swiftly erased by the waves.

The burros took one look at the breakers, laid back their ears and turned right around. Did we think they were crazy? They were certainly not going anywhere near that water. When we found stout sticks and began to apply them, the donkeys reluctantly took a few steps, but they would not walk down near the waves, not if we killed them. Their swim across the Balsas must have been vivid in their minds, and they probably were afraid we were going to make them swim to the Philippines. At any rate, they would not approach the firm sand near the water, but stubbornly plowed through the deep hot sand at the top of the beach, forcing us to do the same.

The shore on which we walked, or rather labored, was absolutely straight, and stretched for miles ahead of us, losing itself finally in the haze of distance. There was nobody in sight in either direction—nothing but sea and sand. We removed our shoes and took turns minding the burros, so that the one who was free could paddle along the fringe of the surf. The one who was acting as arriero had to keep his mind on the job and walk between the burros and the top of the beach, whirling his stick where they could see it and administering a rap if they began to edge higher. One moment of inattention and the two of them were off into the underbrush at a trot.

It seemed as though our walk on the beach, which we had been anticipating so eagerly, was going to be nothing but exasperation, and our impression was confirmed when, at about eleven o'clock, the bottom of one of Evita's boxes began to fall out, and little cans of paté and sausages plopped into the sand. The reata kept the board from falling out entirely, but there was a big gap and it was obvious that repair work would have to be done immediately. Since this meant unloading Evita and dumping out the box, we decided to call a halt for lunch.

There was no shade at the top of the beach except that provided by the bushes. Palm trees, we discovered, do not grow just anywhere on the shore, but only near the *esteros*, where they can get water. Between the river mouths nothing grows but brush and scrubby trees. We had no choice but to carve ourselves a retreat under a thicket, where we were able to sprawl in the shade but not to sit upright.

I set about driving the loosened nails back into the box with the butt of a knife while Fred supervised the job. (He conveniently professes no knowledge whatever of matters relating to tools and repairs.) We had our standard lunch of rice (this time with canned sausage), and washed both the dishes and ourselves in the surf. A doze in the midday heat under our bush refreshed us for the afternoon's walk, and we determined to make the burros walk on the hard sand if it was the last thing we or they did.

"They have to learn," said Fred with determination, clouting Perón on the side of the head. (Salud had advised us in his burro-management classes back at Arócutin that when a donkey is really ornery, a few blows on the head are highly effective.) There seemed to be no other way to teach them, so I joined in and gave poor Evita a good bang between the ears. By this method we forced them inch by inch toward the breaking waves. The unfortunate beasts were terrified, and the sound of the thumps on their skulls had me almost in tears—but it worked. After half an hour of the sternest punishment, they were walking submissively along the hard sand. At first they tried to run away every time a wave larger than the others would rush up the sand toward their feet, but after a few wettings they came to see that it was not going to hurt them. In a short time they were trotting along confidently, their hoofs scarcely denting the firm-packed sand. Perón even seemed to take

135

pleasure in the waves that sometimes swirled around his legs, and would splash through them like a small boy, telling Evita, "Pooh, that's nothing." During this phase of the trip, we changed his title from *general* to *almirante*.

Except for the pelicans that swooped along the wave crests looking for fish, we and our donkeys were the only living creatures in sight. The beach itself did not seem to support any life; the only things we found on it were dead—shellfish and the carapaces of turtles and crabs. The shells were a delight, and we soon had our pockets full of them: fragile pink double shells, like those of a clam, so thin that the wind would blow them away; scallop-shaped shells with bold plaid designs in black, orange, and white; curly spiral ones with mother-of-pearl inlay. We had been told to look for turtle eggs, but somebody, either a man or a dog, had been there before us, for every time we found a set of turtle tracks and followed them hopefully up the beach we discovered a big hole where the eggs had been removed.

Even in the heat of the day it was cool on the beach, for there was always a steady onshore breeze which came up so strong in the afternoon that we had to fasten the chin straps of our sombreros not to lose them. Since nobody was there to see, we both walked along comfortably in nothing but sombreros and shorts.

It was about four o'clock when we sighted our first man on the beach. He was sitting on a fence which enclosed a coconut plantation, and informed us that we would have to hurry if we wanted to reach Playa Azul by sundown. When we asked him to get us some coconuts, he disappeared among the trees and soon came back with two big ones just right for drinking. They were not his, he said, but since he had gone to the trouble of getting them for us we could give him a peso if we liked.

One nut we tied to Perón's pack for future reference, and the other we opened on the spot, hacking off the fibrous outer skin until we had made a hole to drink from. The cool sweet liquid was wonderfully refreshing, and the burros seemed to enjoy nibbling on the thin layer of delicate meat in the shells. The poor beasts had not had any water since morning, and were not going to get any until they reached Playa Azul. They had already snuffed at the sea water hopefully and spat it out with disgust, and the occasional esteros which we passed did not tempt them either, for they were briny and stagnant.

In addition to their thirst, the animals were tired from the morning's struggle along the beach, especially Perón, who was developing a little sore on his back. The sore did not look like much to start with, just a bald spot where the hair had rubbed off; but we had been warned to take care of it, for a sore on the back is the hardest to cure, especially when the animal must work every day. In order to ease him, we had placed two pads under the suadera, so that the load would not rest on the raw place, but by the end of the day the pads were flattened out and the sore looked painful.

We ate our second coconut as the sun was dropping into the sea. Before long it was quite dark. Still no Playa Azul. Then, far ahead, we saw a light flickering, and steered for it like sailors making for harbor. Unable to see a thing, we stumbled up and down dunes and at last began running into wire fences.

We could now see that the light was a lantern hanging from the porch of a white house set by itself on a dune over the sea, but a fence prevented us from reaching it. Fred had to scramble under the wire and make inquiries. We were soon headed the right way and came out on Playa Azul's main (and only) street, at the end of which was the hotelito which had attracted us by its light.

Stumbling into the lamp's glare, weary and sunburned, we found a well dressed group of city folk sitting around a supper table. They were a Mexico City family with three small children, vacationing in this out-of-the-way spot, having come down by airplane. As for the hotelito, we did not care for it, but it seemed to be the only place to stay and we were too tired to make any further effort. Before we could get our burros unloaded, they too demonstrated their fatigue and collapsed, carga and all, in the courtyard.

This so-called hotel was built in what the owners fondly imagined to be American style. It was a cottage with five or six tiny rooms, separated by flimsy partitions which did not go up to the ceiling, and it had "modern plumbing," that is, a toilet and faucets which

137

did not work for the very good reason that they were not connected with anything.

In addition to the family from Mexico City, the little place was inhabited by a group of engineers who were engaged in preliminary surveys and studies to see if a harbor could be made at Playa Azul. One of the engineers was away for the week end, and we got his room—same sheets and everything. Since the house was built within reach of the sea mist, everything was damp, including the bedding.

The señorita who ran the place, a slacks-wearing spinster from the city, felt that she was doing us a great favor by allowing us to have this frightful little den for six pesos per night (which was pure profit for her, since the absent *ingeniero* certainly must have been paying a weekly rate for it). When we asked for food, she gave us half a glass of milk and a tiny dish of beans, informing us that there wasn't a thing more to eat in the place. If we were hungry, it was just too bad; we could have a nice breakfast in the morning, verdad? The donkeys fared no better: they got a little water which we drew for them from a well, but no corn or rastrojo was available.

We slunk off to our quarters, determined that the first light of day would find us somewhere else and that the lady would not get another peso out of us.

13　Fish Stories

IN THE EARLY HOURS OF THE MORNING, FRED DISAPPEARED from our cubicle in the hotelito, to return in half an hour with the news that he had fixed everything: we had a new place to stay, breakfast was being cooked for us, and a medida of corn had been procured for the animals.

We "checked out" of the hotelito by driving our burros past the dining room and answering "No!" when the proprietress wanted to know if we were not staying for breakfast.

A few houses down Playa Azul's sandy main stem was Doña Julia's place, a shack of twigs and shingles, thatched with straw, but boasting the best cuisine and the most entertaining hostess in town. A tiny room with a burlap catre was our sleeping place and the kitchen was our salon. In the yard, where copra was spread to dry in the sun, Perón and Evita were tethered with their noses in a pan of corn.

Playa Azul, even more than Melchor Ocampo, has delusions of grandeur. A brecha from Apatzingán, one hundred miles to the north, brings trucks, and even wheezing, protesting old buses, down to Playa Azul during the dry season; and there is air service, too, with little planes from Urupan coming down on the beach between two flags which mark a runway. In addition to these links with the great world, there was the new excitement of a port. If the clever ingenieros could figure out how to make a protected harbor for boats to land, Playa Azul would become the capital of the Michoacán coast. Already there was a hotelito; soon there would be real

139

hotels, ships coming in, tourists spending money, beautiful homes going up, new stores being built.

Doña Julia told us that if we should return to Playa Azul in a few years' time, the place would be very different.

"People traveling with burros!" she said with mock disdain. "We won't even speak to you. Anybody who is anybody will be traveling in ships."

The settlement, which gets its name of Blue Beach from the dark color of the sand, is built right along the shore. A couple of arroyos come down to the coast at this point and form a big estero which partly blocks the way from the houses to the sea. It was a wonder we had not fallen into it, when we arrived in the dark. Doubling the end of the pond, you find yourself on the open beach, which continues on to the northwestward, exactly like the stretch which we had already covered, straight, level, and deserted as far as the eye can see.

How they were going to make a harbor on the open beach was more than we could imagine, for no concrete structure, however well built, could stand up to the pounding of those seas. We had an opportunity to see what the giant Pacific rollers could do. The day after our arrival a speck on the horizon materialized into a small motorboat, and half the town ran to the beach to see what the lancha was going to do. It came as close to shore as it dared and launched a canoe, into which three men climbed, two paddlers and one passenger. He was the ingeniero whose room we had occupied the night before, and who had come down by sea from Manzanillo. As the little craft approached shallow water, where the towering waves gathered themselves for their assault on the sand, the paddlers backed water for a while, hoping for a calm spell. Then, choosing their moment, they raced for shore. They had not taken three strokes before a big lazy wave reared up and broke on top of them, dumping crew and passenger into the sea. The surf brought them flying to shore, along with their boat, paddles, and two dripping suitcases. Spitting out salt water, the ingeniero picked up his ruined bags and plodded off toward the hotelito, where I suppose he got the same sheets we had had.

In addition to ourselves, there were two other guests at Doña Julia's house who had the sense to pass up the hotelito in favor of this humbler but more cheerful hostelry. They were a beer salesman from Mexico City, who was taking a swing through the hot-country settlements on behalf of "*Corona, la cerveza mas fina de Mexico,*" and an artist friend of his who had come along for a holiday.

Mario Goudinoff (for that was the salesman's name) was of Russian and Spanish descent, a burly good-natured young fellow who was enjoying his job because it allowed him to travel all over Mexico, to the most out-of-the-way places. It was an easy life, for Mexican salesmanship is anything but high pressured; it consisted, in Mario's case, of drinking lots of little half-pint bottles of Corona, buying them for as many friends as possible, and telling everybody who would listen that it was the very best beer in the country, if not the world. He was touchingly devoted to his product and, if a store did not happen to carry it, would refuse to drink anything else.

Mario and Fred had something in common, because long years ago Fred worked as a wine salesman in France and Spain. But Fred did not have Mario's loyalty to the hand that fed him, which is why he is not a prosperous wine merchant today. According to the story, Fred was entertaining a table full of prospective clients at a French night club, when a vaguely familiar-looking gentleman came in and joined the party. When the stranger reached for a glass of the firm's champagne, Fred whispered in his ear: "You don't have to drink that swill. I have some real champagne right here," and pulled out a bottle of Mumm from under the table. Next day he had no job, for the stranger turned out to be his boss.

Though Mario thought the story a very funny one, he was a little bit shocked, too. For him, Corona was all that its advertisements claimed, and the brewery was clean enough to eat off the floor. The stuff we preferred, he claimed, was bottled under the most filthy conditions.

Mario and his friend, Umberto Guevara, had been crab fishing in the estero and invited us to dine with them, after we had all taken a swim. Doña Julia boiled the crabs and cooled them, and

141

they were delicious with peppery chile sauce. We fed the scraps to Doña Julia's two dogs: a big police dog named Remember and an elderly little brindled mutt with some bull terrier in his ancestry that was known as Kaiser. Remember, a pompous and serious-minded dog, had been named to commemorate the visit of an American who had told Doña Julia that if she gave the pup that name she would always remember his visit. She did, too. As for Kaiser, who was to become our special friend, he was the Number Two dog, sleeping out by the pig pen, instead of in front of the mistress' door, and eating only what Remember did not want. Doña Julia told us that Kaiser had arrived with a guest, liked the place, and stayed after his master left.

It was in Playa Azul that we discovered what those "funny sores" on the bottoms of our feet were, for we happened to mention them to a man who, by the description, knew immediately that we were harboring niguas.

"You must have them taken out," he said. "There is a señorita here who does it very well."

Armed with our first-aid kit, we looked up the young lady, who turned out to be a plump, giggling girl of about fifteen. When we bared our feet and exhibited the soles for her inspection, she nodded and said we most certainly did have niguas, and big ones, but she would get them out for us. Her operating equipment was a rusty razor blade, a pin from her hair, and a rag of dubious cleanliness. The operation consisted of cutting away the hard blister with the razor blade and then poking the niguas out with the pin. When the top skin was removed, a huge blob of black stuff welled out of the wound which (a doctor later told us) was decayed tissue. Along with the black stuff came the nigua and its young, too small to see, and at last a clean but bloody hole was left about a quarter of an inch across and a third of an inch deep. I had one nigua and Fred two. The operation completed, accompanied by much giggling and observed by quite an audience, we poured disinfectant into the holes, bandaged them, and hoped for the best. Our "surgeon" told us to watch out that new niguas did not enter the holes left by the old

142

ones, for that is a favorite trick of theirs. The señorita refused to be paid for her services, but accepted a refresco.

Even with my parasites removed, I still had a foot problem. On the walk so far, I had developed all the usual blisters that a tenderfoot is apt to acquire and that, in the course of time, had hardened into callouses—except for one spot at the tip of each heel where I kept getting blister upon blister. This was a mystery to me until I examined my boot soles. In making ready for the trip, both Fred and I had had our boots tipped at toe and heel with steel plates, with the idea that the reinforcement would preserve the parts which get the most wear. My boot heel had been worn down to almost nothing, leaving a steel rim at the back which was supporting all the weight. No wonder I had blisters.

When I communicated my discovery to Fred and said that I was going to get new heels and have the plates removed, he was dubious, saying that his plates were perfectly comfortable and that he would leave them on. The result was that I left Playa Azul on good new heels and never had any further trouble, while Fred, the day after we departed, began developing the telltale blisters on the tip of the heel. I am afraid I said "I told you so," which of course did not help matters a bit.

We had the nigua operation on the afternoon of our first day at Playa Azul and allowed ourselves another day to recover. On the third day, when we woke up early with the idea of moving on, we found that it was raining. Rain! We had not seen a drop of it since we arrived in Mexico and did not expect to see any until May, but there it was. There was no question of leaving, for it was a torrential downpour that obviously would last all day. Even the two steps from our room to the kitchen (they were separate shacks) were enough to get drenched.

Doña Julia told us that the storm was a *cabañuela*, and that one or two such rains always came in the dry season during January or February. For people with growing corn they were a blessing, but those who had copra in the sun cursed the cabañuela that soaked their drying coconuts just as they were ready to bag for the market.

143

We spent the day discussing the route that lay before us with the postmaster, who had made several trips up the coast to Manzanillo on muleback and was able to give us the name of every ranchito and coco huerta along the shore. He warned us that we were entering a region where food was scarce and houses were few and, in a week's walking, he said, we would be in the territory of the Pómaro Indians.

This was the first we had heard about the Pómaros, and none of it was good. According to the postmaster, they were a very clannish group, living by themselves and hating everybody from the outside; they spoke the language of the ancient Aztecs, Nahuatl, and apparently were an Aztec tribe which had migrated centuries ago to settle on the coast.

"They will not harm you," the postmaster said, "but they won't help you, either. Most of them would not even give a drink of water to a traveler, much less food."

There was a doctor staying at the postmaster's house, a wealthy young fellow of about thirty-five called Flores Gutierrez, who had never seriously practiced his profession, but used it as a springboard for his political aspirations. As things turned out, however, he had fallen into disfavor with the Mexico City politicos and decided to retire and become a country gentleman there on the coast, where he owned some property. The local people came to him when they were sick, and he advised them at little or no charge; but medicine was only a sideline for him. His real interests, he said, were hunting, fishing, and drinking beer in a hammock. He was building a big brick house at Playa Azul where he planned to bring his wife and stay every year during the pleasant season.

It was the doctor who told us that we must stop a day at the next settlement up the coast, Las Peñas (The Cliffs).

"It is the most beautiful spot for miles around," he said. "*Precioso!* There are great cliffs going down to the sea, and if you wade around the bottom you can catch lobsters with your hands in the little grottoes. There are oyster beds where you can pick up the biggest oysters you ever saw, and all the fish in the world for the catching."

He told us that the dueño of Las Peñas was in Playa Azul and that we would probably meet him at Doña Julia's to forewarn him of our projected visit. Sure enough, Don Agripino of Las Peñas came to the house for comida and said he would be delighted to have us visit him and most certainly he would take us fishing for oysters and lobsters. We got another invitation at the same time from a handsome boy of about sixteen, Felix Melgoza, who told us we would be very welcome at his father's coco plantation at Chuta, about a day's walk from Las Peñas.

The cabañuela was a one-day affair, and by the following morning it had diminished to a light drizzle. With Perón and Evita fat and strong again after a three-day rest, we said our goodbyes and headed up the beach for Las Peñas, our animals trotting along beside the breakers like old salts.

At our heels was Doña Julia's dog, Kaiser, coming along, as we thought, to accompany us a few steps on the trail, like a polite host. After an hour he was still there, walking sedately at Fred's heels, and no amount of stern admonitions to go home had any influence on him. He was, he claimed, our dog.

When we had made all suitable efforts to get rid of him and he still followed, we accepted him as a new volunteer for the expedition. Fred declared that no dog of his was going to be named Kaiser, so he was rechristened on the spot Julius Caesar, or in Spanish, Julio César. We were pleased to have another dog, especially one who appeared to be so mature and responsible, for we counted upon his doing guard duty at night, and performing other useful canine tasks. We had not got far, however, before Julio César made it clear that he was accompanying us as a friend but not as a servant.

He was the most completely useless dog imaginable, not because he was stupid but because he did not want to work. Rather than keep watch at night, he curled up and slept like a baby, and in the morning, instead of being eager to depart, he had to be wakened. We could have been murdered in our sleep, the burros could have been kidnaped, our equipment stolen—and César would have slept right through it. On the other hand, he did not cause any trouble, following soberly at our heels when we walked, resting when we rested, accepting whatever he got to eat with gratitude, and never fighting with other dogs. The biggest and meanest dogs would not attack César, for he had a knack of approaching them, a certain combination of dignity and modesty, which never caused offense. He also had a way of sidling up to señoras at their kitchen doors which seldom failed to produce something to eat—a dish of old tortillas, if nothing else. The señoras all thought him very simpático.

So self-effacing was César that we sometimes forgot about him for hours at a time, and would suddenly ask, "Where's the dog?" only to discover that he was padding along quietly in our shadows. As Fred said, having César was the nearest thing to not having a dog at all.

The beach, which had appeared endless, by afternoon could be seen to terminate in a series of black, craggy rocks. The mountains at Las Peñas come right down to the sea, where the breakers batter their flanks and carve out wonderful caves, towers, and pinnacles. Between the mountain ridges lie little isolated beaches, not broad and hard like those we had traveled on, but steep, with soft deep sand and ridges of round sea-beaten stones. We were excited to be approaching such wild grandeur, not thinking at the time that we would have to pay for the scenery by the most arduous type of travel we had yet encountered.

Las Peñas was perched on top of the first of a long series of rocky promontories. The great beach on which we had walked for more than thirty miles came to an end, and we found a path that took us up over the cliffs to Don Agripino's door. He lived, with two daughters (his señora was away on a visit), in a tiny shack of the simplest construction, overlooking the most spectacular view we had seen thus far on the coast. Right from his dooryard a sheer cliff dropped a hundred feet down to a tiny beach walled off at either end by rocky spires on which the rollers piled up in jets of foam.

Of all this beauty Don Agripino was the master, for he and his family were the only residents of Las Peñas. There was one other shack on the cliff top, but it was abandoned and the people who had lived there were not expected to return. Don Agripino hoped he would get another neighbor some day, for it was lonesome living there alone, and he did not like leaving the women by themselves when he had to go to Playa Azul overnight.

Since we had arrived in midafternoon and our host was eager to show us over his bailiwick, we got into bathing suits and clambered down a rocky path that brought us out on the little beach. The pale gold sand was soft and cool on our feet, and the deep-sea rollers, somewhat moderated by the outlying rocks, broke with less violence than on the long beach we had come from. Here one ought to be able to launch a canoe, I told Don Agripino. He agreed that it was possible and had even been done, but as for himself he did not care for the idea of putting to sea. He was afraid of *el mar*, and did not mind admitting it.

Don Agripino's pride and joy was a cave which the sea had hollowed out at the foot of the cliff. It was a perfect smuggler's den, with a sand floor and a dry arched roof, big enough to shelter twenty or thirty people. Everybody loves a cave; perhaps it is a reflection of the delight felt by our primordial ancestors when they found a home prepared for them by nature where, by putting a rock in the doorway, they could be safe from every outside danger. At any rate, the three of us sat there like children, listening to the muted roar of the surf from the outside and the hollow sound of our voices reverberating in the rocky chamber.

"Now," said Don Agripino, "we will go and look for lobsters." And he was off across the rocks at a fast trot. I made after him, for, having been raised on the Maine coast, I don't admit that anybody can gallop over broken rocks faster than I can. The rocks were, in fact, quite easy to get around on, because there was not a trace of seaweed or slime on them. I suppose the temperature of the water has something to do with it, but there you do not see streamers of kelp such as we have on the New England coast, or rockweed, or eel grass, or any marine vegetation, but only translucent water so clear that it is easy to spot a fish swimming far below the surface. And the sea in these latitudes has the beautiful turquoise- and robin's-egg-blue shades which we never see in northern waters. The wild rocks and the tons of spray flung up against the blue sky would have well repaid our excursion with Don

Agripino, even if we had not found any lobsters—which in fact we did not.

The technique of lobster fishing, Las Peñas style, is to go along the rocks looking into every little pool, in the hope that an extra big wave may have tossed up a lobster which will be trapped in the pool until another bigger wave scoops him out again. Don Agripino assured us that lobsters *had* been found this way, many of them, but today the sea was not very cooperative. As for clambering below the surf-swept ledges in the manner described by the doctor, it looked like a suicidal idea. Our host kept insisting that it was very unusual, the sea being so high; but it did not look to us any higher than it had been for the past week.

It was tantalizing in the extreme to be so near a teeming supply of seafood and not be able to get our hands on any. Don Agripino, taking us to another little cove, showed us the spot where oysters could be found, but it was covered with angry breakers. Never mind, he told us, why not wait until tomorrow, when we could devote the whole day to the pursuit of the sea's game? He was sure that the ocean would be more *manso* (tame) in the morning. We allowed ourselves to be persuaded.

All the while we were on the shore, we were tormented by tiny gnats which bit like horseflies, especially on the calves of our legs. The only way to get rid of them was to submerge in the water, which we did several times, and we resolved to cover ourselves as much as possible for tomorrow's expedition.

Don Agripino very proudly claimed that there were no pests at Las Peñas. By that he meant scorpions and snakes, I suppose, for the black gnats certainly were troublesome on the beach, and when we returned to the shack for supper we found that we had traded the gnats for something worse. We began scratching, scratching all over our bodies.

"Fleas, *nada mas*," said Don Agripino, extracting one from his armpit and cracking it with his nail. Like the gnats, these apparently were not pests, just members of the family.

The daughters of the house must have been counting on our bringing home something to eat from the sea, for it turned out that they had nothing to offer us but tortillas. We each got a dish of pieces of tortilla in chile sauce, accompanied by other tortillas on the side and followed by cups of ersatz coffee made with the seeds of a tropical fruit called *jamaica*. The fruit, which is bright red inside, is also mixed with water and sugar to make a rather pleasant soft drink.

Don Agripino had a shot of alcohol with his jamaica coffee and waxed talkative. He was a one-man chamber of commerce for Las Peñas. If only, he told us, he could lay his hands on a little capital, he would build a hotelito on the cliff, and tourists would come down to enjoy the beauties of his rocks and coves. Soon there would be roads and a harbor at Playa Azul. Why, Las Peñas would be worth a million pesos to the man who could put a hotel there.

Since we did not seem very much interested in turismo, he changed his tack and began talking of the possibilities of a tienda at Las Peñas. There were many rancheros up in the mountains, he said, and all of them had to go to Playa Azul to shop. If he could put up a little store on the cliff, they would be very happy to trade with him; and then, well, one could begin to buy and sell corn, copra, sesame. Oh, it was a grand life, that of a tienda keeper.

We said that if we lived there, we would get a boat and fish, and he thought that, too, would be a good idea, if one liked the sea, which he did not. But supposing we came to live there and brought a boat, he said; we could bring goods for the tienda from Manzanillo at a much lower rate than the commercial carriers, and carry back corn and copra to sell. He would manage the tienda and we would take care of the boat part. A regular business partnership, verdad? Then, if we wanted to branch out a bit, he knew of good land we could buy for bananas. Not cocos, for that would take too long, but bananas, that will yield a crop in nine months' time and, with the boat, we could take them to market ourselves and avoid the middleman. How about it? Did the señores have a little money they would like to invest?

By this time Don Agripino had taken about three shots of alcohol and saw before him a glorious future in which, working in partnership with the rich Americanos (us), he would become the biggest

149

man on the Michoacán coast, co-owner of a tienda, a banana huerta, and a lancha.

The night was cool, the ocean boomed against the cliffs, and for a while we too were deluded by dreams of glory. Borrowing here and there, we could scrape up a thousand or two, maybe. How much would a lancha cost? What prices were people getting for bananas? Where would we sell our fish? When we stumbled off to our hammocks, we dreamed of a neat little lancha loaded with bananas and copra, with Fred supervising the engine and me at the helm.

We woke up, however, to the realities of life at Las Peñas. After dozing half an hour, the fleas got to work on us so thoroughly that we both wakened to spend the whole night scratching and daubing ourselves with mosquito dope which, although it had worked before with fleas, did not seem to do any good with the fierce Las Peñas variety.

Next day, from the top of the cliff, the sea appeared to have moderated, and again we sallied forth hopefully, accompanied by a couple of boys from a nearby rancho as well as by Don Agripino. Once on the beach, however, it was apparent that the sea was no more manso than yesterday. The oyster beds and the grottoes of the lobsters were swept by huge breakers, and any attempt to get at them would have been foolhardy. We walked a mile or so up the shore, peering into all the pools in hopes of finding a trapped lobster, but . . . nada.

"Never mind," said Don Agripino, the incurable optimist. "We will get fish instead."

He took a stick of dynamite from his pocket and explained that the customary way to fish at Las Peñas was to stand on a high rock where you could get a good view into the water, and when a school of fish came in sight, light the fuse and kill them with the explosion. Of course, it was forbidden by the government, but everybody did it. In our present frame of mind, we were ready to get seafood by whatever means, so we acquiesced to his most unsporting proposition.

The whole party stationed itself on a ledge of rock about six

150

feet above the sea and peered into the agitated water. In the calm spells between waves, we caught sight of an occasional fish hurrying to get out to sea before the next wave swept it to shore.

"Of course," said Don Agripino, "since the señor does not swim, you will have to get the fish."

"Who, me?" I said. To pursue a dead fish among those huge waves with the possibility of being tossed against the rocks was not my idea of how to go fishing.

"Nobody else is going?" I asked, looking around at all those big, strong men. Apparently no one was, so I peeled down to my bathing suit and stood there at the edge of the rock, ready to dive at the signal. Don Agripino unwound a length of stout cord which he carried with him and roped me around the shoulders. I could imagine how much help that was going to be, but at least it might serve to recover the body.

We kept looking for fish, while Don Agripino held the dynamite in one hand and a lighted cigarette to touch off the fuse in the other. As we watched, a magnificent striped fish that must have weighed fifty pounds came nosing past us. The excitement of the hunt gripped me, and I yelled to Don Agripino to throw the dynamite quick, but he shook his head. Either the fish was no good, or Don Agripino wanted more and bigger ones. The beautiful striped fellow turned and swam out to sea again. After that, fish came and went, but not in great numbers, and none of them were very big. The dynamite had cost something, and Don Agripino obviously was not going to use it unless he could kill a ton of fish with it. After an hour of this, we told him that perhaps, since there was no fish, he would do us the honor of eating some of our rice and jerky for dinner, and he graciously accepted.

I untied the rescue cord and got back into my clothes with mixed emotions—half angry at Don Agripino for not having thrown the dynamite and half (perhaps more than half) relieved that I had not been called upon to plunge into the frothing sea.

That night Don Agripino again tried to get the conversation around to our possible investment in a business venture, but the spell had worn off. Obviously paradise was not here. One got sea-

151

food, perhaps, on some blue-moon occasion when the sea was as quiet as a millpond, and the rest of the time one fed on beauty and perhaps a few tortillas. The fleas were, if anything, worse than the night before, and, if it had not been so late, we would have been tempted to move on at once. As it was, we had to wait until morning—eaten alive again.

Before retiring, we told our friend Don Agripino that his plans for Las Peñas were indeed interesting, but that we did not have any money to invest. His face, when he bade us goodbye, had the same expression it had borne the day before when he stood on the rocks watching the big striped fish swim away—sad but philosophical. Perhaps some day other Americanos would come, less susceptible to fleas; and if the sea should be manso, they might get their lobsters and so decide that Las Peñas was a good place to settle down with a little tienda and a hotelito and a banana huerta and maybe a lancha . . .

14 Cocos, Chiggers, and Costeños

LIFE AT THE COCONUT HUERTA OF DON DAVID MELGOZA
was a very different affair from that at Las Peñas. Don David, whose
son Felix had invited us to Chuta, was a former truck driver from
Guerrero who, having saved his pesos over the years, had purchased
a plantation upon whose fruits he hoped soon to retire.

His house was built on a high and breezy hilltop overlooking the
massed green foliage of his cocos and commanding a fine view of the
beach. Here he and his wife and sister welcomed us, apologizing for
their simple palm-thatched house, which they said was soon to be replaced by a real ranch house of adobe. Indeed, they gave the impression of people who were camping, rather than permanently settled, for the huge one-room structure was bulging with clothes,
trunks, and belongings, stacked up or hanging from the rooftree.
Catres with mosquito nets were lined up as in a dormitory, and there
were many evidences of a former, more metropolitan life: aluminum
utensils, chinaware, coat hangers, fountain pens.

We sat on the cool porch looking out over the palm trees. Don
David leaned over the porch railing, cupping his hands around his
mouth, and shouted:

"Oye, Felix! Your amigos have arrived! Come up and bring some
cocos with you."

"Bien, papá!" came an answering shout.

In ten minutes our friend Felix came toiling up the steep hillside.
No longer attired in his "city" clothes, he perfectly filled the role of
the plantation owner's son, stripped to the waist, with sweat running

153

down his broad chest, an old palm sombrero set jauntily on his black curls, and two huge coconuts slung over his shoulder. He wiped his sweaty hand on the seat of his pants and shook hands with us, saying that he was very happy we had come. With a few expert strokes of his machete he opened one of the cocos for us. The technique is to cut off a slice of the husk diagonally at the stem end, which, if properly done, lays bare a little circle of the white coconut meat without breaking through to the juice. This circle of meat is then neatly cut out, and you have a hole to drink from, while the slice of husk is used as a spoon to scrape out the meat when the milk is drained and the nut cut open.

In coco-growing country nobody would dream of eating the hard old nuts that are sometimes shipped to northern markets; those are good only for copra. When just right to eat, the husk is green and full of liquid, with a delicate lining of tender meat no more than a third of an inch thick. On the hottest day coco milk is cool, and a big nut will produce almost a quart of the refreshing drink.

While we worked on the cocos, and the women set about preparing comida, Don David told us something of his plans for the future. He had bought the huerta a year ago, he said, and planned in a couple of years to turn it over to Felix and his other son (who was not at home), so that he and his wife could retire in comfort to some pleasant town. In addition to the boys, he had one employee, a man who used to work for him on the truck route and in whom he had great confidence.

Don David had about seven hundred palms of various ages, and said that he was planting as many more as there was room for. A coco palm does not begin to bear fruit for four years, and it is five years before it bears in sufficient quantity to make money for its owner. Mature palms are worth about two hundred pesos apiece ($25) and live to be eighty or a hundred years old, giving more nuts all the time. During the first five years, the trees have to be watered, unless the ground is unusually damp, and wire fences have to be put up to keep cattle away from the young trees. Apart from that, there is nothing to do but wait and collect the nuts when they come, which is twice a year: a large harvest in January and another, smaller, one

154

in April or May. When the nuts are fully ripe, with little juice and a thick layer of meat, they are split and left to dry in the sun, the meat then being scooped out and bagged for shipment to buyers who extract the oil.

Don David probably paid $6,000 or $7,000 for his huerta. The poor man's way of doing it is to buy the land, do his own planting and watering, and during the five years that he has to wait for the nuts plant corn or sesame between the young trees to bring in a little ready money.

To own cocos is the highest aspiration of most costeños, for the man with a huerta of a thousand palmeras is rich by Mexican standards. If he likes, he does not need to live on the insect-plagued, malarial coast, but can put the whole enterprise in charge of a custodian and come down twice a year for the harvest.

Don David, Felix, and the rest of them were getting a tremendous kick out of this new life of theirs, and babbled on about cocos just as a retired stockbroker will talk your ear off about his Angus cattle. But the Melgozas were going to make their huerta pay, whereas the retired businessman in America seldom breaks even at farming.

Señora de Melgoza gave us the best dinner we had eaten in a long time: soup, chicken, pork, fried bananas, frijoles refritos, and rice. Among their other virtues, the family had the sense to eat well. In Mexico it is not always poverty that causes people to eat badly; sometimes they just do not know any better. We ate with many people who had herds of cattle or fields of palm trees, and who ate like paupers because it was too much trouble to keep supplied with staples from town, to plant kitchen gardens, to hunt, fish, keep a cow, or tend properly to their chickens. In addition, some of them are misers and would rather bury their pesos in the ground than buy food with them. In general we found that, among people with prosperous ranches, those who had migrated recently from urban centers lived a far better life than those who had always lived in el campo; they were used to a decent standard of living, and maintained it, however much work it cost them.

Don David was interested in current events. He told us he had heard that there was a new war going on in Korea, and he wanted to know what it was all about. We explained where Korea was and what had been going on there between north and south before the United Nations stepped into the picture, but the idea of a menace from Russia was too remote for him to imagine.

It was around Chuta that we picked up some traveling companions that were to torment us for the next two weeks—ticks and chiggers. They infested the coast, and there was no way to get rid of them except to bathe in the sea, an expedient which was only temporary, for once on the trail again we would be reinfested with them immediately. The ticks were not so bad, for they were large enough to pick off, but chiggers are almost invisible to the naked eye, and quickly bury themselves in your flesh, where they will go on itching for days. Our bodies under our clothes were soon repulsively covered with scores of itching pimples which we could not help scratching, though of course that made them itch worse than ever. We were to have many almost sleepless nights until we got out of chigger country, nights of lying awake, smoking, and gritting our teeth to keep from scratching, until, unable to stand it, one or the other would say, "Damn it, I've just got to scratch," giving himself a few minutes' relief for another hour of intensified torment.

A spray gun full of DDT would have helped, but we had not thought to include it in our equipment, and the mosquito dope was no good at all. The only thing which helped slightly was a box of antihistamine pills, which, according to the label, were supposed to be helpful, not only for colds but also for itching caused by allergy. In desperation we tried them. I do not think they had much effect on the itching, but they did make us drowsy, so we used them as sleeping pills.

We were not the only members of the party that suffered; the burros were in torment, too, especially their noses, for they picked up a lot of chiggers from their fodder. They walked along rubbing their faces on every stump on the trail. César had them, too. At night, as we lay awake, we would hear the donkeys rubbing frantically at their noses and the *thump-thump* of César's leg as he scratched himself.

We had picked up our first ticks and chiggers on the trail from Las

156

Peñas to Chuta, for it was at this point that we left the clean open beach to clamber through the woods over the coastal mountain spurs. The trail from that point on, until we left the coast, was tougher than anything we had encountered, for it was a series of continual climbs and descents, broken only by occasional short stretches of beach where the sand was deep underfoot and the sun glaring. Instead of making the trail up along the mountain slope, where the climbing would have been less hectic, the people of the region had chosen to go as near to the shore as possible, making use of every tiny beach. At the end of each of the beaches, we would have to cut up over a mountain spur and come down again, then plod through deep sand, up again, down again, out again to the next beach, and so on. The minute the sea breeze was cut off by trees, we would begin to sweat heavily; our clothes were dripping all the time, which increased the itching of the insect bites.

The burros found it terribly hard work, and it was at this stage that Perón began to weaken. Evita was a tower of strength, but the little burro went ever more slowly up the steep climbs and at night often collapsed into a dead sleep without even a glance at his food. The sore on his back was red and obviously uncomfortable, but when we treated it he would simply roll in the dust until he rubbed off the medication, making it rawer than before.

We began to wish that we were not burdened with donkeys. Had we been experienced hikers, used to carrying heavy packs, it might have been easier in many ways to travel without pack animals, for we always had to worry about their food, their rest, their health, as well as our own. Walking with packs we could, for instance, have paused any time we liked to take a swim, with nothing to do but slip out of our clothes. It was not fair to the animals, however, to leave them standing with their carga for half or three-quarters of an hour, and if we unloaded them and repacked them, we wasted another half-hour, which changed the pause from a brief one to a very time-consuming affair. The result was that we generally had to hurry on without getting any pleasure out of those beautiful little beaches, so delightful for swimming and so man-killing to get to, that dotted our trail along the coast.

In the morning the burros had to be fetched (sometimes from paddocks a long way from the house) and packed up with their heavy gear; at noon stops for lunch they had to be unloaded and fodder had to be found for them; at night, the same thing. And there was never a time when one or the other of them was not suffering from some wound or sore that required treatment.

That is the difficult side of donkey travel. On the other hand, they carried all our gear and enabled us to walk with unburdened backs and empty hands, which was a great blessing. Back-packing our gear, we would have had to get along with the barest essentials. Still, if there is a "next time," I would seriously consider designing a pack of the lightest possible equipment—dehydrated foods and a minimum of clothes and medicines—in order to be free of the tyranny of pack animals.

Our friends at Chuta had advised us to make our next stop at Chuquiapa, a coco plantation where we were to ask for a certain Don Manuel Mendoza. Whereas in the desert and the mountains, we almost always found our stop for the night right on the trail, on the coast we often had to go a mile or more out of our way to reach the house or settlement where we planned to spend the night. This was because people built their homes on the hillsides above the stagnant, mosquito-breeding esteros that furnished water for their cocos. Unless we happened to meet someone who could show us the way, it was difficult to find the path around the estero and up to the houses. Frequently the sun would be sinking and darkness would be threatening, as we plunged wildly around the marshy shores of a great smelly pond, looking for a path, while our burros cooperated by getting caught in the underbrush, and the ticks dropped off the trees down our necks.

This was how it was at Chuquiapa until somebody appeared at the other side of the estero and shouted to us to walk back a quarter of a mile, where we would find a path leading up through the coconut plantation.

Don Manuel Mendoza was not the owner of the magnificent stand of palms along the beach, but acted as caretaker for an absentee landlord. He was an elderly man with many grown sons and daughters, and when we arrived everybody was uneasily pacing up and down the porch, discussing what to do about a sick baby. The child, a little girl of two, had been put to bed in the adobe central room, generally sacred to the father and mother of the house, where she lay, bright-eyed and feverish, wondering why she was getting so much attention.

Don Manuel's worried face cleared when he saw us come up to the porch, for visitors from El Norte surely would know about illnesses and carry remedios with them. We did, in fact, have several remedies for fever but, not being doctors, we had no idea what effect they might have on a two-year-old. There was terramycin in our medical kit, as well as sulfa tablets, but we did not know how much to pre-scribe. After a consultation, we decided that since the fever did not appear to be very high, we would begin with half an aspirin at four-hour intervals and, if that did not help, we would let them have some terramycin. The baby took her aspirin with a cup of cinnamon tea, and went to sleep. Everybody felt her forehead and agreed that the remedio was beginning to work, so we went off to supper in good spirits.

The conversation, as always, got around to the Estados Unidos and the big salaries that a man could earn there. We pointed out that, while the pay looked very good in terms of Mexican money, it actu-ally was not as much as they thought, because the necessities of life were generally more expensive in El Norte.

"But tell me," said Don Manuel, "how does it happen that our Mexican money is not worth so much as your money? I mean, some years ago an American dollar was worth two pesos, but now it is worth a lot more."

We were suddenly up to our necks in a discussion on economics and the relationship of money and goods and natural resources, which soon had everybody, including ourselves, hopelessly confused. You may take it for granted that you know about such matters, but when you try to explain them to a simple and direct person you find that you actually know very little.

By the time we went to bed, the baby's temperature appeared to be down to normal, and in the morning she was sitting up and drinking her *atole* (corn gruel) with a good appetite. We left some

159

aspirin in case the fever returned. When we were ready to leave, Don Manuel brought us a letter for a man in the next settlement we were to pass and asked us to be good enough to deliver it. Since there is no mail service to these remote stretches of the coast, letters are passed along from ranch to ranch, and to be entrusted with such a mission made us feel like real costeños.

The letter was duly delivered to Don Guadalupe Cervantes at La Manzanilla (The Linden Tree), after the most exhausting day we had thus far spent—a day in which we never had a stretch of easy going, even for ten minutes. We arrived at sundown and were so tired that we fell into bed immediately, without the strength to converse with our host beyond the minimum that politeness required. I was never so done in on the whole trip as I was that night, so much so that I was afraid I might be coming down with something, but it was just fatigue and, despite the chiggers, I got enough rest to feel like myself by morning.

The people at La Manzanilla admired our dog, and I suspect that they tried to lure him away from us. When we and the burros were a hundred yards from the house, Fred noticed that César was not with us and went back to look for him. Don Guadalupe's daughters had chosen that moment to set out a dish of food for César, and he was so busy wolfing it down that he had not seen us leave. The girls had their arms around his neck and were whispering sweet nothings into his ears while he gulped the tortillas, but when he heard Fred's whistle he shook off his admirers and bounded after us. He made it clear, by much cavorting and animated wags of the tail, that he did not intend to be left behind—not there, at any rate.

It was February 5th, the day before my birthday, and some sort of celebration seemed indicated for the morrow, but how to celebrate in a land without food, without drinks, almost without people?

We did not know that Providence had placed an ideal holiday stop in our path—Caleta de Campos, where we were to find good friends, good food, and blessed relief from bugs; Caleta, which was to take its place with Reparo de Luna as one of the unexpected, and therefore all the more delightful, oases of our journey.

15 Holiday

We got a house all to ourselves in Caleta de Campos and, if we had wanted, we could be living there still, rent free. It was a one-room shack with walls made of interlaced twigs, a palm thatch, and a dirt floor. There was a crumbling adobe stove on which we could make coffee on a fire of corncobs gleaned from other people's dooryards.

We luxuriated in the sense of independence and privacy which our house gave us, although the privacy was more conventional than real: you could see right through the walls. The people of the village, however, maintained our illusion of dignity by very formally knocking at our door and calling in a loud voice to ask if we were at home, even though they could see that we were. Our latticework walls, moreover, furnished splendid cross-ventilation.

Caleta de Campos, or Campos' Cove, is one of the most beautiful places in Mexico or in the world. We came for one day, stayed for three, and contemplated settling there for the rest of our lives.

The village, if it can be dignified by that name, is nothing much: twelve or fifteen palm-leaf houses, half of which are tiendas serving the needs of ranchers and planters for twenty miles around, a *campo de aviación,* and a lighthouse that doesn't light. The settlers of Caleta have not got around to laying out a plaza or planting any trees, so the village just sprawls in the sun and the sea wind, feeling that it has no need to beautify itself, since so much beauty is visible from everybody's doorstep.

From the high, bare promontory where the settlement perches, the whole Pacific is spread out before you, a vast field of blue, unbroken except by ships that pass far out against the horizon. Westward the coast continues rocky and forbidding, but east of the point where the beacon stands the shore line curves back into a welcoming cove, a half-mile semicircle of sand fringed with palm trees.

The slight shelter which the rocks at the upper end of the beach provide has been increased by the construction of a cement breakwater and a jetty where boats can discharge or load cargo on calm days. It is not a real harbor, by any means, but so far it is the nearest thing to it that the coast of Michoacán affords.

The breakwater was a project carried out by Mexico's beloved former president, Lázaro Cárdenas, who, since his retirement in 1940, has devoted himself entirely to the betterment of his native state. Throughout Michoacán, wherever you see a road being built, a dam constructed, an experimental farm, you will learn that it is a project of Don Lázaro. To the people of the state he is a god, and the proudest boast any rancher can make is to inform you that "Don Lázaro slept here." He apparently slept in more places than George Washington did, for there were few settlements where we were not told of a visit of "mi general."

Caleta, however, was a bit disappointed in Don Lázaro because the work of creating a harbor in the cove was suddenly suspended after the construction of one small breakwater and a jetty. The engineers, who had built little brick cottages in the expectation of a long stay, packed up and departed, leaving some of their machinery to rust in the salt wind. Instead of a real puerto, which was what the people had been led to expect, Caleta got only the breakwater and jetty. It is helpful for launching canoes, and small boats can put in if the sea is not too rough, but it is in no sense a puerto.

Apparently it was decided that Playa Azul, being nearer to civilization, would be a more suitable place to make the harbor. The people of Caleta suspected that there was some political chicanery behind it on the part of the big plantation owners near Playa Azul, who, of course, wanted cheap sea transportation for their copra. However, they had not given up hope that some day the ingenieros would come back and take up the job where they left it. Meantime, there was the breakwater and jetty, which were certainly impressive, even if the cement of the latter did already show one ominous crack.

We found the jetty a convenient place to swim and fish. In all the time we sat there dangling our lines, we caught only one small fish, but it was pleasant to look down into the clear water at the bright-colored fins and tails which continually played about the little pier. There were schools of striped zebra fish, angel fish with floating plumes, and scores of minute blue and orange fellows that darted about our bait, stealing with little bites every periwinkle we lowered to them.

The man who loaned us our house, Don Manuel, was in a sense a countryman of ours, for he came from Lake Pátzcuaro. He was a soldier who, although technically on duty with the small garrison at Caleta, had been given permission to run a tienda in his spare time. His term of enlistment was almost over, and he intended to stay on with his wife and children and make a life engaging in commerce on the coast. He came to drink coffee with us on the night of our arrival and told us how he would soon leave the army, collect his discharge pay, and settle down to become a costeño for good.

Caleta was a very hospitable place. Not long after we had moved in, another tienda keeper, Don Pancho, knocked on our door and brought us a catre, saying that he knew the house had no bed and that he would be happy to have us use one of his as long as we stayed. While we were getting out the coffee cups for Don Pancho, there was another knock on the door, and an old gentleman, more than a bit tight, appeared with half a case of beer as a housewarming gift. He was a builder from Guerrero who had been hired to put up a brick house for one of the most prosperous storekeepers, and was generally referred to, out of respect for his trade, as the "maestro." When we spoke of fish, the old man proposed to take us on a fishing expedition that very night, by moonlight, at a point farther up the shore, where a river runs into the sea. We would fish with a net, he said, and he could promise that we would catch plenty, for he was a real costeño from Guerrero, not one of these Michoacán settlers who did not understand the sea.

Since the expedition was planned for 2:00 A.M., and we felt sure that he would have passed out by then, we declined the invitation. Much to our surprise, at about eight o'clock in the morning he appeared at our door again, still tight, and presented us with half a dozen small fish for our breakfast.

"I told you I would get fish, didn't I?" he said proudly. "Soy costeño, yo."

My birthday was a fiesta entirely devoted to food and relaxation. We went to the beach after breakfast and stayed there all day until comida. To get to the shore of the cove, you have to stumble down a very steep path which brings you out in a coco huerta, where a big well, the source of all the village's water, is situated. Since the climb is so difficult, Caleta is one of the few places where women do not fetch water. Instead it is brought up by boys with donkeys that carry four five-gallon oil cans on a trip. We watered Perón and Evita there and left them tied under a palm tree, while we explored the beach, first buying a couple of cocos from the custodians of the huerta.

The beach at Caleta is a perfect half-moon, and the rollers conform to its shape as they surge in from the open ocean. Looking down from the village, you see the deep-sea swells moving along in an unbroken semicircle to fling themselves thundering on the sand. We bathed, scouted the pools for lobsters (without success), fished ineffectively from the jetty, and speculated about what a fine place this would be to pitch a tent and spend a beachcombing vacation.

The idea is not patented, and for the benefit of anybody who cares to try it, it would not be a very expensive affair, for Caleta can be reached at moderate cost by means of the little airplanes which come in to the campo de aviación once or twice a week from Arteaga, to the north. The ideal equipment would include a tent with roll-up sides, a folding boat, surf-casting rods, and a few cans of meat, jams, and so forth, to supplement the rather simple fare of the village. A dollar a day per person would take care of expenses.

One day at Caleta was not enough for us, especially when in the evening Don Pancho suggested a fishing and lobstering trip for the following day. He had a visor for goggle fishing and could borrow a canoa to go after the big fish that bite in deep water. Surely we were not going to leave so soon? We stayed.

A lot of things happened the next day, however, to prevent Don Pancho from keeping his promise. When in the morning we went to the tienda of our friend Don Manuel to make some purchases, we found half the men of the village standing around, while Don Manuel, assisted by Don Pancho, made an inventory of the entire contents of the tienda. Don Manuel looked rather glum. There had been a game of monte the night before, we were told, and Don Manuel, after losing all his money, had thrown his tienda and all its contents into the pot. He had been cleaned out and was now in the act of turning over the shop to its new owner, a black-browed tough-looking young fellow of about twenty-five, who stood behind the counter with a revolver in his belt, offering free beers to his friends.

When the inventory was finished, Don Manuel called on us and said that he was going back to Pátzcuaro with his wife and the chamacos (there were five of them). Yesterday he had been full of plans about his future life on the coast; now he said he really didn't care, he would find something to do in Pátzcuaro, his wife would be happier there among her own people, the kids could go to school. . . . He shrugged his shoulders. That was life. If he had been destined to become a successful trader on the coast, he would have won the card game, verdad?

Don Pancho also called to apologize for having broken our date, and begged us to wait one more day. Somebody had to act as umpire when the value of the tienda was being estimated, he explained, and being a friend of both parties, he was picked for the assignment. He had managed to salvage enough from the wreck so that Don Manuel and his family would have money for air passage back home and not be forced to hike it. He said that gambling was the curse of Caleta. There was nowhere to spend money, and after a few drinks the stakes would go up and up, until the man who finally came out the heavy loser would often be left completely broke. He himself did not gamble, just a friendly game for centavos now and then. If we would care for a friendly little game . . . We quickly said No, thanks.

"What about the man who won?" Fred asked. "Will he run the store now?"

Don Pancho said the winner didn't know the first thing about shopkeeping and would just sell off everything in the tienda and then close it. He didn't need the money anyhow, being the son of one of the wealthiest planters in the district.

The happiest person in Caleta that night—much happier than the winner of the tienda—was Don Manuel's wife, whose eyes were sparkling with joy at the thought of going back to her "tierra." She was a Tarascan woman, and she could never feel at home among these costeños, not if she stayed fifty years. She missed the cobbled streets and shady plazas of Pátzcuaro, the cool mountain air, the bustle of the market, and most of all the comfortable big adobe house where her papá and mamá lived. To lose the shop was a pity, but she would have been glad to lose a dozen shops if it meant going home.

There were many things about Pátzcuro that we, too, missed, but the spell of the coast was on us and, at that point, it would have taken very little to persuade us to settle down and become planters in Caleta. Don Pancho thought it would be a wonderful idea, and the three of us spent several hours talking about the copra business and the possible income to be derived from a coco huerta.

Don Pancho told us that with about $1,500 we could buy enough land to plant a thousand palm trees. The best way to do it, he believed, would be to go halves with a native costeño, who would be responsible for caring for the trees until they matured. We would buy the land, the nuts for planting, and the wire fencing, while our partner would do all the manual labor. At the end of five years, we would divide the trees, each taking five hundred. And a huerta of five hundred trees, Don Pancho claimed, would support us for the rest of our lives.

We got our pencils to try to estimate the expenses and profits of such a venture, and concluded that when the trees were mature they might net us about $100 a month, which in Mexico is enough to live on in a modest way. It is a wonder that we did not make a down payment on the spot, for Don Pancho claimed he knew of just the piece of land for us, but some instinct of caution prompted us to defer such an important decision to the end of our trip. We could always come back to the coast if we still wanted to become planters, and perhaps it would be well to find out a little more about the business before we plunged—not to mention finding the money.

Discussing the question with another acquaintance in Caleta, we were informed that Don Pancho didn't know a thing about cocos and had bought some very second-rate land himself, which he was probably trying to unload on us. Now if we wanted good advice, we would look at a piece of land which our informant could assure us was absolutely perfect . . . and so on. We concluded that a disinterested expert's advice would be essential, and nobody in Caleta was disinterested.

Cocos are big business on the coast, and many a fortune has been made from them. While there are a number of relatively small plantation owners, such as Don David Melgoza at Chuta, most of the best land is the property of a handful of dueños who are, at least in terms of pesos, millionaires. Some of them are absentee landlords, but several of the wealthiest prefer to stay on the coast and supervise their huertas in person. One of them is Don Melitón Aguirre.

We were chatting with Don Pancho across the counter of his tienda one day when an old man rode up on an ancient mule without a saddle and dismounted to make a few purchases. He was barefooted, dressed in a white cotton suit such as the Indians wear, but dirtier, and carried the little *costal*, or shoulder bag, which the old-fashioned Mexican prefers to pockets.

167

The old fellow bought a kilo of beans and a little salt, and was very much upset when Don Pancho told him that he was short of small change and would have to owe him thirty-five centavos (about a nickel).

"I will give it to you next time you pass by," said Pancho.

The old man would not agree, no, indeed. He peered about the shelves for several minutes and finally selected a box of matches and two aspirins to make up the difference. Then, as he was about to mount his mule again, his eye was caught by a pile of sombreros, and he inquired about the price. Don Pancho handed him one of the hats to try on, remarking that the price was eight pesos.

"What?" said the old man, handing back the sombrero and clapping his own broken old hat back on his head. "Eight pesos! I have never paid more than five pesos for my hats." And swinging aboard the mule, he kicked its lean flanks with his bare heels and trotted off in a huff.

"Do you know who he is?" Don Pancho inquired. "That is Don Melitón Aguirre, the dueño of half a million palm trees. Do you know what he carries in that costal? A roll of thousand-peso bills big enough to choke a horse."

"But what does he do with his money?" we wanted to know.

"Lo entierra," said Don Pancho with a shrug. "He buries it. He is a widower, and lives alone without even a housekeeper to cook for him. Once a day a woman comes over from the next ranch with a pile of tortillas."

Don Melitón is not an oddity, for there are many others like him, not only on the coast but throughout rural Mexico. They are men who have worked hard since childhood, saving their money, buying more land or more animals, never spending a cent on themselves, until, when they become rich, they have no use for their money except the pleasure of watching it accumulate in a hole under the floor or a secret niche in the rocks. Since their sons and daughters would be only too happy to spend the hoarded pesos, the location of the cache is usually known only to the old man, who often dies without having an opportunity to pass on the secret. The heirs go crazy digging up the house and grounds, and sometimes call in professional treasure hunters, who can detect the cache with instruments if there is gold or silver in it. Since gold, the favorite metal for burying, does not circulate legally in Mexico any more, and silver coins are too bulky, the old misers try to get brand-new bank notes, which will last longer underground, and they have been known to offer a 10 per cent premium to anybody who will take their tattered old bills in exchange for new ones.

In addition to Don Melitón Aguirre, there lived in the vicinity of Caleta another barefooted millionaire, Don Pedro Málaga, who was a former brother-in-law of General Cárdenas, his first wife having been the general's sister. When Cárdenas became president in 1934, so the story goes, Don Pedro decided to take a trip to Mexico City to visit his famous relative.

He arrived in the capital in his old white cotton suit with his costal over his shoulder and, scorning to pay the price of a breakfast at one of the big restaurants, went to the market to save a few pesos by eating at a cheap stall. Since he looked like an old beggar, a standkeeper hailed him.

"*Oye, viejo*, if you will take this broom and sweep in front of my stand, I'll give you twenty centavos." Other merchants in the vicinity joined in, more out of pity than need, until there were five of them offering Don Pedro the magnificent sum of one peso to sweep around their stalls. Without a word, the old man took the broom and carefully swept the required area; but when they handed him the money he flung the coppers to the ground, and, reaching into his costal, pulled out a huge roll of bank notes which he shook under their noses.

"Do you know who I am?" he shouted. "I am Don Pedro Málaga, and if I wanted to I could buy all of you, and your wives and daughters as well. Next time, perhaps, you will know a gentleman when you see one, fools!" And throwing down the broom, he stalked away.

Later on in our trip we stopped one day at a wretched mountain shack where an old man and his sons and daughters lived in what appeared to us to be utter poverty. Happening to mention the district in conversation with an Aftosa man, we were surprised when he burst out laughing at our mention of the "poor family."

"You should be as poor as that old man!" he said. "Why, the mountains are teeming with cattle that carry his brand. It takes days to round 'em up when we make an inspection. You'd be surprised how many of these 'poor' people have a fortune stashed away in a hole in the ground."

The younger generation of planters and ranchers, however, look upon money as something to spend, and the old millionaires are probably a vanishing race. When their children get hold of the hoarded pesos, the money promptly begins to circulate.

On the third day of our stay at Caleta de Campos, the fishing expedition finally came off. Don Pancho appeared in the morning with fishing goggles and a pair of denim gloves. He explained that they belonged to a friend of his who was expert at diving for lobsters, but unfortunately his friend was out of town and we would have to do our best without him.

On our way to the jetty, Don Pancho whetted our enthusiasm by telling us about two fishermen from Manzanillo who came to Caleta and in two days caught enough lobsters to load a special plane which they took up to Morelia, where seafood brings a fancy price.

"Of course," he added, "it is all a question of knowing how to do it."

After a few tries from the jetty, I appreciated the truth of his observation, for I dived myself silly without bringing up a single lobster. I am not a particularly good diver, and the water was about fifteen feet deep. By the time I got to the bottom, I would have but a moment to glance around before the pressure pushed me back to the surface, and, from what I could see, not a lobster was around. I finally gave up the effort and contented myself with drifting about face-down in the shallower water, watching the antics of the rainbow-colored fish. Don Pancho made some dives, too, but had no better luck than I did. Fred, who had his mouth all fixed for lobster, was disgusted with us, but in spite of his exhortations we crawled out panting on the cement and announced that the lobster hunt was off; we would try fishing instead.

Don Pancho and his brother-in-law had borrowed a canoa, which they managed to launch from the beach without difficulty, and picked us up from the jetty. It seemed an unstable craft to be riding the Pacific swells in, and leaked like a sieve. One of us had to be bailing constantly with a half coconut shell in order to keep the boat afloat. Our friends paddled us across the cove and threw over a stone anchor to hold us over a submerged rock which they claimed was a good fishing ground. In this case, at least, their claims were justified, for within an hour we had a number of small fish and two huge ones weighing at least eight pounds each. They were a beautiful pink color and looked something like carp, but the local name for them did not mean anything to us and we never did find out what they were. At any rate, they made a magnificent comida for the four of us.

The dinner party was held at the brother-in-law's house and consisted first of a sort of bouillabaisse à la Caleta, followed by fried fish and accompanied by beer. We were happy at least to have proved that the Pacific had fish in it. As to the lobsters, the tales about how easy they were to catch were certainly highly exaggerated, but I imagine that a skilled goggle fisher could have brought some up without difficulty from the places that were too deep for amateurs like Don Pancho and myself.

We did get one oyster on the coast. When we left Caleta on the next stage of our journey, Don Pancho accompanied us for a few miles to put us on the trail, which led out through an arroyo to another beach west of Caleta where, according to Pancho, there was a big oyster bed; but we were shy of fish stories by that time and were not inclined to spend a couple of hours in a vain search for oysters. Don Pancho proved that they were there, however, for he picked up one huge oyster which had washed in with the surf, and Fred, who ate it, said it was the best he had ever tasted.

We shook hands with Don Pancho, who left us to return to his tienda.

"Come back again," he said. "Come back and plant a huerta, and we will have great times fishing and hunting together."

"*Si Dios quiere,*" we told him.

16   The Devil's River

THE COAST FROM CALETA ONWARD WAS A NIGHTMARE— beautiful, but hellish labor for man and beast. Houses became fewer, food scarcer, and the trails rougher every day, while we ourselves were beginning to be tired with a fatigue that was not relieved by nights spent frantically scratching tick and chigger bites.

We were more than a month from Pátzcuaro now, and still a long way from Manzanillo, our original westward goal. Back at Caleta, Fred had diffidently advanced the idea that perhaps we had seen enough of the coast and might turn inland, for there was a northward trail there that would have taken us up to Arteaga, one of the big towns of tierra caliente. I have a stubborn streak in my nature, however, and refused to admit that things were getting too tough for us. So on we went up the coast.

No sooner had we gone too far to turn back than I wished that I had listened to Fred's councils of moderation, for the little expedition seemed to be foundering. Fred developed terrible blisters on both heels (due to the steel plates) and could scarcely manage to hobble along, while Perón, whose back was getting worse all the time, had a new sore on his rump where the tail strap chafed him. Evita, César, and I were just plain exhausted.

It was at a place called Guahua, two days' walk from Caleta, that we reached our low ebb. It had been an infuriating day of painful ascents and descents, of tiny beaches that blinded our eyes with their glaring white sands, and rocky trails where more than once Perón had to be heaved from behind to keep him going. When we

173

sat down to rest and drink at the top of one climb, I managed to leave behind our one-quart canteen, which, since we had not bothered to fill the big one, was all the water we had. Fred did not take this kindly, but decided that I was trying to murder him and suggested that it would be more merciful to use the pistol than to wait until he expired from thirst and sore feet.

Guahua was a couple of families living outdoors under ramajes, and our quarters for the night were two giant trees between which we slung our hammocks. Since Fred's blisters were broken and inflamed, we stayed over the following day in an effort to get him in better shape for traveling. As to our itinerary, I capitulated and proposed that we turn inland at the next place where we could find a trail north.

The women at Guahua had told us that in the morning there would be fresh beef, for they were planning to slaughter an animal. We waited all day for the beef until, in the afternoon, we were informed that the men had gone looking for the animal in the hills and presumably had not found it yet. It was at this low ebb in our affairs that I found in the carga a half-package of dried peas, still wearing their original cellophane wrapper. We stewed them into a thick pea soup, and it was strange to think that peas purchased months ago at the A & P on Atlantic Avenue in Brooklyn had come so far with us and now were saving us from going to bed without supper.

The next day we began inauspiciously by climbing the same mountain twice. It was a long ascent of more than an hour, and when we got to the top we were dead sure that we were going in the wrong direction. There was nobody around to advise us, so, after a long and inconclusive discussion, we turned the burros around and went back down the mountain. At the foot we met a man who told us that we had been on the right trail, and that if we stayed on it we would get to Tisupa, the first of the Pómaro Indian settlements. Back up again we climbed.

We did not get to Tisupa that day. The double climb had taken the heart out of the party, and we compromised on a rancho that lay midway on our route. For the last hour the trail was very steep, almost perpendicular, and Perón was in a state of utter exhaustion. He had to be pushed and pulled all the way. Pushing a donkey up a mountainside through the steaming hot woods is not much fun—not what you think of when you answer the call of the open road. I do not know how we got him as far as we did, but finally, with only fifty yards to go and the rancho in sight above us, Perón suddenly folded up and just lay there on the trail with his eyes closed. There was nothing to do but let him lie until he felt like getting up, so we loosened his cinch and ourselves carried up the bags and hammocks which were his only burden. He didn't look after us, but lay like one dead for the next three hours, until at length he arose and tottered up to the ranch in search of food.

The ranch was a tiny shelter of the most primitive sort, overlooking the sea, and was poetically named La Higuerita (The Little Fig Tree). We found the master in bed trying to fight off a malarial chill. He welcomed us hospitably, told his wife to cook us some deer meat, and asked why in God's name we were undergoing such hardships, instead of traveling by boat like sensible people. At that point, it was a hard question to answer.

Our malarial friend told us that he was going to Manzanillo himself as soon as a lancha arrived—probably tomorrow or the next day. Why didn't we come along? A boat trip, even in an open one-cylinder canoa, was a very tempting suggestion, and we might have done so had we been sure that the boat would really come. Knowing Mexico, however, we imagined that it might easily be a week's wait, and in a week we could be up in the mountains, not far from civilization. Besides, what would happen to our burros? The boat certainly would not be large enough to carry them along, too? Our host said that it was not, but that we could easily sell the burros, for there was a shortage of donkeys in the vicinity. Perón, even in his present state of collapse, would bring seventy-five pesos, and Evita would sell for more than a hundred. We could buy other burros in Manzanillo, if we wanted to continue our walking trip from there.

Apart from the question of whether or not the boat would really come, we were deterred by a certain sense of responsibility for

175

the burros. They were Tarascan donkeys, after all, and they suffered as much as we did from the heat and insects. It did not seem fair to condemn them to an alien life for the rest of their days just so that we could ride comfortably to Manzanillo. We were all in this together, for better or worse. *Adelante!*

The next day Perón was on his feet, though far from sprightly, and we transferred most of his load to the patient Evita in order to give him a rest. It was at this point that we noticed that the sore on his stern, which had been only an abrasion a day or two before, was developing into an abscess, and that there were worms in the abscess. We needed "kill-worm" and we needed it in a hurry, for worms can create a terrible wound on an animal in a very short time. Such are the problems of arrieros.

The territory of the Pómaro Indians, those reputedly unfriendly folk, lay ahead of us. Would they feed us and doctor our poor burrito, or would they shut the door in our faces, as the *gente de razón* back in Playa Azul had predicted?

The first Pómaros we met on the trail seemed just as friendly as any other Mexicans, and their manner of dress was cleaner and neater than that of most of the settlers on the coast. The Pómaro men wear what is practically a uniform of white cotton pants and jacket with a bright red sash wound around the waist. This is the old-fashioned hot-country costume in Mexico, but is worn today only by old people and Indians; the younger men prefer overalls or army-style khaki pants. Many of the Pómaro women wore white as well, and their skirts, like those of the Tarascans, swept the ground.

These people of ancient Aztec origin are allowed by the Mexican government to run their own lives according to their traditional customs. The government has given the Pómaro community perpetual title to their ancestral territory, which runs about thirty miles westward up the coast by some twenty miles northward, an oblong of land which, though it contains some mountains, has plenty of good fertile soil and pasture, far more than is needed by the fifteen hundred Pómaros who today make up the tribe. The Indians live under the benevolent dictatorship of two caciques who are elected for life terms and who also handle the Pómaros' relations with the Mexican government. Since basically all the Pómaros want from the government is to be let alone, these relations are easily conducted.

Our first night with the Pómaros was spent at the house of one of the chiefs, who, unfortunately, was away working with his sons over the copra, so that we did not get to see him. His wife and younger children made us welcome in their scrupulously neat adobe house, and the señora apologized at length for not having anything to eat. She had sent all the food out to the men in the huerta. If we would like to wait a day or two, the *señor grande* would come home and kill a pig to celebrate the end of the copra harvest, but for the present, well, she had tortillas, and we were welcome to use her kitchen to cook anything we had with us.

One thing which impressed us in the chief's home was that life seemed to be lived there almost exactly as it was lived centuries ago. Everything was made by hand, and could have been there at the time of the Conquest. In fact, examining all the household possessions, we could see only two which could not have existed long before the Spaniards came: a saddle (for there were, of course, no horses before the Spanish introduced them), and a zinc bucket.

Tisupa, the tiny settlement where the house was situated, was in the heart of a very fertile area surrounding the mouth of a big arroyo. There was water everywhere, and the Indians not only used it where they found it, but had dug irrigating canals that made a network through their fields, which were green with cocos, bananas, and papaya trees.

San Pedro, one of the main Pómaro villages, about twelve miles north across the mountains, is equally well watered and intensely cultivated, lying in a green valley at an altitude of about 3,000 feet. We were not surprised that the Pómaros loved their land and wanted to be left in peace to enjoy it.

Our slow ascent of the mountains behind Tisupa was a pleasure compared to the constant ups and downs of the coast. The first we saw of San Pedro, as we came down into the valley, was a blinding-white adobe building which turned out to be the church, or *el templo*, as the Indians say. There was no resident padre, but the people held Sunday services themselves, and once every few months a priest on muleback would come down from Coalcomán to hear confessions, marry, bury and, if possible, collect the 10 per cent tithe which the Church still levies on the people of this backward region. Although it is supposed to be voluntary, most of the Indians paid it as a matter of course.

San Pedro is a large village of about one hundred families, all Indians, for the Pómaros do not permit non-Pómaros to live in their villages or, if they can help it, to marry their daughters. We found the village prosperous, clean, and hospitable. Many of the houses were of adobe, and all had large porches and walled yards where dogs, chickens, pigs, and brown babies lived amicably amid the dust and corncobs.

We immediately met a couple of men who brought us to the nearest tienda for a warm beer and undertook to find some killworm for Perón's wounded rump, which they examined with many shakes of their heads. When the creolin was applied on a feather, worms fairly seethed out of the abscess—a loathsome sight, but Perón did not seem to feel it at all.

Our friends walked with us through the village to a large adobe house where they told us we would be well taken care of for the night. It was the home of Don Juventino Reyes, one of San Pedro's leading citizens, a dark, plump man in his forties with a round moon-like countenance and beautiful white teeth. His blunt features and the shape of his head suggested that there might be some truth in the legend that the Pómaros had mingled their blood centuries ago with that of runaway Negro slaves who fled to this part of Mexico from Spanish settlements during the early colonial days.

Don Juventino seemed very glad to receive us, and told us that comida would be ready right away. It was a luxury, for a change, to sit and wait for dinner, instead of being told there was nothing and having to rustle up a meal from our iron rations. In due course the señora put bowls of steaming chicken broth in front of us, and then, just as we were wondering if we would get a bit of chicken as well, she brought in the whole bird, beautifully stewed and cut in pieces.

178

The Pómaros do not know very much about themselves or their history. In search of information about their migration from the land of the ancient Aztecs, we looked up the schoolmaster, a señor called Huerta, who upheld the dignity of his profession by wearing a store-bought striped shirt and a tie.

"All that we know," he told us, "is that we are a branch of the Aztecs that emigrated from the *altiplano* (the central plateau) in the days before the Conquest, but why our ancestors came here, whether because of wars with other tribes or in search of new land—*quien sabe?*"

All the Pómaros speak Nahuatl among themselves, and some of them know very little Spanish. Their native tongue has been corrupted through the centuries, so that it is considerably different from the pure Mexican that is spoken still in some parts of the altiplano, such as in Tepoztlán, near Cuernavaca.

"Profesor" Huerta told us that about fifty years ago an epidemic of smallpox almost wiped out the tribe, which shrank to a mere five hundred people, but that now there were more than twice that many, and the birth rate was going up all the time. The Pómaros have in their communal territory far more land than they can work themselves, and at present much of it is rented out to "foreigners," that is, non-Indians. The rent money is collected by the caciques and probably buried in a hole in the ground against the time when the clan might need it. The communal land is held in perpetuity by the tribe, but is not worked collectively: each man may cultivate his own fields, plant what he likes and where he likes, and pocket the profits.

These Pómaros, even more than the Tarascans, seemed perfectly content with the life they lived in their backwater of Mexico. They need very little that civilization has to offer, and do not have any desire to come into closer contact with the outside world. At San Pedro we heard none of the talk that was on everybody's lips at Caleta, Playa Azul, and Melchor Ocampo—talk of roads and harbors, tractors, jeeps, hospitals, and motion-picture houses. About the only thing the Pómaros thought it was worth going out of their territory for was to buy liquor. A Pómaro with a thirst will trot

179

fifty miles in two days to buy himself a bottle, and then trot back again without even stopping to look around.

At San Pedro we reached a point where a decision had to be made: Should we head for home and travel straight north, or explore a little further into Pómaro territory by taking the westward trail to the Rio de Cachán and the Indian villages of Pómaro and Coire? Either way would bring us eventually to the city of Coalcomán (which meant hotels, hot showers, cold drinks, and beefsteaks), the northern trail in five days and the westward one in two weeks.

We were tired and dirty, and the comforts of Coalcomán had a powerful allure; on the other hand, we did not want to spend the rest of our lives wishing we had seen the Rio de Cachán. We pulled out of San Pedro in the morning, still undecided, each of us trying to read the other's mind. At length a fork presented itself, the right branch leading north to the high sierras, the left down to the sea again. We halted the burros and sat down. Prudence dictated the right-hand trail and adventure seemed to council the other. Let the fleshpots wait, we finally decided, and, turning the burros' heads to the west, took the trail for the Rio de Cachán.

Cachán is doubtless some local word, for it is unrecognized in Spanish lexicons, but there is a word *cachano*, meaning the devil, which is well suited to this particular region. To get down to the river we had to lose all the altitude which we had gained with so much effort coming up from Tisupa the day before. First, the trail took us up another thousand feet or so, where among beautiful pastures and stands of oak trees we found a settlement of three or four houses known as Las Encinas (The Oaks), and where a plump young woman cooked us a breakfast of boiled eggs. The eggs were to be all we got to eat that day.

From there onward it was a steep descent all the way, and from the highest point of the trail, looking out over the flat, wooded land of the river mouth, we could see the old Pacific again, shining serenely in the sun, laughing at our efforts. Fred hobbled along on his bandaged blisters, Perón dropped worms from his hideous wound, Evita walked wearily under the greater part of the carga, I

180

had some kind of kink in my knee which gave me a sharp pain every time I bent it, which was continually, and César scrambled along with lolling tongue and dejected tail.

When we had lost perhaps four thousand feet of altitude, the path leveled out through a tick-infested wood, where we caught glimpses of scarlet poinsettias and heard the chattering of parakeets in the branches.

Our watch had stopped back on the coast, so that we could no longer estimate distances very accurately, but we knew from the position of the sun more or less what time it was when we started and finished a day's hike. Our conservative estimate of the distance from San Pedro to the Rio Cachán was eighteen miles. We had not started particularly early, and the sun was very low when at last we stumbled out of the woods and across a dry arroyo.

Here we were stumped, for the trail split into several small paths and we had no way of knowing where the settlement, if any, might lie. Not a house or a trace of a person was visible. Back in Playa Azul, our adviser, the postmaster, had told us that the trail around the Rio Cachán was very difficult and that we would do well to hire a guide. We had not done so because our decision to go that way was made when we were already on the trail—and now it was too late. Fred said that he could not go a step farther, and the donkeys indicated that they felt the same way, so César and I left them resting on the bank of the arroyo and went on to reconnoiter, following various little paths in the hope of discovering a settlement. At long last, on a path somewhat larger than the others which I concluded must be the main trail, I found a house perched on a hillside. It was empty, and apparently had been empty for some time, but it would shelter us for the night.

The rest of the party managed to totter along to join us, and we bivouacked under the porch of the deserted house, while the sun went down, speedily plunging into obscurity the somber landscape of the devil's river. The rancho was tenanted by only one living creature, an old broody hen that made her home in the kitchen, where she was jealously guarding half a dozen eggs that she had laid in one of the stove holes. My hopes were raised by the eggs, but they turned out to be so old that they were virtually petrified inside. There was a strong temptation to kill the old bird and stew her for supper, but she was our hostess, after all, and there was something comforting about her fluttery presence around the silent kitchen.

The hen and the two or three bags of copra piled in the yard made it clear that the ranch was only temporarily abandoned. Probably the dueños were camping out in their coco plantation and would return at the end of the harvest. We fervently hoped that they would not return while we slept.

We built a huge fire in the yard in an effort to dispel the haunted atmosphere that an empty house has, and slung our hammocks under the porch roof. Since we were very tired and our supplies were scanty, we went to bed hungry. We had a little rice left, but if we cooked it we might not eat the next day. It was an eerie night and we did not sleep much, but watched the stars wheeling over the mountains we had come from and listened to the coyotes howling in the woods. The burros wandered around the yard all night restively, foraging for food in vain.

I got up before dawn and cooked our remaining rice and some coffee, not a very appetizing breakfast, but enough to keep from starving. I found a few old ears of corn that had been left in the kitchen for the hen and gave them to Perón and Evita. Their need was greater than hers.

Without a guide, with no idea if we were on the trail or not, we set out despondently and soon became hopelessly lost. The trail took us as far as the Rio de Cachán, a shallow wide stream which we forded with ease, and then deserted us completely. For four or five hours, while the sun got hotter and hotter, we wandered around the banks of the river looking for some sign of a trail. Nothing. Our hopes were continually raised by paths which, after a mile or two, would simply disappear, leaving us more confused than ever.

The hotels and cold beers of Coalcomán seemed very remote. What had possessed us to come down again to sea level when we were well on our way into the cool, delightful, chigger-free mountains?

"Well," said Fred finally, as we sat drearily smoking on a stone by the riverbank, "we can either starve here or try to get back to San Pedro."

We turned east again and fought our way downriver through brush and over rocks. Somehow, though we missed the trail on which we had arrived, we found another path which brought us toward noon to a remaje where children were playing and a woman was washing clothes in the river. People at last, praise the Lord! There was fresh meat drying on a line, and we rejoiced at the prospect of a good dinner. We were to be sorely disappointed, however, for the woman was one of those Pómaros who give their tribe a bad reputation. First she lied and said she had no food, and then, when we pointed to the meat, she claimed that she needed every bit of it for her family. In what was clearly only an effort to get rid of us, she said there was another family across the river and they would have food for us.

Wearily crossing the river, we found another ramaje, but there was no one at home and no way of getting food, for the place was protected by several big fierce dogs. Back to the first woman again.

"Can't you see that I am busy washing?" she said angrily when we again begged for food, pointing out that we were lost and had eaten practically nothing for two days. This was the worst reception we ever got in a Mexican home, and when we spoke of it later to people we met on the trail, they were horrified, declaring, "*Que barbaridad!*"

I think that at that point Fred was ready to demand some food by force of arms, but the woman, slowly and with great irritation, got up from her kneeling position on the riverbank and began poking around the stove, to present us in due course with half a dozen cold tortillas. That was all she could spare.

What about some meat? we wanted to know. She shook her head stubbornly. Please, just a little meat, señora, for the good

God's sake. She at last relented enough to add a few strips of beef to the pitiful stack of cold gray tortillas, and for this kindness she charged us plenty.

We whipped our tired donkeys and got away as fast as possible. We had an idea, when we first saw the ramaje, of resting there until the next day, but the cold reception we received put a different face on things. Tired and hungry as we were, we decided to start back for San Pedro at once. Perhaps we could make Las Encinas before sunset, but if not (and it did not seem likely), we would rather spend the night with the jaguars of the sierra than the hardhearted folk of the Rio de Cachán.

As we started on the long trail back, we realized that it was indeed time for us to head for home, because, once we had crossed the big dry arroyo, we did not recognize a thing on the trail, although we had come over it only the day before. It was so strange to us that we were afraid for a long time that it was not the same trail, until, late in the day, we came upon a few poinsettia trees in a damp gully that we remembered having seen on the way down. We had come all that way so tired that we had plodded along, looking down at our feet, without seeing anything of what was around us. True, the scenery was not especially diverting, being only trees and lianas, but we had expected to remember something besides one flash of red at the side of the trail.

The sun was setting as we began to reclimb the mountains, and it was obvious that we were not going to get to Las Encinas before dark. No matter, we would camp at the first water we found and push on in the morning. As dusk was settling in, we crossed a little brook at the foot of a very steep ascent and decided to go no farther. It was a bad campsite, damp and sloping and cluttered with small saplings, but it would have to do.

Our spirits were high again, for we were on the homeward trail, and every step from now on would take us nearer to Lake Pátzcuaro. We felt that if the good Lord had intended us to see the westward settlements of the Pómaros, He would have guided us up the Rio de Cachán. We had tried and failed, and we could now turn back without regrets.

184

17 The Downfall of Peron

WE FACED OUR NIGHT ON THE SIERRA WITH THE DETERMI-
nation to keep a bonfire burning and stand watches against the
possibility of wild beasts.

In the spooky light of dusk we collected all the wood we could
find, spread out our blankets, and got set for a long night. The
burros were tethered a few feet away from us for protection, for
jaguars are far more likely to attack a donkey, particularly a weak
one like Perón, than a man. They seemed to realize their danger
and to be glad of our company and the fire, although there was
nothing whatever for them to graze on. César, too, was nervous,
and kept as near us as possible, pricking up his ears at every sound
from the woods.

I stewed our small ration of meat, cutting it in little pieces to
make it go further, and we ate it from the frying pan in order not
to lose a drop of juice. We ate one tortilla each, gave two to
Perón and Evita, and saved the remaining two for breakfast. It was
a slim supper for half-starved people who had walked God knows
how many miles, and an even slimmer one for the poor donkeys,
but it was something.

At about nine o'clock, when we had finished our meal and
were scouting for more wood in the dark, we were startled by the
sound of voices. Presently a flaring light appeared on the trail below us and, as it came closer, we made out the figures of two
women mounted sidesaddle on donkeys, followed by a man on foot
who was lighting their way with a torch of ocote. They were as

surprised to encounter us on the trail as we were to meet them, but our big fire made it clear we were not waiting to ambush late travelers. Everybody said Buenas noches, and the trio stopped to find out what we were doing there.

"You mean you are going to spend the night *here?*" the man inquired. "But the place is infested with *tigres* and with *leones* as well."

We had not realized that the mountains harbored mountain lions in addition to the more common jaguars, and did not particularly like the idea of their company. What were the lions like? we asked.

"Son grandes, rojos," said our informant, his eyes gleaming in the firelight. "They are big and red, very dangerous. Why do you stop here?"

We replied that we and the burros were too exhausted to go farther and that, anyhow, we would rather take our chances with wild beasts than run the risk of a bad fall, climbing a mountain in the dark. They said we would be welcome to come along with them, but we did not have the strength to repack all our gear and climb for another three hours, so, wishing them good luck, we turned back to our campfire. For a long time we saw their light weaving back and forth as they followed the curves of the upward trail.

To keep the fire going, we had to make a wood-gathering expedition every half-hour, for the stuff we found was punky and burned in a moment. Fred told me to get some sleep while he kept the fire up. It was cold. An animal screamed somewhere in the mountains above us. A tigre or león? César came and lay down as close to me as possible, curled in a tight ball. The burros shifted their feet and tossed their heads. I dozed, and presently Fred was climbing under the serape with me—just for a minute, to get warm, he said.

We were awakened by a voice saying, "Buenos dias!" and, opening our eyes, found ourselves looking up into a horse's face a couple of inches above our own. His rider, a big fellow with a huge sombrero and a pair of pistols in his belt, was leaning forward in the saddle to peer down at us inquisitively. We had slept the night through, and so had César, who now tried to stifle his yawns and pretend that he too had not just been awakened. There was a faint light in the sky which we thought at first was moonlight, but the horseman told us that it was day. Our fire was a heap of embers.

"Did you see any tigres or leones?" he wanted to know.

We said that we had not, although they may have smelled us all over in the night, for all we knew.

"Tienen suerte," said the horseman. "You were lucky. Of course, you had a dog. Es bravo, el perrito?"

César, playing the role of man's best friend, was busily padding about the encampment to see how the burros and the carga had passed the night.

"Bravo?" exclaimed Fred, "Es una fiera!" He did not want to admit that we had been so stupid as to sleep soundly the night through without even the protection of a good watchdog, so he made César out to be a paragon of canine virtues and a regular terror with tigres and leones.

The horseman looked with respect at our bow-legged, brindled companion and repeated that we were lucky. He refused our invitation for coffee, saying that he had to get on to San Pedro and that he might see us there later in the day.

Our coffee was quickly made on the embers of the bonfire, and in a couple of hours we were at the top of the steep climb, seeking breakfast at Las Encinas. On the way, we had come close to losing our burros over a precipice. It happened at a fork of the trail, one branch of which went up over the top of a mountain ridge, while the other skirted the slope. It was obvious they were alternate routes of the same trail and, being lazy, we chose the path which eliminated the ascent.

Proceeding in single file in our usual marching formation (Evita, myself, Perón, Fred, and César), we went briskly along the little path for fifty yards or so, when suddenly Evita stopped short. The trail in front of her had washed out completely. On our right was an almost perpendicular hillside, so steep that the burros' carga rubbed the side of the slope, and on our left a precipice where a false step would have meant a quick end for the whole party. Evita was scared, which made matters worse.

If there is a Tarascan donkey command for "Back up," we never learned it. The only way we knew to make a donkey back was to wave our hands in front of his face, but in this case I was behind the burra and could not see any way to get ahead of her. We decided to start with Perón. Taking him by the halter to keep him from trying to turn around, I waved my sombrero before his eyes and told him, "Anda." With gentle pushes and words of encouragement, we thus got him back to a wider point on the trail where he could turn. Fred gave him a slap on the rump to hurry him along to safety, and the two of us went back to Evita, who was tossing her head and rolling her eyes back at us in a panic. She saw Perón trotting off and, since burros hate to be separated, she decided, before we could stop her, to turn around and follow him. We got there just in time to grab her nose as she wheeled about and fell, with her hind legs over the edge of the precipice. There she hung balanced with seventy-five pounds of carga pinning her down and her hind legs pawing frantically for a foothold in the empty air. There was no time to remove the carga, so Fred got hold of the rope that secured it and gave a mighty heave, while I pulled at her head. This way we inched her up a bit, until she managed to get one hind foot back on the trail. We all three tottered there for a moment and then, with a last shuddering effort, she was on her feet and trotting back down the trail.

San Pedro revisited was a different cup of tea from our first stop there, for our friend Don Juventino Reyes had gone away on a trip, and we had to seek other lodgings. Our host this time was a man whose chief business seemed to be selling little bottles of tequila to his fellow townsmen. There was plenty to drink in his house but nothing to eat, and it took us two weary hours of combing the town before we found a señora who was willing to sell us a chicken and another who let us have some bananas. The tequila merchant's wife plucked and cooked the chicken, which took another two hours, but by nightfall we had eaten and were able to turn in.

Our night on the sierra had infested us and our bedding with new legions of chiggers and ticks, and in desperation we broke one of our rules (to stay away from strong drinks except in large towns) and bought a pint bottle from our host. By the time we had downed the fiery stuff, the chigger bites had subsided in a general sense of well-being and we were able to get some sleep.

From San Pedro north to Coalcomán is about eighty miles by the old mule trail, though probably half that as the crow flies, for the trail winds around and about through rugged mountainous country. The first half makes a gradual ascent, following mountain arroyos along valley floors, and the second half moves up to the high ridges of the Sierra de Coalcomán, part of the Sierra Madre del Sur. There you are really up in the clouds, traveling along the spine of the mountains at an altitude of from eight thousand to ten thousand feet, through forests of gigantic pines, as yet untouched by lumberers or charcoal burners.

Nights were cold in the mountains after the tropical air of the coast, but there were compensations—ticks and chiggers are not found above six thousand feet. It is far better to be cold than to be bitten.

By the time we set out from San Pedro the second time, we were a shabby and tired party. Our boots were wearing out, to begin with. Fred had worn holes through both his soles, while one of my boots was completely open on the side. Sleeping in our clothes had been a heavy strain on our supply of old shirts, and most of them had been discarded along the way in tatters. The last stage to Coalcomán was made with one filthy shirt apiece; we did not want to take the time to wash and dry them, and if we had they probably would have come apart; the dirt held them together. As for supplies, we were completely out of everything except coffee and sugar, and we were smoking whatever we could pick up in the local tienditas—sometimes homemade cigarros wrapped in cornhusk.

We were both thinner than Pharaoh's lean kine. I had cut three new holes in my belt. Fred's jeans, which had originally fit him like paper on the wall, now hung in folds around his skinny flanks. We were as black as Indians with sun and dirt; our nails were cracked, our hair was full of dust and chiggers, and Fred was adorned with a ten-day beard.

The donkeys were in need of a rest, too. Their noses were almost hairless from rubbing at insect bites, their once-round bellies were flat, and their ears hung at a perpetual dejected half-mast. Evita continued to be a tower of strength, but Perón was in a bad way, being worm-eaten now not only on his rump but on his spine, where the almost cured pack sore had opened up again. We kept down the worm population with creolin, but he would need a long rest and treatment to heal the sores, and all we could do for him was to pack him lightly and encourage him with promises of a week in pasture when we reached Coalcomán. During this stage of the trip, for most of the time we carried the gallon canteen and the cameras ourselves, to spare the animals, and even that little weight was a sore burden on our weary shoulders.

We made the eighty miles in five days by forced marches, which was not bad going, considering our fatigue and the amount of climbing that had to be done. There were kind people and pleasant places along the way, where earlier in the trip we might have been tempted to linger, but our minds were fixed upon hot baths, clean clothes, and big meals in restaurants.

The trail from San Pedro took us up over the peaks that surround that village and down again into another green valley where we had the good luck to find a flourishing cattle ranch and an abundant lunch. Our hosts were people from Coalcomán who leased their property from the Pómaros and who, at the time of our arrival, were engaged in the butchering of a pig. Don Laureano Mendoza and his wife were people who really knew how to treat weary travelers, for they quickly piloted us into comfortable chairs, told us that their men would unload the burros, and set before us a comida that began with soup, progressed through chicken and pork, and ended with sugar candy and coffee. When we left, the good people tucked a package of jerky and a half-dozen eggs into our pack boxes, in case we had trouble finding food on the trail ahead.

It was lucky that they did, for we found nothing to eat at our

190

night's stop. It was a ranch settlement of five or six houses, and the first thing that met our eyes as we entered the yard of our hosts for the night was half a dozen huge scorpions hanging upside down from strings tied to a post. Some of them were alive, and they were the biggest we had ever seen—about four inches long.

"What's the idea?" we asked the middle-aged man who came out to greet us. He smiled at his grisly captives.

"Oh, I like to see them suffer," he said. We couldn't blame him. He told us that he had caught them around the yard by means of string lassos. We crossed our fingers as we prepared to spend the night there, but we did not see any of the terrifying creatures.

If the ranch people did not have food for us, they had good hearts, for they offered us one of the family catres to sleep on—an offer which we gratefully accepted, for we were bone-tired and the evening was chilly for hammocks. Only after we had retired on the porch, snugly wrapped in our blankets, did we discover that our couch belonged by rights to the grandfather of the clan, a handsome old man of seventy or more, who at bedtime flung down a petate on the floor and stretched himself out to sleep there. We started to get up, protesting that we had not realized that we were putting him out of his bed, but he insisted upon our staying where we were. He was perfectly comfortable, he said. At dawn he sprang up as lightly as a boy and prepared to set out for a day's work in the fields, apparently none the worse for a night on the cold ground.

Our last stop before the high sierras was San José de la Montaña, a large village that nests in a deep hollow between towering peaks, ringed about with emerald-green fields. There we were warned to make an early start in the morning, for we had before us the ascent of the Cabeza de Toro (Bull's Head), a stiff climb straight up into the sierra, which everybody is careful to take before the heat of the day.

In order to reach San José, we had skirted the Bull's Head by a precipitous path along the mountain slope where, we were told, not a few horses and donkeys had been lost by taking a careless step and rolling down the steep incline. San José, as it opened out before us, looked like a metropolis, for it boasted a church, a cobblestoned plaza with a fountain, and numerous well built houses grouped upon little streets. As far as food goes, however, it was no better than the meanest rancho, and we were again forced to dine on the Mendoza's carne seca.

Before sunup we were off for the Cabeza de Toro, the longest and hardest climb of the whole trip. There were no rests on the way, for the trail went straight up, most of the time in short zig-zags. It was hard for us, but it was much harder for Perón, who was now in dire straits. Apart from the sore on his back, which the pack must have made very painful, he was plagued with a new and most unpleasant difficulty—constipation. The abscess on his rump went so deep that any activity in that region caused the poor beast great anguish, and for that reason his digestion was all tied up. He made very hard work of the Bull's Head, and we were doubtful if he was going to make it at all. Walking behind him and prodding him onward was a nasty job, for with his sores and his digestive troubles he smelled terribly. We felt very sorry for the little fellow, but there seemed nothing to do but go on and get him to Coalcomán as fast as possible.

The ascent was interminable and, despite our early start, the sun began to get uncomfortably warm before we were halfway up. Fred and I are not mountain climbers, and even our 450 miles of difficult walking had not prepared us to take that sort of thing in our stride. Toward the end we had to stop and pant every ten min-utes, then labor forward a few more yards, croaking encourage-ment to the burros. The system of holding the animals' tails could not be used any more, for Perón was too sick and Evita too heavily loaded; another ounce of weight to pull would have made them fall over in their tracks. All four of us looked with disgust at the carefree César, who, with only his own twenty-five-pound self to carry and four legs on which to carry it, clambered up energetically and turned back every now and then to ask why everybody was so slow.

It was noon before we scrambled up the last feet of the ascent and threw ourselves down on the pine needles at the top. San José was a little circle of green below us. To the south we could trace the valley through which we had come and the distant summits of the range where we had spent the night with the tigres and leones.

In every direction, as far as we could see, rose mountain after mountain, not the bare, eroded sierras that you see in the north, but slopes still timbered with virgin pine and oak. There is a story that Cortés, trying to describe Mexico to the Spanish sovereigns, seized a sheet of paper and, crumpling it, flung it down before their majesties, saying, "Mexico is like that." It was like that looking down from the Cabeza de Toro, and we spent an hour or more trying to carry away with us some of the spectacular view in the form of photographs. For the photographer there was the added satisfaction of towering cumulus clouds rising from the north, pure white against the deep blue sky.

We had some difficulty taking up the trail, for there were a number of little paths wandering off in different directions; and since the pine needles and rock underfoot did not leave much trace of passing feet it was hard to tell which was the most-traveled branch. Since we were going north, however, we took the trail that seemed most likely to carry us that way, ascending to the backbone of the ridge, where on the right hand we had a shallow saddleback and on the left a steep slope that plunged down three thousand feet or so to a river valley, where we could make out an occasional tiny ranch house.

Beguiled by the view and inhaling the sweet smell of sunbaked pine needles, we nonchalantly strolled along for some time before the notion began to creep into our minds that we might be on the wrong trail. Our route had never taken us so high in the mountains, and on previous occasions, when we had climbed, the ascent had usually been quickly followed by a descent into the next valley. Was it possible that we had missed the path down into the valley at the left? We could see the gash of an obviously much-used trail leading north among the scattered ranchitos below us. Should we be down there, and if so, how were we going to get there? Our joy in the scenery began to be clouded by the thought that we were without water (we had been told we did not need to carry it), on top of a wild sierra, following what might turn out to be only a cattle path.

Then disaster struck. Perón, who had used the last of his strength climbing the Cabeza de Toro, began to waver in his stride. Before we could reach him to prevent it, he lay down on the trail. We got him up. This is done with a loaded animal by standing one on each side of him and lifting the carga, thus lightening the burden and giving the animal's belly a lift by the upward pull of the cinch. He went on for another five minutes, then stumbled and went down again. Five times we got him up and five times he fell again. The sixth time he did not get up.

We removed his carga (he was only carrying bags and hammocks which did not amount to more than forty pounds) and stripped off his heavy aparejo. He was lying on his side with his head pillowed on the pine needles. Lightened, we managed to hoist him to his knees, but no further. He lay there with his legs folded under him and looked at us sadly from under his bangs.

What to do? We were afraid of being lost; the sun was moving down the sky, and from previous experience we thought it unlikely that Perón would be able to travel until the next day, if then. We loaded his pack on the patient Evita. It was a grievous burden for her, but she accepted it with resignation, and we drove her a little way along the trail, hoping that Perón, free of his load, would get up and follow. But he just looked after us and raised his furry ears. Back we came and held a council.

The decision was that he would have to be left behind. Even if we had a place to stop for the night (which we did not), and even if he should be able to walk on the following day, he would probably collapse again, possibly in even worse circumstances. The question was whether it would be a mercy to shoot him (for come nightfall he would be scented by prowling animals and might come to a most painful and terrifying end) or whether, if left to his own devices, he might later stumble along the trail and find his way out of the mountains.

Putting ourselves in his place, we decided that we would rather face the wild beasts than be shot, so we patted his head and said

194

goodbye, and told Evita to say goodbye. For a long time we could see his ears, and we kept hoping that he would get to his feet and follow us. But he did not move, just gazed after us with his big brown eyes until at length a curve of the trail lost him to our view. We felt sad. Perón had never been a very good burro, but he had come a long way with us and we had hoped to bring both of the animals safely back to their home in Arócutin. To think of him alone and helpless there when night came on, with jaguars screaming in the sierra . . .

We had not walked an hour, thus despondent, before we suddenly and, as it appeared, miraculously, came upon a ranch. We had never seen a ranch in such a high place before, and did not expect to see one, but there it was, a little wooden shack with children playing in the yard and smoke coming from the kitchen door. The rancheros invited us·in and were able to reassure us about the trail. We were going in the right direction for Coalcomán.

"Would you like a donkey?" we asked, explaining about Perón's collapse. The children jumped around us excitedly as we recounted the story of the burrito who was too tired to go on.

"*Pobrecito!*" everybody exclaimed. Certainly they wanted him, and they were grateful to the señores. Never mind if he had gusanos, they could cure him, and he would be very useful, for they didn't have any burros, not even one. The señora gave us some beans and tortillas and, while we were eating, a little boy and girl started off up the trail to find Perón, carrying a dish of corn and a pail of water with which to revive him.

We pursued our way feeling much better. Perón would have a nice home in the mountains, with children to ride him on trips for wood and water, and a little corral near the house where he would be safe from wild beasts. He would probably live to a ripe old age.

The party seemed very small without Perón, but also more intimate. Previously we had been walking in single file to keep the burros out of trouble, but with only Evita, Fred and I were able to walk together behind her. We made better time, too, for the burra was a sensible animal who figured that the faster she walked, the faster she would reach her night's repose. She was overburdened, there was no question about that; but we judged she could make it with the double carga as far as Coalcomán, where we planned to send half the equipment back to Erongarícuaro by mail.

Fred and I beguiled ourselves with a game, familiar to anyone who has ever been hungry, of describing various wonderful dinners we had eaten, or would like to eat. Fred, having traveled and eaten widely in Europe, was better at this than I was, so the game fell into a pattern whereby I would describe in great detail some imaginary inn in Barcelona, the Côte d'Azur, or the Italian Piedmont, and Fred would then tell me what the innkeeper might give us for dinner.

We had just polished off some minestrone and were settling down to a fritto misto, when a ranch came in sight. Descending from the high ridge, we had dropped about a thousand feet in altitude, and the ranch was halfway up the ascent to the next ridge. Spurred by hopes of a meal, we drove ourselves up the rocky trail, to arrive panting in the dooryard of a comfortable-looking house. The illusion of comfort soon vanished, however, for we found the lady of the house in a state of distraction. She had four children down with chicken pox, she told us, and could not keep them in bed; there was nothing to eat, her husband was away, and how she was going to manage the good Lord only knew. Various pantless children covered with red spots were hanging about dejectedly, and a baby was crying from inside the house.

I had had chicken pox, but Fred was not sure that he had, and in any case what if it were not chicken pox but something worse? We asked the señora if there were houses on top of the ridge, and she replied that there was a settlement called El Corral up there.

Evita was disgruntled at having to continue, and we couldn't blame her, but the rancho was just too dismal as a stopping place. With the last of our strength, the three of us slogged up the winding path (which was as steep as the Cabeza de Toro though only a quarter as long) to come out once more gasping among the pine trees of a high ridge.

El Corral was three tiny houses, very simple and very poor, but the rancheros seemed warmhearted and glad of company. They told us that few people ever stopped with them, and that they had no place to put us for the night except on the porch of one of the huts. We didn't care. It was clean and healthy in comparison with the chicken-pox pesthouse down below.

Looking southwest over the mountaintops, we watched the sun going down in clouds of fire that seemed to be reflected below upon a shining surface. Surely that could not be the Pacific, four days' journey away and still visible? Our hosts nodded and smiled, proud of their spectacular vista. Yes, it was *el mar* shining down there. The old Pacific, which had blandly viewed our struggles along its shores and washed out our tracks after us, singing to itself.

The night was cold on the porch floor, but we were huddled together out of the wind and slept much better than we had expected. In fact, we congratulated ourselves on having made that last effort to get to El Corral instead of staying below with the chicken pox.

It was not until some days later that we discovered we had spent the night with lepers, and that our nice clean mountain settlement was a real pesthouse, compared to which the chicken-pox rancho would have been a health resort.

We made the discovery in conversation with an Aftosa inspector in Coalcomán who knew every inch of the trail we had followed from the coast and who was curious to find out which of his friends we had met and stopped with. When we mentioned El Corral, he frowned and asked just which of the three houses we had visited. We explained that it was the highest one, and he seemed relieved, saying that he guessed that one was all right; the lepers lived in the one just back of the high ridge.

"They try and keep them out of the way when people come past," he said. "There's an old man whose face is all bandaged up and a younger one that's lost his feet. All three houses belong to the same family, of course, but as far as I know none of the rest of them are infected—yet."

The trail from El Corral to Coalcomán had been described to us as a long two-day march, and we didn't really expect to make it in that time, but we were going to try. By noontime, after leaving El Corral at dawn, we came out of the high sierras and stumbled down a precipitous descent toward a shallow, swift river, one of the northern branches of our friend the Rio de Cachán.

Fred was plagued by foot trouble. His blistered heels were still raw, and he had a new development on the sole of one foot which he suspected was either an infection of his old nigua hole or a new nigua which had entered the same place. It pained him considerably, but he did not want to open it up for fear that he might only succeed in crippling himself. His concern over his new difficulty was not relieved by our host for the night, an old man who took great delight in telling us about a friend of his who had lost a leg from a nigua infection. I fed Fred a few terramycin pills and tried to rent a horse for him for the next day's march, but it seemed that there were not many horses around and they were all in use. Fred would have to hoof it, nigua and all.

Our last day journeying toward the pueblo was a forced march. We did not unload poor Evita all day, but kept her going up and down, over bare foothills and jungly river flats in the heat of the sun. Her heavy double pack kept slipping to one side or the other, and we made any number of exasperating halts trying to rope it in some manner that would keep it steady. Dust and stones kept getting into our feet through our broken boots. To save time, we no longer bothered to take off our footgear to cross rivers and arroyos, but simply waded in and let our feet dry on the trail. We made two short stops in the course of the day, once to eat crayfish (the nearest we came to lobster) at a hut on the riverbank, and once to buy limes at a citrus grove. We bought some sugar cane, too, and chewed the pulp as we walked along, hoping to derive extra energy thereby.

The last ranch before Coalcomán was a place called Ixtala, which we reached about half an hour before sunset. Much as we wanted to cover the rest of the distance, we did not see how it could be done until the next day, for both Evita and Fred were done in.

At Ixtala, however, we found a savior in the shape of a bright boy of eighteen called Ramón, who said that he had two donkeys the señores might ride and thus get to the pueblo that very evening. He would be our guide and bring the animals back. Our fallen hopes revived and we put ourselves in Ramón's hands. While we were discussing terms, Evita quietly folded up her legs and collapsed. She was not, she said, going to carry the double pack a mile farther, no matter how much we wanted to get to Coalcomán.

Since I seemed to be the strongest member of the expedition, apart from César, who did not count for anything, I gave up my chance to ride a burro so that Evita might have some help with the carga. The rented donkey took the lion's share of the load, and Evita, with only a couple of bags to carry, managed to shake off her fatigue and trot down the trail once more. Meanwhile Fred, after making all the indicated chivalrous protests about my walking, allowed himself to be persuaded aboard the other burro. Gaunt and hollow-cheeked, with his stirrups almost touching the ground, he looked like Don Quixote coming wearily home from tilting with windmills.

After two hours we rounded the curve of a hill and saw lights below us and a tall illuminated church tower with a clock.

"There it is," said Ramón. In a few moments we were clattering between rows of houses over cobbled streets, blinking at the unaccustomed electric light that streamed from doorways and shops.

18 The Americans of Julius Caesar

COALCOMÁN IS A REAL TOWN WITH BUSES AND TRUCKS arriving every day from the great world of Apatzingán, Uruapan, and Morelia, with plane service in all directions, two hotels, three or four restaurants, a doctor, a cockfighting ring, a one-man uniformed police force, and a clock that chimes the quarter-hours.

There is a beautiful little plaza in front of the church, shaded by palms and citrus trees and planted with carefully tended flower gardens, where in the evening, in the old Spanish style, the young people promenade round and round, the boys going one way and the girls the other. At noontime the town bakes in the sun, but toward evening the air is cool and flower-scented and the stars are very near and bright.

Nobody works very hard in Coalcomán. There are cockfights every afternoon which all the men and a few of the women feel obliged to attend, and when the cockfights are over the school children parade around the plaza, paced by three or four solemn little girls beating drums. Then it gets to be time for a cool drink and a chat with one's friends. . . . And so the day passes.

We were quite the oddest thing that had struck Coalcomán in a long time, when we drew up before the little hotel on the plaza with our burros and packs, our filthy clothing and broken boots. The old maid who ran the place was doubtful whether to take us in or not, for she did not cater to the burro trade, but our being Americanos made it all right. Everybody knows that Americanos are crazy. She was familiar with the absurdities of people from

200

El Norte, for her hotel was headquarters for the Aftosa teams that worked out of Coalcomán. In fact, people in town said that the hotel, which was brand-new, had been built with Commission money—the profits she had made from rooming and boarding cattle inspectors and their families.

César cased the joint with a quick trot around the inner patio, a sniff at the kitchen door, and a couple of laps at the central fountain, and came back to report that it would do. Always clever at handling señoras, he cozied up to the proprietress so successfully that long before we got our belated dinner he had been served a brimming plate of scraps and was snoring happily at the old girl's feet. The dog seemed to make more impression on her than we did, for although she forgot our name she did not forget that the dog was called Julio César.

We later heard her instructing the cook to prepare some "bistecs" (beefsteaks) for "los Americanos de Julio César," and so that became our name in Coalcomán—the Americans of Julius Caesar.

The boy Ramón had taken his burros back to Ixtala, and with them Evita, who was to be boarded in his pasture and fed a half-medida of corn daily until we were ready to leave, which would be, we figured, in about a week. We wanted plenty of time to taste the pleasures of civilized life.

The most active social center in Coalcomán was the paleteria, which not only kept all the children in town supplied with ices, but did a flourishing business in cold beer and refrescos. At one of the two tables in the establishment, the Aftosa inspectors could generally be found whenever they were in town, especially a big burly Coloradan called Walter Goddard, who became our special amigo in Coalcomán.

Walter had an odd reason for being in Mexico. A soldier in the prewar army, he had been officially listed as dead when the Japanese took over the Philippines, and it was only after years of imprisonment that his family discovered he was alive and about to be repatriated. By the time he got home, he found that all his property in Colorado had been divided up after his supposed death. The idea of trying to get back his own was too complicated and depressing to face, so he had come to Mexico with the Aftosa Commission in order to save money for a new ranching venture in Colorado. Living entirely on his Mexican salary, he was able to save his $10 per day from the United States, which in the course of time amounted to a tidy sum.

Walter was always in the company of a Mexican boy of about nineteen who served as his *mozo*, or groom, and whom he planned to take back to Colorado with him when he left Mexico. The boy was very proud of his relationship with the big American, and used to dress in Western ranch style and walk with the same horseman's stride as his boss.

Since cockfighting was the major sport in Coalcomán, we went to see the show the day after our arrival. The boom of a gun signaled the start of the first bout at around three in the afternoon. A peso entrance fee admitted the spectator to a former stable yard where a circle of chairs surrounded a simple ring with a two-foot wooden barrier. One of the most active and energetic of the local cockfight *aficionados* was the town doctor, a neat little man with a military mustache upon whom we had called earlier to have Fred's nigua removed. We had been told to come back after the cockfight. The doctor was presiding over the weighing-in of the various birds, several of which he himself handled in the ring.

The cocks that were to engage in the first bout were carried around the ring for the inspection of the audience, and then the betting began, mostly ten- or twenty-peso bets, but occasionally wagers running up to a hundred or two hundred. The handlers laced on the cruel spurs which are used in Mexican fights, razor-sharp little knives which can inflict terrible wounds, even from glancing blows. The two cocks were held face to face, to tease them into anger, and after they had nipped at each other with their beaks a few times they were placed on the ground and the handlers stepped back.

It was all over in a couple of minutes. The two birds flew at each other, striking so fast that it was impossible to tell when a blow went home and when it did not. Then suddenly one bird was down and the other was on top of it, and the bout was over. The handlers

202

picked up the bleeding birds, squirting water into the cocks' faces from their mouths and blowing on the ruffled feathers to separate them and examine the wounds. The loser died in a moment, but the winner, it appeared, would live to fight again.

All the bouts looked the same to us, and after four or five of them we left, unable to understand why people get so excited about these contests. In a bullfight there is art and drama, but a cockfight, at least as it is done in Mexico, is just a way of gambling. In other countries the birds do not wear the sharp-bladed Mexican spurs, but instead are fitted with spurs that are sharp only at the point, so that they kill by stabbing and not by cutting. This prolongs the fight and is said to make it more interesting. But the aficionados of Coalcomán claimed that their fights were thrilling spectacles, and went back day after day to sit through the interminable affairs or, sometimes, to handle their own birds. Almost every patio in town had one or two cocks tied by the leg, crowing fierce challenges at the world in general, and ranchers brought them in from the country for sale at thirty or forty pesos apiece.

At other than cockfight times, the little doctor, locally known as El Médico Chico, to distinguish him from a former, larger physician, was generally to be found in his office, where he dispensed optimistic advice to the somber-faced folk who consulted him. Going to the doctor for Mexicans is not at all the casual affair that it is in the United States: they put on their Sunday clothes and sit perfectly still in the waiting room, generally accompanied by a mother, sister, or friend for moral support. If there are magazines in the anteroom, nobody reads them; it is much too serious an occasion for that.

In treating Fred's nigua, the little medico rubbed his hands, sterilized a number of wicked instruments, and then proceeded with an operation which, apart from being sterile, was exactly the same as the one which the giggling señorita had performed in Playa Azul. The nigua apparently had died; there was a little infection in the cavity, but nothing to worry about. Five pesos was the modest charge.

We had another medical problem, however, which had been on

our minds for the past three weeks or so, and, after batting it around between ourselves for a few days we again sought the opinion of El Médico Chico. Did he, we wanted to know, have any means to determine whether a señora was *embarazada* or not? No lady ever seemed less embarazada than I, for I was as lean as a greyhound and absolutely unaffected by any of the frailties that are supposed to manifest themselves; nevertheless there had been signs and portents that could not be ignored.

Needless to say, it had not been planned that way at all. No woman in her right mind would pick a three-month walking trip as the time to start having a baby. The medico had no laboratory facilities for making tests, and there was no sure way to determine what the situation was. Should we continue the trip? Why not? he said. If I felt like it, walking fifteen miles a day wouldn't hurt me in the least. His only caution was not to stray too far from truck and bus routes in our homeward trip, so that if I had any difficulty there would be vehicles to get me to medical aid.

Having consulted the doctor, we then asked the advice of Walter, himself a father, who told us that his wife rode horseback practically until her baby was born, and suffered no ill effects.

"The walking will probably be good for you," was his conclusion, and he sent his mozo out for a bottle of brandy to celebrate the occasion. Since news travels fast and mysteriously in small towns, it was not long before everybody in Coalcomán knew that the "señora de Julio César" was expecting, and all the old ladies of the market greeted me with nods and winks when we passed by.

The actual fact was not confirmed until after we returned to the United States, although as we went on it seemed more and more evident that I was pregnant. I was as strong as an ox, however, and the niña herself (it was a girl!) must be a very tough specimen to have stood up under the starvation and exhaustion that her mother imposed on her from the time that she joined the party (which was somewhere around Melchor Ocampo). She thus walked some five hundred miles in her first two months of life, subsisting largely on corn and beans and strong coffee.

After long weeks of inadequate food, I had developed a passion for fruit which happily I was able to satisfy in Coalcomán. In all the hot country we had passed through, we had eaten no fruit except coconuts and, very occasionally, bananas. The town market displayed heaps of big juicy papayas, and I was in the habit of consuming a whole one—four or five pounds of it—at one sitting. If you expect a papaya to taste like a cantaloupe you are disappointed, because it has a touch of that exotic, decadent flavor that is common to many tropical fruits, but once you accept it for itself it becomes a very special treat. After the papaya, I would eat half a dozen bananas to top off with. Perhaps my passion for fruit was a "craving," but I think it was just plain hunger.

As for Fred, he regarded my orgies with tolerance. His own craving was for rivers of ice-cold beer, occasionally preceded, followed, or interrupted by tiny glasses of tequila. Because the pestilencias that we had encountered during our sojourn on the coast had soured him on the idea of becoming a coconut planter, in Coalcomán, sitting at a table in the paleteria, he toyed alternately with the notion of setting up in business with a paleteria of his own, or of going into partnership with one of the Mexican Aftosa men in a mule-breeding enterprise.

What with melons and beer, hotel bills, the purchase of new shirts, and the repair of our boots, we suddenly found, toward the end of our stay in Coalcomán, that we would have to go more carefully with our money if we were to get back to Pátzcuaro. We had started the trip with 2,500 pesos (about $215), which was intended to cover all the expenses of the trip (including the fitting out and our preliminary stay in Erongarícuaro). When we left Coalcomán, we had about 600 pesos left, and thus had spent 1,400 in the course of two months, an average of almost $3 a day in American money. There had been, of course, many days when we spent little or nothing, but they were more than balanced by our stops in such places as Reparo de Luna, Melchor, and Playa Azul, where we had enthusiastically made up for lost time and run through our pesos like drunken sailors. In the larger settlements, furthermore, there were always supplies of food and cigarettes to be replenished. If we had been teetotalers, the trip would have been cheaper, for the beers which we enjoyed so much when we found them were apt to be expensive in remote regions where they had to be brought in by burro load.

We might, of course, have sent for the five hundred pesos which we had left with a friend in Erongarícuaro for emergencies, but waiting for it could easily have held us up a week or more. We decided to make do with what we had.

Since time was getting on and the weather was getting warmer, our intention had been to cut northward from Coalcomán and get into the cool hills as quickly as possible; but the doctor's recommendation to stay on truck routes made sense, and we therefore changed our itinerary to follow the dirt road that runs northeastward about one hundred miles, to link Coalcomán with Apatzingán, one of the biggest cities of southern Michoacán. On this route, however, we faced the unpleasant necessity of returning to tierra caliente, for although Coalcomán is relatively high and enjoys a comfortable climate, the terrain to the east drops down once more into arid desert country, where the midday heat is just about as bad as in the Rio Balsas area.

Pouring over our maps with the advice of all the clientele of the paleteria, we found that we at least did not have to go all the way to Apatzingán, but could strike north from a town called Buena Vista, some thirty miles west of Apatzingán. This route would take us into Tarascan country by way of a brecha which runs up into the hills to Peribán. And from there to Lake Pátzcuaro would be just a matter of cutting across country, through the heart of the old Tarascan domain, the towns of Charapan, Paracho, Cherán, Sevina, and so over the mountains to Erongarícuaro and our journey's end. Three weeks at the outside should see us safely there.

There were many things to do before our departure. The entire carga had to be reexamined and half of it eliminated, so that Evita could travel in comfort and we could avoid the bother and expense of buying another animal. We accordingly mailed back to Erongarícuaro our hammocks, cooking utensils (except for the faithful coffee saucepan), lantern, half the medical equipment, extra film, and so forth, leaving only the barest necessities for the homeward trip. We would sleep on the ground (being out of nigua and chigger territory), and count on buying meals along the way, for settlements are much more frequent and better supplied in this part of the state than in the isolated regions from which we had come.

The boy Ramón brought Evita in from pasture the day before our planned departure, and to our amateur eyes she looked very fit after her week's rest; but as she was led up the street to a mesón for the night, Walter Goddard studied her with a professional eye.

"She favors her right front leg," he said, and it was true.

We had to postpone our departure while Evita was treated with cold compresses and other remedios of doubtful efficacy. Fortunately the limp must have been caused by nothing more than some knock she had given herself in the pasture, for in three days she was ready to travel.

In the meantime, to save money, we moved into a little hotel which had more flies but less racket than our former billet on the plaza. Small hotels in Mexico are all alike, one- or two-story structures built around a central patio, with a dining room in front and generally one very inefficient toilet somewhere in back. The sleeping accommodations vary from catres to real beds with mattresses, and there are sometimes sheets and sometimes not. Most of them are clean and perfectly comfortable for the guest to whom plumbing is not the most important thing in the world. A room for two in such a hotelito ranges from two to six pesos, compared to fourteen to thirty-five pesos charged in the tourist hotels.

We were quite content with the change, but Julio César was not. The proprietress of the other place and all of her numerous female staff had thoroughly spoiled the dog and made him the pet of the kitchen. We continually had to fetch him from his comfortable lair next to the old maid's stove. He showed no interest in our preparations for resuming the trip, and would sulk about the patio in front of our room, intimating that this was not the sort of thing he was accustomed to. Whenever we took our eyes off him, he fled.

Came the morning of our departure. Evita was loaded and ready

207

at the hotel door; the bill was paid, and the goodbyes had been said. No César. As we walked past the plaza, we whistled long and loud, but no ridiculous brindled dog answered the call. He had deserted us.

We had picked him up in a hotelito in Playa Azul and lost him in a bigger and better hotelito in Coalcomán. No doubt he will eventually join some other traveler and go on to even better hotels —the Virrey de Mendoza in Morelia and the Reforma in Mexico City. Some day, perhaps, we will hear that he has taken up residence in the Biltmore or the Waldorf-Astoria.

If ever a dog was an opportunist, it was Julio César, but we missed the ungrateful wretch as we went forth from Coalcomán. Perón had left us, César had left us. Who next?

19 Collapse of the Jefe

TEPALCATEPÉC, CALLED "TEPEQUE" FOR SHORT, IS A newer, noisier town than Coalcomán. For miles around there is nothing—a few ranchos in the white-hot desert dust. Then, for no particular reason, Tepeque suddenly appears, a cluster of adobe houses, a church steeple, and the raucous sound of music.

The traveler, coming down a slight decline in the road, has no warning that a town is nearby, for there are no outlying houses or suburbs. All at once, there it is, as though somebody had accidentally dropped a seed and the seed had flowered into a town.

Perhaps the people in Tepalcatepéc love noise because it is the only way they can assert themselves in the face of the brooding heat and stillness of the desert. There are six or eight juke boxes (*toca discos,* as the Mexicans call them) in the plaza, and the folk of Tepeque are never happier than when they are all playing different tunes fortissimo. It keeps them from being lonely.

We were two and a half days coming from Coalcomán, a trip that was hard because of the heat, but that otherwise presented few difficulties. We arrived, in fact, much sooner than we expected, because the last leg of the trip took us over a long, hot stretch where there were no houses, no water, and no shade, so that we were forced to keep going whether we liked it or not.

We told the proprietor of the mesón where we left Evita that we would be leaving Tepeque the day after tomorrow.

"Not with this burra you won't," he said. "She will not be able to carry carga for a week or more." He ran a brown hand lightly

209

over Evita's back, and she winced with pain. On either side of her spine, where the weight of the load rested, there was an ominous swelling.

"Why don't you sell her and buy another?" the mesón keeper suggested.

Abandoning our shaggy Tarascan donkey to labor the rest of her days in that heat was unthinkable. Perón, at least, had been left in the cool mountains where the climate was not unlike that of his home. We asked the mesón keeper if she would be able to travel without a load, in which case we would buy another burro for the carga and take Evita along as a lady of leisure. He asked us to give him a couple of days in order to treat the swelling, and, it being then Friday, promised that we could leave on Monday. We glumly settled down for the week end in Tepalcatepéc.

Buying a burro in a strange Mexican town is not so easy as it might seem. Although Tepeque was full of donkeys, they were all in use, and their owners asked absurd prices because they were not especially anxious to sell. They assumed that money was no object with us gringos. We spent a hot and frustrating Saturday morning wandering from house to house and indignantly turning down animals that were offered at from 125 to 200 pesos. It was late in the day when a bright-eyed little bootblack in a military cap came to our hotelito and informed us that his uncle had two donkeys for sale—a burra for seventy pesos and a burro for one hundred. We could take our pick of the two. We sent the lad for the mesón keeper, in order to have professional advice, and the four of us sought out the uncle, who paraded his two animals before us. The female was larger, but she had a mean, stubborn head and lean flanks, whereas the little male was well filled out and looked as strong as a bull.

We bargained a little and finally paid out eighty-five of our remaining pesos for the burro, the seller agreeing to feed and water him for us until we departed. The parties to the transaction then sealed it with a beer at one of the plaza stands, and it was there that our eye was caught by a gaudy bullfight poster announcing a marvelous *corrida de toros* to be held in Apatzingán *el dia Do-*

mingo, 9 de Marzo. That was tomorrow. We counted our money. Could we afford bus tickets to Apatzingán and *barrera* seats at the bullfight? We decided that we could, and that a diversion would pick up the morale of the expedition.

The bus trip to Apatzingán took us three hours over desolate, hot flat plains, part of which we would have to retrace on foot in going to Buena Vista. It was an ancient, almost springless vehicle that ground along over the rough road at fifteen or twenty miles an hour, tossing the passengers about like corn in a popper. The open windows admitted the ovenlike breath of the desert and bathed everybody in clouds of dust.

When we pulled up in Apatzingán at noon, we stepped out into the plaza bewildered to find ourselves in a modern city—office buildings five and six stories tall, shops with plate-glass windows, buses and cars running every which way. There is much money and trade in Apatzingán; new buildings are going up and old ones are being torn down, and the place is halfway between a sleepy provincial town and a bustling twentieth century metropolis. We had to pay twenty-five pesos for a lunch of steak and fried potatoes, a clear indication that we were back in civilization.

The *plaza de toros* at Apatzingán is a sad affair, a jerry-built structure of hastily assembled boards and benches, out of keeping with the splendor of the rest of the town. We were there long before the rest of the audience, and watched the four bulls being persuaded out of their corral and into the pens from which they would go to the ring. The persuading was done by youths with long poles from the top of the corral fence, while we and an audience of small boys shouted advice and commented knowingly upon the qualities of the beasts. There were three good-looking black bulls and one ugly reddish-brown one with a big silly cow's head. Fred said that the red one, which was named Indio, would be the bravest. He could not explain why; he just felt that it was a *toro bravo.*

Under the grandstand two bony old picador horses, already wearing their saddles and protective pads of quilting, were quietly munching corn. The red bandages they wore over one eye—to keep them from seeing the bull's charge—gave them a rakish look. The chapel, where in motion pictures the toreros kneel in prayer before statues of the Virgin, was an open-faced shack of wood with a dusty, unframed holy picture nailed to the back wall, and the toreros, when they arrived, did not kneel but only crossed themselves mechanically. The place did not encourage lengthy devotions. Adjoining was a similar shack which constituted the infirmary; it held a not very clean narrow bed upon which some children were playing. It was a sad backstage scene, made incongruous by the flashing costumes of the bullfighters, who lounged about on the hard benches waiting for the strains of "La Macarena" to signal their proud entrance into the arena.

Fred was busy with his camera everywhere, and had succeeded in getting himself mistaken for a press photographer, so that when the *corrida* began he was permitted to stand with the fighters and their attendants in the aisle behind the ring. He was so excited at being separated from the bulls only by a thin wooden fence that he forgot about taking pictures, and it seemed to me that in a minute he would run out into the ring waving his khaki jacket and shouting, "*Ho, ho, toro!*" with the matadors.

The corrida was a disaster. The bulls did their part, but the matadors were bad, or were having a bad day. Our friend Indio, the first bull of the program, put on a magnificent show, and charged about the ring chasing men over the barrier and upsetting horses. The toreros did not like him; the bull was too clever for them. While he did not gore any of the fighters, he came so close to it on several occasions that they abandoned their fine poses and ran pell-mell for the fence, to clamber over a split second before the sharp horns crashed into the wood at their heels. The toreros claimed that Indio had been fought before, because he seemed to know all the tricks and was always able to guess where the man's body was to be found behind the fluttering cape.

The kill, where the fighter profiles before the bull and goes in with his sword over the horns, is the highest moment of the bullfight—the moment of truth, as the Spaniards say. Indio, however, would not give the matador a chance to execute a quick, clean, and beautiful stroke, and so he was butchered by a number of thrusts from the side, to the accompaniment of loud boos and the throwing of empty pop bottles from the stands. When at last the brave beast, wounded in six or eight different places, sank to his knees and died, there was no applause for the fighter, who, wiping the sweat from his face, plodded back to his friends, muttering that it was a bad bull. The audience did not think so, for when the mule team came and dragged out the carcass there was a mighty cheer for Indio.

The rest of the corrida was not much better. Of the three remaining bulls, only one was properly killed; two were hacked to pieces by the matadors, who apparently had been demoralized by the disaster of Indio. They were all good animals, and deserved a better end.

Because of the coming elections, there was a 10:00 P.M. curfew on the sale of beer and liquor in Apatzingán. Apparently political feeling ran high in these parts, and the police were afraid of drunken arguments leading to general brawls. Roaming about the already dark and deserted city after supper in search of a nightcap, we found all the cantinas closed and the restaurants selling only food and soft drinks. Fred felt sure that there must be a way to get a beer, and led me across the plaza into the market section, where we stumbled about among the darkened booths and vegetable stands in search of an illicit pub until at length we bumped into a police post.

"Buenas noches," said a polite little Indian policeman. "What are you looking for?"

When Fred explained that he wanted a beer before going to bed, the policeman nodded gravely and said he thought it could be managed, if the señores would care to accompany him.

The understanding little cop piloted us to a locked but still lighted cantina and ordered the proprietor to serve us a couple of beers. He himself modestly drank nothing but a refresco, being on duty. He then steered us back to the center of town, wished us good night, and returned to his post. He was a very sensible and friendly guardian of the law, and we hope he gets to be chief of police some day.

Returning to Tepeque at noon on Monday, we visited Evita at the mesón and received instructions about her care. She must always wear her suadera, or sweatcloth, to keep off the sun in the daytime and to protect her from the moon's rays at night. We knew, did we not, that moonlight had a disastrous effect upon animals with sore backs? Before the start of each day's march, the suadera should be removed and the swelling washed with cold water, to keep it clean and cool during the day. If we observed these precautions, she should be able to make the trip back to Erongarícuaro.

The new donkey was loaded with Evita's carga in the morning, and we were once more a two-burro expedition. Theoretically, his name was Perón II; but the name never seemed suited to him after it had been carried so long by Evita's shaggy companion, and we got into the habit of calling him Macho, which simply means "male." It was complimentary to him, because male mules are known as machos.

We were amused to see how quickly Evita put him in his place. Being, unlike Perón, a full-grown burro, he was interested in Evita as a female, and made the mistake of expressing this interest when they first met. She gathered up her hind legs and kicked him neatly and accurately in the face, which disposed of that question permanently.

Once on the road, Evita made it clear that her place was that of the lead donkey, and that the other fellow was to fall in behind her at a respectful distance. Since the burro was carrying carga and she was not, she quite logically concluded that he had been engaged as her mozo, and she always treated him like a servant. With Perón she had been motherly and affectionate, but with Macho she was arrogant. It was impossible to feed corn to the two of them out of the same vessel, for Evita would drive the burro away with bites and kicks. Corn was too good for the likes of him, she informed us.

214

Macho turned out to be a very good donkey, except for one fault: he was infernally slow. He could carry a huge carga all day without fatigue, but no amount of prodding would make him go at anything faster than a weary shuffle. At this stage in the journey, however, speed did not matter so much, for we were tired and were usually content to amble along at the burro's pace. In all other respects he was a well behaved animal who would halt on command, keep to the road, and stand still while being loaded. One cannot ask much more of a donkey.

The burro problem was a very minor affair, compared to the next calamity which the expedition was called upon to face: the collapse of Fred. In the course of our stay in Tepalcatepéc, he had developed a touch of intestinal trouble, which we had not worried much about, ascribing it to overindulgence in spicy food and beer. A shot of paregoric from our medical kit had fixed things for the time being.

As soon as we were well out of Tepeque, however, the trouble came back, ten times worse, and we were forced to conclude that it was not just an "upset stomach" but some tropical bug, probably amoebic dysentery, the price we paid for not being careful about our drinking water.

About five miles out of Tepeque we were thankful to come upon a little settlement where we could rest over the hot midday hours and talk about what to do. Fred took some more paregoric and went to sleep on a catre, while I sat gloomily on a bench in front of the tienda which had taken us in, and wondered if the expedition had come to an end in this desolate and broiling corner of Mexico.

Late in the afternoon, Fred woke up, saying that he still felt dizzy and weak, and that he guessed we would have to spend the night where we were. We had at least twenty miles of arid desert country between us and Buena Vista, and our original idea had been to do it by moonlight. Would Fred be able to travel on the following day, and would he be able to make twenty miles in the heat of the sun? I did not think so.

"There will be a full moon rising in an hour," I said, "and it will

215

be almost as bright as day. You catch a bus to Buena Vista and let me take the burros on alone." Fred did not like the idea of his wife wandering around a Mexican desert at night with two burros.

"Besides," he said, "you are going to have a baby."

"I am not going to have it tonight," I said, and set about packing the carga.

"I wish you wouldn't . . ." he said weakly, and I knew it meant surrender. He knows very well how to lay down the law when he wants to.

I left him a serape for the night and a bag of clothes to carry on the bus, thus lightening Macho's load for the long journey. Since there would be no more buses to Buena Vista that night, Fred would be taking the morning bus, and would probably pass me on the road somewhere near Buena Vista.

"Here is the revolver," he said, passing it to me. "Do you know how to use it?"

"Of course I do," I replied, but he decided that a little target practice would not be amiss. Before an interested group of spectators from the rancho, I fired five shots at a nearby tree (nicking it once). It was a bad display of marksmanship, but at least I had demonstrated that I could pull the trigger.

The burros were ready, Macho with his carga and Evita in her suadera, and a round orange moon was rising. We said goodbye, and I was off down the road, alone with the two donkeys.

20 Fire in the Desert

THE PISTOL FELT BULKY IN THE HOLSTER CLIPPED UNDER
my belt, and I practiced drawing and aiming it a few times to get
the feel of it. The road was white in the moonlight, and a light
cool breeze had sprung up. It was strange being alone, for I had
depended on Fred, not thinking about it particularly, but just
knowing that he was there to cope with anything that came up.

Now I was jefe, or head man, of the expedition. As a woman,
although in trousers, I had been accepted courteously by everyone
we met, as long as Fred was present to vouch for me. I was not
sure how the Mexican country folk would react to a solitary gringa
with two burros. Indeed, I was not particularly anxious to find
out in the middle of the night, but hoped that I might simply go
my way without any encounters.

Between me and Buena Vista there was only one settlement on
the road, a place called Piedras Blancas (White Rocks), on the
Rio de Tepalcatepéc, where a dam and reclamation project were
under construction. It had been pointed out to us on the bus journey to Apatzingán as one of General Cárdenas' enterprises, designed to open up new fertile lands in arid country. There were
temporary barracks, crowds of workers, bulldozers, cranes, electric
lights, noise and confusion.

About an hour after leaving Fred, the burros and I topped a
bluff at the river's edge and followed the road down to a long
earthen dike that traversed the boggy river bottom and ended at
a rickety wooden bridge across the main channel of the stream. We

had proceeded about fifty yards on the dike when Evita decided that she did not like it, whirled around, and trotted back, followed by Macho. It was a bad spot to be alone with two ornery burros, but when it comes to stubbornness I do not admit that any burro can surpass me.

First, I tried leading them across by their halter ropes, a system that worked all right with Macho, but not with Evita, who dug in her feet and refused to budge. Back we went once more, for I could not leave them standing where a truck might want to pass at any moment.

I finally got them across by the strategy of divide and conquer, tying Evita on the far side and shepherding the burro across the dike first, tying him, and returning for the recalcitrant female. Even so, she gave me a lot of trouble by plunging down into the bog when we were halfway across. To keep my feet dry, I mounted her (sitting to the rear of her swollen spine), and in that fashion we splashed along under the dike until she finally realized that she had picked the hardest way of getting across and allowed herself to be coaxed up to the roadway again.

There was still the wooden bridge to be faced; but there I was in luck, for a group of workmen lounging on the other side saw my difficulty and came over in a body to help, picking up the burros' rear ends and shoving them across in a moment. I thanked them with handshakes all round, as is usual in Mexico, and if they were surprised to see a lone American woman appear in such fashion they were at least most polite about it. A couple of them, young men of eighteen or twenty, accompanied me to a tienda where I bought refrescos for them and explained, in my halting Spanish, that my husband was *enfermo* and that I was to meet him in Buena Vista tomorrow. When I thought the amenities had been sufficiently observed, I bade them good night and headed my burros up the road. In a moment the settlement was out of sight, and I was alone again, congratulating myself upon having come through Piedras Blancas so creditably.

It was not yet time for congratulations, however. After ten minutes of solitary walking, I saw, in the moonlight ahead, two men sitting at the side of the road. What were they doing there at

218

night? I prodded the donkeys to go faster and, as I drew up to the two figures, called out a gruff "Buenas noches" in the most masculine voice possible. One of the figures arose and came toward me. There was nothing to do but stop and see what he wanted. The pistol suddenly felt good against my ribs.

"Don't you recognize me?" It was one of the boys for whom I had bought a refresco. He said that he and his friend wanted to talk to me some more and had taken a side trail in order to "surprise" me. Would I perhaps give him a cigarette and sit down to talk for a while? I gave him the cigarette, but did not sit down, saying that I had a long way to go and must move on. We talked for a few minutes of desultory matters, and I again bade him good night.

"Perhaps the señora would like me too accompany her on the road?" the youth suggested, pointing out that he had nothing to do, that it would give him great pleasure . . . I said No, thank you, and he seemed downcast, and began to mutter something about not having any girl of his own and how it was nice to talk to a girl, especially an American.

All this time his friend sat quietly at the roadside.

"You may not have a girl, but I have a husband," I said, and gave Evita a prod to get her moving, calling "Adios" over my shoulder as I hurried off up the road as fast as dignity would permit. I made a point of not looking back, but loosened the little .32 in its holster in case my young admirer did not know how to take No for an answer. He did, as it turned out, but I spent an uncomfortable half-hour wondering if there were another side trail by which he might again "surprise" me. That was the only hint of difficulty that I ever had with a man in Mexico, but the same might happen on a New York subway or anywhere in the world. The night and the solitude were what made it frightening.

With Piedras Blancas behind me, I walked on steadily through the moonlit, level plains, and did not meet a soul. Not a truck passed, not a horseman or donkey driver. We went along, the burros and I, in a kind of trance. Somewhere ahead there was a light in the sky, either a grass fire or a forest fire in the hills that rimmed the bowl of

219

desert. In the inhabited parts of Mexico there is always a fire some-where. Every night in the dry season you will see fire in the moun-tains where somebody has thrown a cigarette on the trail or a char-coal burner has been careless. When it does not rain for six months, everything is tinder-dry.

I did not give much thought to the fire when I first noticed it, but as the hours passed and the red glare in the sky kept growing brighter I began to wonder if the fire might be in my path. It was hard to tell, for the road curved, and first the glow would be on the left and then on the right. There was a light but steady breeze from the north, so that when the fire was on the right-hand side I felt satisfied that it was traveling away from me; but then the road would turn and I could not be so sure. Perhaps it was coming toward me.

There was tall dry grass on both sides of the road. Cattle did not come that far to graze because there was no water, and the prairie grass was left in its thick natural state, perfect fuel for a fire.

It is hard to judge distance at night, and I had no idea how far away the fire might be. I decided fatalistically that it might be just as dangerous to stop as to go forward, and so we continued on. Occasionally I got a whiff of smoke.

I was on top of the fire before I knew it. Coming up a slight in-cline and around a bend in the road, I saw a big bonfire on the road-side ahead and concluded that it must have been lighted by some night travelers, like myself, who perhaps were waiting until it would be safe to go ahead. What to do? I did not particularly want to encounter people, much less have to pass the night with them, but there seemed to be no way to get past their bonfire unob-served. Hitching the burros at the side of the road, I went forward alone, as quietly as possible, for I had it in mind to reconnoiter the people to see if they looked like honest folk and how many they were. It was really a big bonfire they had lighted for themselves, I thought. In fact . . . was it a bonfire? A few more steps, and I realized that my travelers were imaginary, and that their fire was a blazing and fallen tree trunk.

220

I was on the crest of a low hill, and suddenly there opened out below me an inferno of swiftly racing flame which had already crossed the road and was billowing off to the southward. Great clouds of crimson smoke bellied above the flames, and in the wake of the grass fire the whole valley was dotted with blazing trees and shrubs. The burning tree which I had mistaken for a bonfire was at the extreme western end of the burn. A few yards beyond it, for some mysterious reason, the fire had stopped short in its westward progress and roared on to the south.

It looked as though my burros and I had just missed being caught in the middle of it. Perhaps if the brash youth had not accosted me outside Piedras Blancas and held us up for five minutes, the three of us would by now have been suffocated. I doubt if we would have been burned on the road, but breathing the searing air from the cloud of flame would have killed us more quickly than the fire itself.

It still looked pretty hot down there on either side of the road; furthermore, it was around one o'clock, and both the burros and I were tired. It seemed safe to make camp for the rest of the night in the long grass a few yards from the edge of the burn. If the wind held from the north, the fire would not return, and if it did return we could move over into the already burned area in a moment. In the meantime the burros would have good grazing, and I would have a comfortable bed in the soft pasturage.

I drove the animals off the road, unloaded the burro, and tied them both securely by the neck with their reatas. There was nothing for me to eat, but I had a ready-made camp fire in the blazing tree and quickly made myself a saucepan of coffee. Using a prairie fire to heat my coffee gave me a devil-may-care feeling.

Rolled up in a serape, I drank the coffee and smoked a cigarette. As I threw away the match, I had a lesson in how easy it is to start grass fires, for the dry stuff at my side blazed up furiously. If I had not immediately beat it out with my hands, I would have started a new fire then and there.

As for the big fire, it was rolling away to the southward, where a line of low barren sierras would presumably stop it before long. I

221

intended to stay awake for a while and make sure that the wind did not change, but in a moment I was asleep, not to awaken until dawn.

Looking down from my vantage point in the morning, I could trace the course that the fire had taken, coming down from a point in the hills north of the road and sweeping before the wind straight south, leaving behind it a path of blackened earth and smoking trees about three miles wide. By daylight I could see that the westward progress of the fire had been halted by a tiny path that came up from the south and intersected the road at right angles. Why the fire had been able to jump the road and yet had been stopped by a little track through the dry grass is a mystery to me, but fires behave strangely and, of course, the wind had been pushing it south.

Loading a burro singlehanded is a tricky job. I managed it by emptying most of the heavy objects from the two boxes and replacing them after I had heaved the boxes up onto Macho's back. Since I had nothing to eat for breakfast and did not dare waste my remaining pint of water on coffee, I smoked a cigarette to quiet my rumbling stomach, and before sunrise we were on the road.

The rest of the way to Buena Vista was long and hot but without adventures. At about nine o'clock a cloud of dust behind me on the plain signaled the approach of the first bus from Tepalcatepéc and, as it drew near, I made out a wildly waving hand. Fred was aboard. The bus creaked to a stop and everybody leaned from the windows grinning at me. My pale and weary husband said that all the people aboard the bus had been helping him look for me. They had seen the devastation left by the fire and were beginning to be afraid that something had happened to me. My costume and the knife and pistol I carried in my belt created quite an impression.

"Que carai!" the passengers exclaimed to one another. "Una mujer con pistola y cuchillo!"

Fred promised to order me the best breakfast that Buena Vista could produce, and then I was alone again with the bus bounding away over the ruts ahead of me.

In two hours' time I steered my tired and thirsty animals down the hot main street of Buena Vista and into the portals of the mesón where they and we were to spend the night. We had a little "room" which Fred had arranged by leaning planks against the roof of the portico that surrounded the stable yard, and here, after a big breakfast, we both slept for most of the hot day, awakening occasionally to kick a hen off our bed or brush away a fly.

Like all towns in the really hot country, Buena Vista was dormant in the early afternoon hours. Nobody moved in the streets. The glaring sun held sway alone, striking the whitewashed walls of the houses with such fury that it was physical pain to look outside.

It was a quiet town, where people moved slowly and talked in low voices. Tepalcatepéc fought the desert with noise and bustle, but Buena Vista seemed to have surrendered to torpor. It sprawled at the junction of the east-west and north-south truck routes, treeless, abandoned to the sun, and utterly parched, like a dry white bone.

The local doctor was debonair about Fred's ailment, which he diagnosed as amoebic dysentery. He advised less beer drinking, and administered a number of shots of I-dont-know-what, which, together with pills, were supposed to do the trick. Mexican doctors are great shot-givers, and shove a needle into you for every conceivable ailment. This medico declared that more shots would be given at bedtime and again at noon the next day. Then we could leave, if Fred felt strong enough to begin the northward journey.

Evita was getting medical attention, too. Upon removing her suadera, we found that pus was oozing from her swollen back. With the aid of a stable boy she was securely tied, her back washed, and the hair cut from around the place where the swelling had burst. A mixture of alcohol and lard was administered and the suadera replaced, with a clean wet cloth over the sore place.

"Cheer up, Evita," I told her. "Tomorrow you are really heading for home."

223

21 The Cave of the Caoba

BUENA VISTA'S LEADING CITIZEN WAS AN AMERICAN OF
Scandinavian descent called M. G. Jorgensen, who came to call on us
at the mesón.

"What do you do here?" we wanted to know.

"Well, I am supposed to be a miner," he said slowly, studying us
with his bright blue eyes. "At least, that is what I have told the
people here. Actually," he added after a pause, "I am looking for
buried treasure."

He was a sturdily built man of sixty-five who looked at least
ten years younger. Perhaps the romantic quest for gold kept him
young. He had the right temperament for it—unshakable optimism
and constant good humor. If anybody finds gold in Mexico, he
should find it, for he spent most of his life as an oil-company geolo-
gist and knows the country by heart.

In the course of our wanderings we had heard many yarns of
buried treasure. Almost every village in Mexico has its legend of
a gold cache, but few are the people who find them. According to
Jorgensen, however, the heart of the buried-treasure country was
around Buena Vista, and he knew of at least ten wealthy business-
men in Apatzingán who got their start by finding Spanish gold.

Most of the treasure still underground in Mexico dates back to
the early nineteenth century when the priest Miguel Hidalgo
raised the famous "*grito de Dolores*"—the revolutionary cry for
freedom which first challenged Spanish power in Mexico. The news
of Hidalgo's approaching armies sent scores of wealthy Spaniards

224

fleeing back to Spain, but most of them had sufficient warning to conceal their treasures well and carefully. They hoped, of course, to come back and fetch them, but most of them never returned, and some of the gold is there today for the man with luck and skill enough to find it.

In Spain you can buy for a few dollars descriptions of buried Mexican treasures which have been handed down from generation to generation. They are known as *relaciones*, and while the majority are forgeries or worthless, a few sometimes lead to discoveries. Jorgensen, who approaches his task with a scientific spirit, had gone to Spain and purchased about a dozen of them which, from his knowledge of Mexico, appeared to be genuine. He also equipped himself with the best available metaloscope, gave himself five years for the quest, and selected Buena Vista as his headquarters. The Bank of Mexico agreed to dispose of any treasure he might find. Having become a Mexican citizen, he will not have any income-tax trouble if he does make a find, for the Mexican government is not very demanding in such matters and contents itself with 10 per cent of the treasure.

Jorgensen spent his first year as a treasure hunter following up a series of leads which netted him plenty of experience but no loot. Now at last, he told us, he was really on the track of something big —the Cave of the Caoba.

A caoba is a mahogany tree, and it seems that somewhere in the neighborhood of Buena Vista, according to old stories, there was a cave on a hillside near a huge mahogany tree, where something like twelve mule loads of gold were supposed to be hidden. Jorgensen discovered an old man in his seventies, Don Manuel Chávez, who remembered that when he was a boy of seven or eight, three men had come to Buena Vista claiming to be the grandsons of the Spaniard who had formerly owned a large dye works near the site of the present town. The men offered substantial rewards to anyone who would point out the mahogany tree, which according to their relación was supposed to be located on a hillside strewn with lava rock about three hundred meters from the river that passed below the mountain of Tomatlán.

225

Many people in Buena Vista knew where the tree was, but feeling against the Spaniards still ran high in Mexico, and the townfolk did not see why they should give away the secret to the "Gachupines." Since it seemed likely that the Spaniards might discover the tree by themselves if they searched long enough, a posse of men from Buena Vista went forth one night and cut it down, removing the wood so that it would not lead the Spaniards to the scene. The chief of the posse was the father of old Don Manuel, who told the story.

The Spaniards, after searching aimlessly for some time, gave up and went back to Spain, leaving the treasure of the caoba still intact. The men of Buena Vista, however, even though they knew where the tree had been, had no luck in finding the cave, until many years later Don José Moreno, a resident of the town and an inveterate amateur treasure hunter, discovered what appeared to be the site of the cache. On a hillside covered with huge lava rocks of fantastic shapes, Moreno noticed a spot where for no good reason there was a cluster of totally different rocks. Examination disclosed that the rocks were set in mortar, and some energetic work with a pickax uncovered the mouth of a cave that had been filled with earth and then closed up from the outside. Moreno did not have the funds to continue his work, and was glad to team up with Jorgensen when the American arrived on the scene with his metaloscope and sufficient funds to hire workmen.

Looking over the site, Jorgensen discovered not far from the cave the decayed stump of a large mahogany tree. That seemed to clinch it, and men were hired to set about the excavation. The cave turned out to be full of alluvial soil, totally different from the soil of the mountainside, and when it was cleared the diggers came upon rock and mortar similar to that which had been used to close the mouth of the cave.

When we arrived in Buena Vista, Jorgensen had been at work several months, but it was a heartbreakingly slow job, even with half a dozen workmen and modern machinery. The reason it was so slow was that the cement was no ordinary substance; it was made of blood and bones, mixed with river sand and mud. The supposition

226

is that the Indians who were forced to make the excavation were killed and their bodies mixed up with the mortar, an old trick, Jorgensen said, which the Spaniards learned from the Moors, and which not only ensured the secrecy of the cache but provided the best possible mortar. According to Jorgensen, the stuff has a sponge-like texture, yet is so tough that a strong man does well to make a half-inch dent in it with a pickax blow. Near the top of the excavation only human bones were found, but as the hole deepened many animal bone fragments came to light. In other words, the men who did the work were killed at the end, to take advantage of their labor as long as possible.

When we talked to Jorgensen, the shaft had been sunk to a depth of fifty feet, and the metaloscope indicated that there was certainly something there. Since only fragments of bones were found, he had no idea how many Indians were slaughtered to seal up the treasure; but his workmen have removed numerous boxes of assorted human bones which they insist upon burying so that the spirits of the dead will not return to claim the gold when it is unearthed.

The workmen are a group of tough hombres, hand-picked both for their strength and intelligence and for their ability to guard the treasure. How tough they were Jorgensen did not realize until he got to know them and won their confidence. Of the seven men in the crew, five had at one time or another killed at least one man, while the other two had impressive records of successful self-defense in numerous affrays.

While he waits to become a millionaire, Jorgensen has set himself up comfortably in Buena Vista with a house which, unlike any other dwelling in town, boasts mosquito screening and a ceiling cloth to keep out scorpions. He was still at work fixing it up when we returned his call. In undershirt and slacks, with hammer in hand, he might have been any suburban American taking time off for household repairs. He did not look anything like one's idea of a dreamer, and yet he is, or he would not be searching for Mexican gold.

As for the United States, he said he didn't care if he never went back. Nowadays the government interfered with a man's life too much, snatched all his profits, and poked its nose into his affairs. He told us that the F.B.I. had once showed up at his home in California to demand an explanation of certain letters he had received from Mexico. What business did they have reading his mail?

"After that," he said, "I became a Mexican citizen. In this country a man can still do as he likes."

Jorgensen had married a Mexican woman and had a five-year-old son who was the apple of his eye. It was partly because of having a son, at the age of sixty, that he had decided to become a millionaire by way of the buried-treasure route. Other people had done it, so why not he?

"The biggest find so far," he said with a far-away look in his eyes, "was forty-two million pesos in gold. I personally know the man who found it and the banker that cashed his find. As for me, I'll be satisfied with a million dollars."

We left Buena Vista in the evening with the idea of making five or six miles, sleeping in the open, and getting a good start for Peribán at dawn. That way we would cover the hot desert country by moonlight and be ready to start climbing into the hills on the following day. Our road took us due north, out of tierra caliente and into tierra fria.

We were not more than a couple of miles out of Buena Vista, however, before Fred began to feel dizzy again. Whatever was in the shots he had taken must have been potent, for their effect was, if anything, worse than the dysentery. The moon had not yet risen. We stumbled across a rocky pasture in the dark and flung ourselves down for the night, staking out the burros to find what nourishment they could. Fred slept like a log, but awoke as dizzy as before.

Traveling fast, it would be a two-day walk to Peribán, and from there another four days across the mountains to Lake Pátzcuaro, but Fred couldn't travel fast, couldn't travel at all, perhaps. An added complication was the shortage of funds. We had just about enough to get us back, but not enough to stop long on the way. After my experience with the grass fire on the road from

Tepalcatepéc, Fred had decided that my solitary traveling was finished, but I felt differently. My night in the desert had given me confidence in my ability to act as jefe of the burro train, and I wanted to try again. It was much more practical than forcing a sick husband to plod after me, and as for giving up the trip and going home by bus—at this stage it was unthinkable, when a few days would bring us to the lake.

We got some coffee and tortillas at a nearby shack and learned that a truck bound for Peribán would be coming along the road presently. I gave Fred his serape and clothes bag, strapped the pistol to my belt, and hitched up my pants.

"I'll see you in Peribán day after tomorrow by suppertime," I said.

A bus crowded with standees came toiling up the road against the red sky of dawn and paused to take on the new passenger. Our goodbyes were smothered in a cloud of dust, and again I was alone on the road with Evita and Macho.

It was a long, hot day's journey from dawn to sunset that took me up out of the baking plains into wooded hills, cornfields, and cattle pastures. I made a brief noontime halt at a hacienda, where three old maids gave me milk and cold beans, and provided corn for the burros. They were suspicious of me at first, but when I explained who I was and why I was alone, they warmed up. Their big kitchen was full of towheaded children from one to eight years old. The women explained that they were the niños of their brother, the owner of the hacienda, who had married an American girl, but she, *pobrecita*, had died in giving birth to the littlest one. The older children were studying lessons from tattered schoolbooks; soon they would have to go away to study, for there was no other way to educate them; yet it was a pity, verdad, to send such little ones away from home?

I had a new interest in children myself, so we talked woman talk while I ate my frijoles. Did I have children at home? It was a question that everybody always asked, and when we said No, they regarded us with pity and commiseration. This time I was able to answer, "No, but there is one on the way." They didn't seem to think there was anything unusual about a pregnant woman driving

229

burros through the mountains. Expectant mothers in the Mexican ranch world don't get much coddling. By the time I left, the old girls knew how many sisters and brothers I had, how many children *they* had, and the details of Fred's family tree.

Despite all the talk, I managed to get away within an hour, feeling cheered at the reception I had received on my first occasion of stopping alone at a Mexican home. Had it not been illness which separated me from Fred, I would have enjoyed myself thoroughly in my solitary adventures. For one thing, I was forced to use my none too fluent Spanish, instead of letting Fred do all the talking. I had expected to be tongue-tied, but to my surprise I managed to make myself understood, ungrammatically but adequately, most of the time. In the course of that day I had numerous traveling companions with whom I chatted on the road; a group of four men on horseback rode with me for several miles, and later I met a young chap on foot who accompanied me for an hour or more, telling me of his ambitions to go to El Norte.

During the hottest hours of the afternoon I followed the example of other arrieros on the road and took a two-hour siesta under a tree, eating some bananas and biscuits that I had bought at a wayside tienda. It was a bother to unload and reload the animals; but the three of us were glad of the rest, and we found that we were then able to go on until sunset without a break.

I had selected a place called La Sidra as my halt for the night, as it was supposed to be about halfway to Peribán. The sun had just gone down behind the mountains when I arrived there and began making inquiries about a place to spend the night. It was a little settlement around a sawmill at the foot of a steep mountain slope, a peaceful and friendly place which I entered confidently expectant of a good welcome.

"The captain wants to see you," said a gruff voice in my ear, and looking around I was astonished to see a soldier regarding me inquisitively in the half-light. There I was with a gun in my belt, and "el Capitán" certainly wanted to see me in order to confiscate the weapon. I took off my sombrero as I followed the soldier toward the sawmill, and held it in front of me to hide the revolver.

El Capitán was seated at a desk, engaged in paperwork and surrounded by lieutenants and sergeants. He was a stocky fellow neatly attired in breeches and spurred boots, and to my relief it was not my gun he was interested in, but me. What was I doing, an American woman all by myself, and could he be of assistance? When I told him the story of Fred's illness, he was full of concern and chivalry, ready to mobilize all the resources of the Mexican army to reunite me with my husband.

"I will take you to Peribán myself tonight in the jeep," he said. "As for the burros, we will get a man to bring them along for you in the morning. Then you can be with your *esposo* tonight, and you will not have to worry about him or he about you."

When I made polite protests, he cut them off with a gesture of his wide brown hand. It would be a pleasure to serve the señora.

"I speak a little the English," he added. "On the way we will talk and you will help me in the speaking, no?" He told me that his outfit was assigned to the forestry service, trying to teach the people how to conserve natural resources.

The captain took his place at the wheel of the jeep, and two lieutenants and a sergeant crowded into the back seat, all pleased at the opportunity of going to town. As we jounced along in the cold night air, the captain diligently exercised his English, while I tried hard to stay awake and make suitable replies.

Peribán was dark when, around midnight, we bumped over the cobblestones into the plaza and pulled up before the town's only hotelito. We banged on the door until at last an old lady opened it. Yes, the señor Americano was there. I thanked my rescuers and followed her into the hotel.

Fred was asleep, and a twist of paper with some red pills indicated that he had seen another medico and that sleeping pills had been prescribed. There was a glass vial, too, with the end neatly broken off. Another injection had been administered. I pulled off my boots and threw myself down beside my dormant spouse. Anyhow, we were forty miles nearer our journey's end.

Awakening toward dawn, Fred raised himself on one elbow and regarded me with a puzzled look.

"How did you get here so fast?" he wanted to know.

"In a jeep," I replied, "with el Capitán García-López of the Servicio Forestal."

He really must have been sick, because he omitted the jealous-husband routine which, as an Italian, he generally feels obliged to display, just for form's sake.

"Thank God, anyhow," he muttered, and fell asleep again.

22 Tarascan Country Again

PERIBÁN AND LOS REYES, ONLY ABOUT SIX MILES APART, are as different as though they were at opposite ends of Mexico.

We rested up for a day in Peribán, which is a typical Tarascan town, old, quiet, and dignified. There were street musicos playing guitars and fiddles instead of the blaring toca discos, and, it being market day, country women in long skirts lined the plaza with their tiny heaps of produce, wood, and woven belts for sale. It was cool, hemmed in by pine-covered hills, and the little hotel was the cleanest and cheapest we had ever stopped in. The room with a real bed and sheets cost us two pesos for the night, and at a nearby *fonda* we got beef and chicken and pork for a couple of pesos per meal. In terms of American money, two people can live in Peribán (eat and sleep, that is) on a dollar a day.

Los Reyes, on the other hand, is a big modern town where everything costs three times as much as in Peribán. Neither of these places is much visited by outsiders, for it is a journey of five hours or more over a very bad road that comes down from Zamora and then swings southeast (another five hours) to Uruapan.

The reason for the big difference between the two towns is that Peribán, up in the hills, has no important industry, while Los Reyes is surrounded by fields of sugar cane and has two or three mills that extract the raw sugar. These plantations, formerly the property of one wealthy hacendado, have for the most part been expropriated and turned over to the people as ejido lands, except that, unlike most ejidos, there is some central control that supervises the farmer's work

233

and handles the marketing of the sugar. This we learned from a horseman we met on the road who accompanied us for a mile or two.

Fred managed to stumble along with me behind the burros, but he was making hard work of it. He was weak and skinny and his cheeks were hollow. He could not wear his own blue jeans any more because they fell off him, and even mine, two sizes smaller, had to be tightly cinched around his waist to keep them up. After an hour of walking I induced him to hitch a ride, so as to save what strength he had, for there were trucks and buses passing every now and then. I went on by myself, teaming up with some of the sugar workers who were returning to Los Reyes with donkeys loaded with cane. It was a good thing that I had their company, since there were countless small bridges over irrigation ditches, and at each one my burros had to be manhandled across. Evita enjoyed the walk, for she placed herself strategically behind one of the cane-carrying donkeys and nibbled at the sweet tassels all the way.

Joining Fred in the hotel at Los Reyes (fifteen pesos per night, which was highway robbery), I spread out our maps and examined the route before us. At this point we were to leave the truck roads for two days and follow a trail across the eastern hills that would bring us out at Cherán, on the paved highway that runs down to Uruapan and the volcano of Parícutin.

"You had better meet me at Cherán," I told Fred. He protested, but it was easy to see that he was far from all right. Despite various pills and shots, the dysentery still kept coming back, each bout leaving him weaker than before. The fact that he allowed himself to be persuaded was proof that he did not really feel capable of facing another forty miles of tough walking. My own enthusiasm for solitary travel was beginning to wane, but if we wanted to get back under our own power it seemed the only solution.

In the course of almost three months I had improved as an arriera. Gone was the sentimental approach and the gentle voice. As Fred again pulled out in a bus, I whipped up my burros and, in the tones of command that comes only with practice, ordered them: "Bur-r-r-*ooh!* Va—mo *nos!*" We were on the home stretch.

The first few hours out of Los Reyes took me up a sharp ascent through pine trees over a rocky trail. As usual, I was not long on the road without finding a companion, this time a young man on horseback who was driving two other horses up to fetch loads of wood. He went at a rapid pace, flicking his horses and my burros impartially with his quirt, so that I made far better speed than usual—such speed, in fact, that after three hours I was winded and glad to come upon a shack where I could stop for breakfast, allowing the energetic youth to continue his way alone.

Being among the Tarascans again was like being home. That high country is the heart of the Tarascan agricultural district. Once the climb from Los Reyes is topped, you come out upon rolling farm land, dotted with hills, but practically level as the trail goes. It was late March, the season for plowing, and every field had its teams of yoked oxen laboring to draw primitive hand-made plows.

The scene would have been enjoyable had it not been for the dust that was picked up by a strong breeze and whirled out of every field in dense brown clouds. I was wearing a new sombrero which had no chin strap and kept sailing off into the dirt. The dust stung my eyes and seemed to be filling up my lungs; my original tan was coated by a darker earthen tan that was sticky and could not be brushed away, and my hair was a horror which I kept coiled on top of my head and tried not to think about.

Except for the breakfast stop, I walked steadily, for to make Cherán in two days would require fast travel. Sunset found me, on schedule, entering the old Indian town of Charapan that sits up on a rocky hill above the wheat fields. The cows were just coming home to be milked, women in red skirts were fetching water, and boys were driving burros down to drink. The peaceful sound of church bells welcomed us. It was no use looking for a hotelito or even a mesón in Charapan, but the storekeeper who sold me a refresco said that Don Camilo González sometimes housed travelers overnight.

Seeking a night's lodging in a simple Mexican home, the traveler may sometimes get the impression that the people are reluctant to take him in. In most cases, however, it is not reluctance but embarrassment, because they see at once that you are accustomed to better food and beds than they can offer. Such was the case at Don Camilo's

235

where the women hemmed and hawed about taking me in, until I made it plain that I was used to sleeping on the floor and eating frijoles de la olla. Before an hour had passed, I was practically a member of the family.

Don Camilo himself was a kindly old man with a shrewd face and great pride in his Tarascan lineage. He was delighted when, in the evening as we all sat around the fire in the kitchen shack, I asked him to teach me some words and phrases in the guttural Indian tongue. The señora and I made big pots of coffee for the whole family, for with the end of the trip in sight I had plenty to spare. We sat on benches around the walls, the firelight playing on the flat planes of Indian cheeks and picking up highlights in the shining black braids of the women.

For several hours we amused ourselves with a two-way language class, they teaching me Tarascan words which I wrote down as best I could in a notebook, and I teaching them the English equivalent. The word "pig" was their favorite. It made them laugh to think that a cuchi should be called by such a funny word as "pig." Tarascan is a tough, knotty speech full of *k*'s and *w*'s and *z*'s and, of course, well salted with Spanish words to express ideas and things which did not exist in Mexico until the Spaniards came. By the time the lesson was over, I had progressed enough to be able to say, after consulting my notes, that I was tired and wanted to sleep.

My chamber was a storeroom full of grain sacks and saddles, and my bed a straw petate on the wooden floor. The night wind of the mountains blew in cold gusts through the slatted walls, but I was too weary even to feel the cold.

The next day I got lost. The trail from Charapan was difficult to follow, for it led through fields where in many places farmers had plowed right across the path, obliterating it completely. In the early hours of the day I was lucky enough to have a companion, a young boy on foot who kept me on the trail as long as he was with me, but when our ways divided I promptly got confused. The boy had indicated the general direction, saying that I was to go to the right of yonder cerro and to pass through a village which I would find on that hillside over there . . . but the burros and I soon were confronted with numerous divergent paths, and the one we chose was the wrong one.

We wandered about among rocks and bushes, while the hill we were supposed to leave to the right had mysteriously managed to swing around to the left. Burros do not enjoy exploring. They like to follow well defined trails where they can trot along with assurance. When there is no trail, they don't know what to do, and tend to stop and graze, or even to lie down, pack and all. Furthermore, a burro cannot go everywhere that a man can go, and we were continually running into wire fences which necessitated long detours, patches of brush too thick to pass through, and rocks too steep to climb. I allowed myself to get into a state of complete exasperation, which did not help a bit, but I was hot and tired and had eaten nothing but half a can of salmon all day. The sun was getting past the meridian, Fred was doubtless waiting in Cherán, and there I was with the damn'-fool donkeys, wandering in the heat and dust and getting nowhere.

Evita, being unloaded, behaved worst, and kept taking side excursions, which entailed my running after her, turning her around, and heading back for the point of departure, only to find that in the meantime Macho had strayed away somewhere to wedge his pack boxes between two rocks. In desperation I finally mounted Evita, keeping off the sore spot as best I could, and drove Macho ahead with energetic slaps of a rope's end. In this way I kept them together and managed, by many painful twists and turns, to extricate the party from no man's land and proceed over fields and gullies cross-country toward a village perched halfway up a hillside.

Once at the village I was able to get back on the main trail. Hungry and tired as I was, I did not stop except to ask directions and drink a couple of bottles of nauseous warm soda pop. The next town, Paracho, was another two hours of walking, and Cherán about the same distance beyond. The sun was dropping; I certainly would not get to Cherán, but I might make Paracho, where I could leave the burros at a mesón and hop a bus to Cherán to keep my rendez-vous.

I constantly met people on the trail who assured me that Paracho

237

was cerquita, but it was a long and weary way before I stood on a hilltop and looked out across a broad valley between two mountain ridges. Paracho was down below, at the side of the paved highway, its old church tower catching the last rays of the setting sun.

I did not look at the town so much as at the paved highway. I had seen many towns, but not a paved road since leaving Ario de Rosales. It was a marvel to watch the little cars zipping along so smoothly and with so little effort. Descending to the roadside and shepherding my animals out of the path of the cars, I recalled, like an atavistic memory, the sensation of a well upholstered car seat, the view of mountains and plains slipping past the windows, the casual discussions of whether to eat at this place or go on for another fifty miles. I remembered how one would glance casually at a peasant passing with his donkeys and wonder what went on in his head. I knew now what the peasant's thoughts were, for they were my own: the steep trails, the worry about food and money, the sore back of this animal and the limp of that one, the dust and the heat, the brains boiling under the sombrero at noontime or congealed with cold under the fold of the serape at night, the mixture of patience and envy as the auto speeds past, the shrug of the shoulders and, "Vamos, burros, es dura la vida." Life is hard.

Paracho had a good mesón for the burros, and I just had time to see them fed and watered before catching a bus for Cherán. In half an hour Fred and I were eating supper together in a fonda, a frugal supper because we had about twenty-five pesos between us and two days of traveling still to go.

Fred said he felt better. He had spent the previous night in Uruapan and come on by bus to Cherán in the morning with a precious bottle of paregoric to keep his stomach under control until we should get back to Lake Pátzcuaro. I suspected that Fred's improvement was illusory and attributable to the fact that the town notables of Cherán had been playing host to my esposo all afternoon and plying him with mescal, which certainly was not going to help his dysentery. He had decided to be his own doctor now, however, declaring that he had been practiced on by enough amateurs, and that he wouldn't see another medico until we could find a good one in Morelia. In the meantime mescal and paregoric made an interesting and cheerful combination.

We took the bus back to Paracho and bedded down with our donkeys in a cubicle at the mesón. Fred deposed me as jefe of the expedition and took command himself once more. We were going to arrive as we had left, he said, together.

The country through which we were now passing is famous for its guitar makers and guitar players. Despite the toca disco, the Tarascans still like to make their own music, and almost every village has its little orchestra of guitars, fiddles, and perhaps a trumpet or harp. In Paracho and Cherán everybody makes guitars, either as a business or as a side line, and all along the streets you see thin shingle-like slabs of wood left to season in the sun, and hear the rasp of files and sandpaper and the strumming of chords as somebody tries out a new instrument.

The volcano of Parícutin has been a great boon to these people, for it brings tourists in droves down the road to Uruapan, a side trip that formerly was ignored by most sight-seers. Fred had passed near the volcano while coming by bus from Los Reyes, and I had seen from Charapan faint clouds of vapor in the sky which the people told me was *el volcán*. When we passed, it was no longer in eruption, but just smoking quietly, dying, perhaps, or else resting before a new outburst of fire and lava.

The people in Cherán and Paracho hope that Parícutin will have a long and violent life, for its appearance has enabled them to build big new *fábricas* and shops full of eye-catching native handicrafts. The squeal of brakes as a tourist catches sight of a shop window full of guitars is money in the till, and an easier life for the chamacos than their fathers and grandfathers had.

23 Home

WHEN WE LEFT THE TARASCAN COUNTRY EARLY IN JANU-
ary, the air had been clear and cold, and the foliage of the trees still
fresh from the autumn rains. Now, at the end of March, the sky was
no longer deep blue, but bronzed with dust. It was impossible to take
a photograph at any distance, for mountaintops and valleys alike
were blurred. The few leaves upon trees along the roadside rustled
dryly in the hot wind. Plowmen wore handkerchiefs across nose and
mouth; women patiently tried to wash clothes in arroyos that had
become stagnant mud puddles; babies rolled in the dust, picked
up handfuls of it, and flung it to the wind. Never mind, in two
months the aguas would come.

We walked up one side of the valley, following the highway. There
was a more direct burro trail through the fields on the valley floor,
but it was swept by dust clouds, while on the auto road we walked
in the lee of the hillside. Our relatively easy progress lasted until
Cherán, where we had lunch, and left the camino nacional for a track
that took us out of the valley over a saddleback pass.

Fred was far from his normal self, but with the aid of paregoric he
was able to keep body and soul together and to pick up his feet one
after the other. The end was in sight, and that made all the difference. We walked a conservative twelve miles and stopped for the
night in a village with a beautiful Spanish church flanked by pine
trees—Nahuatzen, our last night on the trail.

It was Saturday, the day before market day in Erongarícuaro, and
as we climbed into the hills from Nahuatzen in the morning we fell

in with groups of Indians bringing down firewood for sale, people who knew our friends in Erongarícuaro and Arócutin, who even knew our burra.

"No me diga! So that is the burra of Don Damian Ascencio that has come all that way with you! She must be tired, and you, too."

They admired our Macho, agreeing that he was *fuerte, bonito,* and that Don Domingo certainly would be pleased with him as a replacement for that perrito of a donkey he had loaned us.

Men, women, and children, all were going to spend the night on the street reserved for woodcutters in Erongarícuaro. They would stack their wood as near the head of the street as possible, put their burros in the mesón, and then stretch out their serapes, sleeping on the cobblestones so as to be prepared for early-morning trade. The women carried cold tortillas and pots of beans to be warmed up over campfires. Everybody had on his best clothes, for as soon as the wood was sold they would go and do their own marketing, mingle with the gay crowd on the plaza, go to mass.

Because they were in a hurry to get the most advantageous spots in the wood market, after talking a moment with us, they pushed ahead at the distance-consuming Indian trot which they seem to be able to sustain effortlessly for miles.

Evita smelled home, and had to be dissuaded from running ahead with the Indians. Her ears were up and her head was high as she breathed in the smell of hot pine needles and caught the fresh-water fragrance of the lake. Macho plodded on with the carga, little knowing that his journey was coming to an end and that he was fated to spend the rest of his days as a Tarascan burro.

Our feet scuffed softly in the dusty pine needles, and the tall trees around us shaded the path so that even in the midafternoon heat we did not find walking uncomfortable. Two men lunching at the side of the trail on canned salmon and crackers invited us to join them, but we did not stop.

The trail began to descend, and a fresh breeze came to us that smelled of water and marsh grass and the cooking fires of our friends. The trees thinned out as the descent grew steeper, until from a rocky prominence we could look down over the fir tops upon the lake,

241

blue and smiling, faintly ruffled by the wind, its flat margins golden with ripening wheat. There below us to the left were the tile roofs of Erongarícuaro, the church tower, and the miniature canoes paddling to and from the landing place; to the right Arócutin dozed in the sun on its rocky cliff—we could almost look into Don Salud's dooryard—and there beyond Arócutin was the trail we had taken almost three months ago, over the mountains to Zirahuen.

I found tears coming to my eyes, just because it was beautiful and because we had made it. We stood there and looked for a solemn moment. The donkeys looked too, their long ears erect and their nostrils quivering. Then, feeling lightheaded and a little crazy, we plunged down the steep slope and through the wheat fields.

We were a disreputable-looking pair, clothed in dust and dirt, still marked by the insect bites of tierra caliente, our shirts in tatters and our pants all fringed out at the bottom. We were as lean as the thin dogs of the hot country, blacker than the Indians, and as poor as the humblest campecinos, for we arrived with two pesos and some odd centavos in our jeans. As for the burros, their harnesses were held together by bits of string; the neat halters that Evita and Perón had started with had been discarded long ago, frayed and useless; we had left one animal on a mountain south of Coalcomán, and the other was returning with a badly ulcerated back; the battered pack boxes had been renailed a dozen times, and bore the marks of the hundreds of trees and rocks with which they had collided.

But we had made it, over seven hundred miles of walking: deserts, rivers, mountains, beaches, towns, villages, and lonely ranches, in spite of fatigue, hunger, insects, heat and cold. We had set out, not to prove anything or to discover anything, but just to see what manner of people and country lay at the end of the "strange road" that goes south from Ario de Rosales.

We might have returned with phials of gold dust, tiger skins, maps of buried treasure, parrots, rare botanical specimens, or clues to fabulous deposits of silver or copper. Instead we came back from the distant hot lands with a handful of broken sea shells, picked up on Pacific beaches, a case of dysentery, and a baby.

In some ways it had been easier than we expected. We had not been forced to hack our way through jungles or battle with wild beasts or wild men; we had suffered from hunger but had not starved; we had been lost, but never hopelessly; no scorpions, snakes, or tarantulas had bitten us; no one had robbed us; as far as we knew, our lives had never been in danger. On the other hand, the difficulties we did encounter, being mostly unexpected and unprepared for, were all the more formidable: the chiggers, ticks, and niguas, the tremendous distances between ranches, the lack of food, the ailments of the burros, the trouble in finding trails and getting correct information.

"Next time," of course, we will have a better notion of how to prepare for such a trip. In the meantime, if there are like-minded adventurers who yearn "beyond the sky-line where the strange roads go down," perhaps this account of our adventures will give them courage to take the plunge. Money, equipment, and special knowledge are secondary; the main thing is to go. Careful preparation is a fine thing, but no amount of planning can foresee the unexpected and inevitable disasters which simply have to be faced as they come and with what is at hand. And if anyone reading this book gets the idea that he does not need to worry about scorpions in the Mexican hot country, he will probably be the one that gets stung. The bad parts of a trip, the times when you are lost, starving, exhausted, and wonder why you ever wanted to leave home, seem to be the times you most enjoy remembering afterward.

Although we did not expect to prove anything, we did demonstrate that the average sedentary New Yorker is tougher than might be expected. The red stuff in the veins is really blood, and the muscles, if flabby, will harden in time.

We made discoveries, too. Mexico is beautiful, as we well knew, but when you toil, as we did, to find its remotest beauties, they come as a benediction upon your struggles: the Rio Balsas at sunrise, rushing southward under its dark bastion of mountains; the deserted sandy coves of the Pacific coast; the mighty Sierra de Coalcomán, with its range upon range of wooded, jaguar-haunted mountains.

Our best discovery was the good hearts of the Mexican people. Among Mexican countryfolk old ways of hospitality still survive, and welcoming the wayfarer is an almost sacred obligation. The red carpet was rolled out for us, not because we were Americans, or because we were journalists or had money, but simply because we were tired, hungry people in need of help.

We made friends we will never forget in tierra caliente, even though we knew them only for a day or two: Don Genaro in Reparo de Luna; Doña Julia in Playa Azul; Don David Melgoza and Felix in Chuta; Don Pancho at Caleta de Campos. . . . As for our Tarascan friends in Arócutin, we knew they were good people, but how good we did not realize until we asked them for help with our preparations and received two donkeys and all their harness free of charge, to use as long as we needed them. And when we returned them a crippled burra and a different burro, with half their equipment lost or ruined, there were no complaints.

"Bien, bien," said Don Salud. "We are glad to see you back safe."

We find ourselves now once more in New York. Our walking trips are taken behind a baby carriage, and the pots and pans that were balanced on so many corncob fires are back on the gas stove. Evita and Macho are carrying loads of wheat or wood up and down the steep hills around Arócutin, and Perón, one hopes, will lead a long and happy life in the mountains south of Coalcomán.

Civilization again has us in its net, but sometimes in our sleep we still walk the strange roads behind the bobbing packs of the donkeys, and wake up with the arriero's call on our lips:

Bur-r-o-os! Vamonos!